John A. Kouwenhoven –

1948

To Keith, Ce

S –

m

(JK copy)

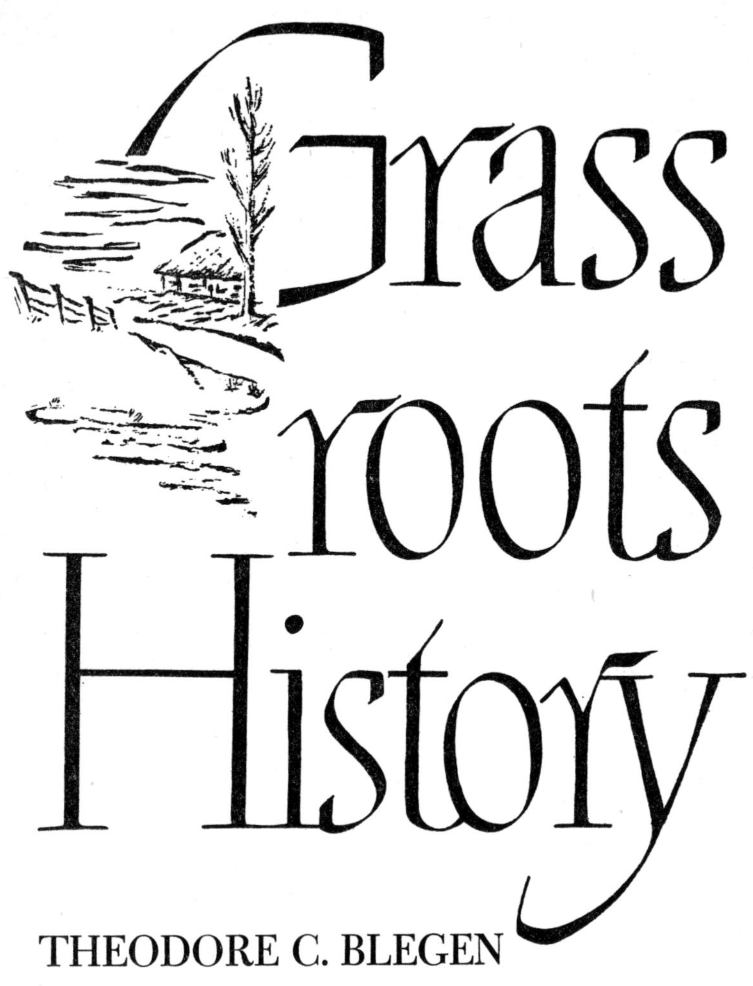

THEODORE C. BLEGEN

University of Minnesota Press, Minneapolis

PRINTED AT THE LUND PRESS, INC., MINNEAPOLIS
MINNESOTA, U.S.A.

London

GEOFFREY CUMBERLEGE · OXFORD UNIVERSITY PRESS

To
CLARA WOODWARD BLEGEN

A Word from the Author

THE pivot of history is not the uncommon, but the usual, and the true makers of history are "the people, yes."

This is the essence of grass roots history. It grapples, as history should grapple, with the need of understanding the small, everyday elements, the basic elements, in large movements. It recognizes, as maturely conceived history should recognize, the importance of the simple, however complex and subtle the problem of understanding the simple may be.

Someone has said that "there are all the colors and forms of humanity in our daily life – the mingling of races and the moulding of a race – the amalgamation of ancient inheritances into a new tradition." Understanding such colors and forms and processes, the very grass roots of our daily life and civilization, is central to the purpose of history.

Without such comprehension, we cannot make our national self-examination realistic. That process of examination, which Professor Boynton believes is "more than keeping pace with national complacency," makes it necessary for us to draw upon all sources of understanding, including community and regional history. Unless we do so, we shall not, in pulling together the national story, do justice to the abundant variety of American culture. Our efforts to synthesize national history have failed to achieve such justice, and one important reason for their failure has been an inverted provincialism which has scorned the simple and steered clear of the near-at-hand.

Grass roots history is an avenue to that "social awareness" which the natural scientists, more boldly than the social scientists, have declared to be the most urgent and compelling need of our day. One of the major responsibilities of the historian is to make clear the backgrounds and nature of social awareness and to help us to understand that, like charity, it begins at home.

This book is made up of papers in which I have tried to express and demonstrate these ideas. They make a whole and are presented to the public as such. The scheme of the book is simple. The first two papers advance certain general ideas which are illustrated by studies and stories in two succeeding sections.

My examples are drawn, in the main, from two fields of research: American immigration and regional history. In exploring particularly the migration from Norway, I have done so with the purpose of illustrating approaches that can be applied not only to other immigrant groups but also to the American people as a whole. We have need to dig into the folk story of America if we are to bring out the pattern of American development and American culture in all its color and richness of texture and design. My other field, that of the Upper Midwest, has to do with a great region of America that contains within itself, as James Gray has said, "the memory of everything that America has been and the knowledge of what it may become."

THEODORE C. BLEGEN

Table of Contents

A WIDENING PROVINCE

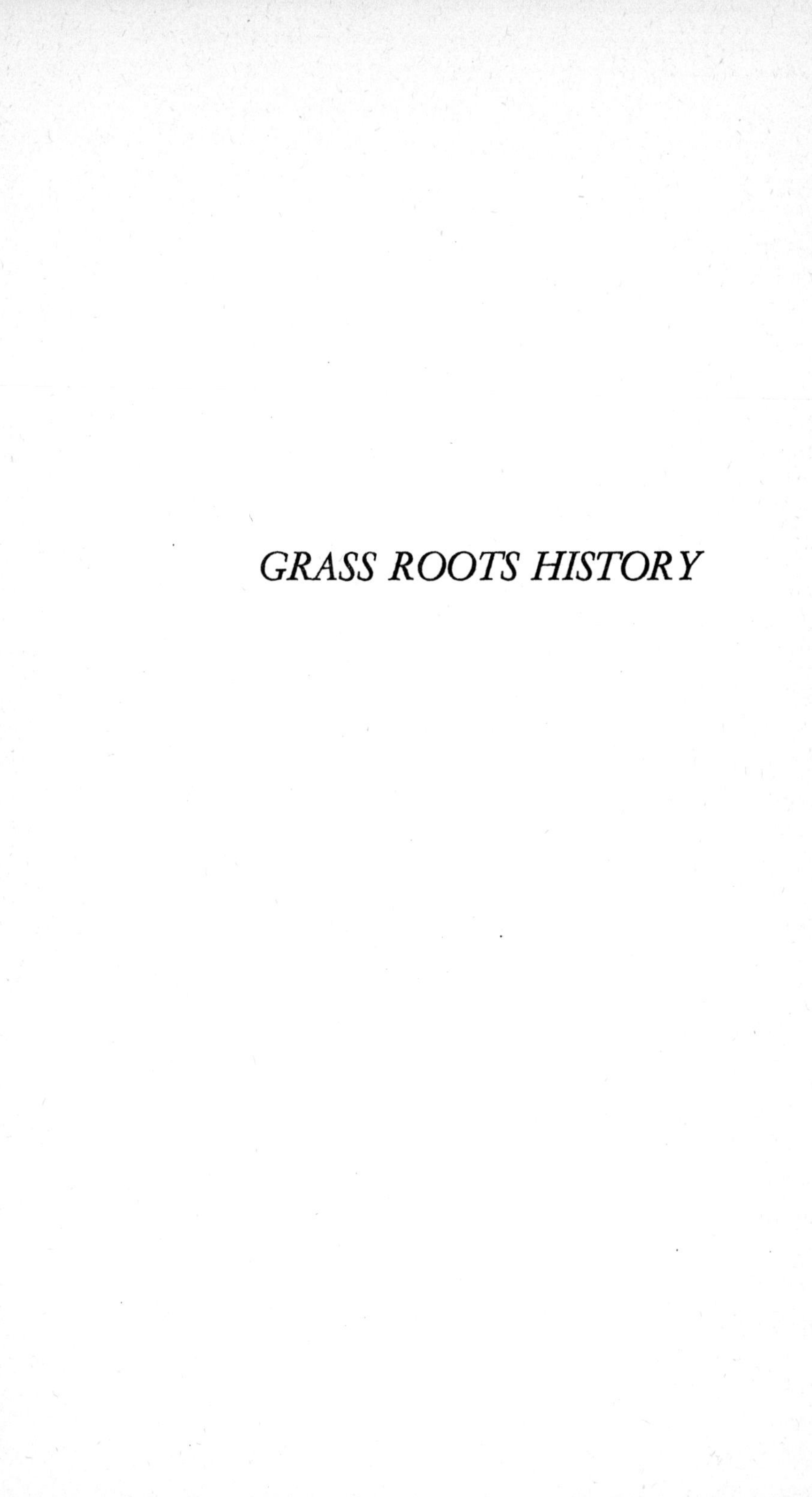

GRASS ROOTS HISTORY

Inverted Provincialism

IN THESE days of grave national and international problems, it is a first essential to take stock of what we are and have, of what we think and feel — even, I venture to say, of our folk culture, though such an acute critic as Margaret Marshall says that anybody who talks about folk or folklore in America has a bear by the tail.

Everybody has his own definition of folk culture — everybody from anthropologist to sociologist and novelist, to hillbilly radio crooner and cookbook publisher — and they all differ. Observe, however, that even when warning us away, Margaret Marshall uses a phrase that smacks of folklore: having a bear by the tail. In questioning that we are a folk, she picks a phrase from the lips of the folk.

Soon after the liberation of Norway, I had a communication from one of the museum authorities in that country. The Nazis had seized the great folk museum of Norway, occupied its buildings, turned them into factories and laboratories. But the museum did not quit. Its friends continued to sustain it, and in 1944 they celebrated the anniversary of its founding. With guards on watch to warn of a Gestapo raid, they held a secret meeting, at which speeches were delivered on the museum's future and Grieg music was played. And a gift of sixty thousand crowns, gathered by secret solicitation, was presented to the director. "The day's events," I was told, "merged with the life of hundreds of years that the museum itself illustrates in its buildings and exhibits."

These devoted folk had a bear by the tail — and they twisted it. To change the figure, a folk museum spoke above the Nazi guns.

This sidelight on the care for folk culture in another country set me to wondering about the cultivation of American folk-cultural interests. Do *we* care? Do we accept responsibility for interpreting the traditional beliefs, customs, folk arts, ideas, and practices that help to explain what we are as a people? Are we concerned about exploring our culture to its roots in terms of the common life? And is this a time for such responsibility and exploration – this time that calls so urgently for international understanding?

My own answer to the last question is an emphatic yes. There is no conflict between the two ideas. They really are not two ideas, but one. Why did we refuse world responsibility and leadership after the First World War? Professor Schlesinger says the League of Nations was rejected by a country which was itself a league of nations, and that a spirit of intense nationalism enveloped a people who embodied many nations. Perhaps we did not really know and understand ourselves. Who had written the story of American culture for us? What textbook really told it? Were the basic materials for self-knowledge available to us?

Today we urgently need to know the "varied patterns of civilization" of other peoples, of other continents. We cannot build peace upon ignorance. By the same token, however, our knowledge must not be superficial. And it will be superficial unless we also understand our own pattern of civilization.

It is encouraging to see that much advance has been made in recent years in the study and appreciation of our national, regional, and home community life. As Tremaine McDowell points out, artists have been busy painting native scenes, authors have recorded native manners, musicians have transcribed native rhythms, historians have explored America afresh to understand everyday life.

What has happened is not wholly new, but it marks a shift of direction. In trying to understand America, our states and regions, and ourselves, we have turned away from what I like to call "inverted provincialism."

This inverted provincialism considered itself urbane and cosmopolitan. It was little interested in the values of folk culture. It rejected the near-at-hand as local and insignificant. It cultivated the faraway, without fully understanding it because it did not understand the near-at-hand, without sensing, too, that the faraway may in its inner meaning be near-at-hand. Imitative because it lacked self-confidence, inverted provincialism in many instances established molds and patterns for our educational and institutional development that have been hard to break.

In art it sometimes scorned the ideas and expressions of native artists, forgetting that Rembrandt drew his inspiration from the near-at-hand in his native Holland and never went outside his own land; that even Cezanne, the founder of modern art, spent his entire creative life in Provence.

In literature inverted provincialism gave small attention to the so-called regional writers, forgetting that the classical writers were often regionalists, forgetting that the masterpieces of Mark Twain are his books describing and interpreting the folk culture he found at home, for in the home community and on the river that he knew he found the universal. There was even a tendency to delay recognition of American writers at home until, in Conrad Aiken's phrase, they had foreign visas for travel in America.

In music inverted provincialism forgot that the classics once were new and that many of the great composers got their inspiration from the hearts of the folk.

In history it devoted itself to the polite and reputable themes. It lifted its eyebrows at those who turned aside from the Monroe Doctrine, the tariff, and presidential administrations to find life and blood and significance in social and cultural themes, whether on national, regional, or local levels.

The arrogance of inverted provincialism masked an ignorance of, and disinterest in, the actualities of the common life. It was an indifference to that culture which shows itself, not so much in the clash of the individual with inner and outer forces, as in his reflection of problems and crises; that changing and growing culture which reveals itself in the standards and ways and tastes of group and community, in what Philip D. Jordan calls our "traditional modes of political, economic, and social activity." That culture – which goes much deeper than the antiquarian concerns that have so largely monopolized "folklore" as we usually understand it – is folk culture.

No one would deny the importance of genius, but no one can understand the whole picture without studying and knowing the strivings and life of the folk behind the genius.

Let me illustrate two approaches or points of view by mentioning two gifted writers in comparison with what I shall call the literature of the unlettered. Willa Cather, who gave us *O Pioneers!* and other novels of immigrant life on the Nebraska prairies, and O. E. Rölvaag, who wrote the saga of *Giants in the Earth*, were writers of intuitive power, possibly geniuses, whose books will be read beyond their generation.

Alongside their masterpieces I often think of a book that has no title and has never been brought between covers. I refer to the thousands of letters written by everyday immigrants through the decades of the nineteenth century. They make up a diary on a grand scale of the Per Hansas who crossed the seas and joined caravans west. They have a sweep from coast to coast, from north to south. Many have an unconscious eloquence, sometimes a stylistic simplicity, that make their reading memorable. I have collected thousands of them and have found in them everything from fire and passion to elation and sorrow – the life of "hamlet, workshop, and meadow," the reflection of folk characteristics in peoples undergoing the transition from one mode of life to another.

In my total picture of America I give a place to these unpretentious pages that reflect and reveal the folk culture that produced the Cathers and Rölvaags.

The inverted provincialism of which I have spoken has been stubborn, but during the past quarter of a century new and vigorous forces have made themselves felt. There has been dissatisfaction with the boundaries set to older inquiries. Fresh research has reached out, as it should always reach out, beyond old frontiers. It has come to light that there is indeed an American art, a regional art, even a folk art; and that they are fields rewarding to high talent.

In the field of literature, the efforts of Vernon Parrington and many another have made an impact, and the English departments in colleges now accept the fact that American literature does not end with Emerson.

Folklore continues, and properly, to go far backward into "the abysm of time," but it has become much broader than it once was in its range of interest and is not limited to narrow concepts of "survivals in culture."

Dr. Jordan, leading the way toward a new folklore, asserts that an antiquarian air has enveloped much folklore research. The reason for it is the simple fact that "a nineteenth century concept of folk culture has continued into the twentieth century without recognition that methods must change to meet new conditions and new types of materials." He boldly calls upon folklore to begin "collection and analysis in fields that not so long ago were considered outside the province of folklore"—such fields as the frontier, manifest destiny, the West, Jacksonian democracy, the philosophy of thrift and hard work, the migration of folk patterns, sport, the folklore of town and country, even architecture.

On the historical side, we have explored the social and intellectual history of our people with a new sense of its importance. We have pushed behind the barricade of statistics to learn that the American immigrant was not a line in a graph, a statistic, or merely a problem, but a human being.

For three decades a new school of historians of immigration and acculturation has given its attention to this field, one of the great themes in national history, unpacking, in Carl Wittke's phrase, the culture in immigrant chests, tracing the processes of transition, seeing the story in terms of the national life.

A broad-ranging and productive newer investigation of the history of nation, region, and community is under way. Some writers have made the discovery that a given American region may contain within itself, to quote James Gray, "the memory of everything that America has been and the knowledge of what it may become."

We have written about social customs and manners, the growth of American thought, farming and industry, folk figures out of the past, and a thousand other subjects that help us to understand American folkways, with all the influences brought to bear upon them by our origins, our pioneering heritage, and the modern forces of integration in national life.

I should not like to leave the mistaken impression that so much progress has been made that a feeling of complacency is warranted. The most promising development is not the stream of books and special studies of recent years, but an increasing awareness of needs as yet unmet.

Let me offer an illustration or two. In the Archive of American Folk Song in the Library of Congress there are now, I believe, at least seven thousand records of American folk songs collected directly from the field. There are said to be a thousand tunes gathered up which are in the nature of American folk hymns, and about five hundred hymn texts are available.

Yet when a new edition of a hymnal widely used in America was issued recently, it contained only a dozen American folk hymn tunes. The editor was eager to print a large number of American hymns. Why did he include only a scant dozen? Because our American hymn texts, though collected, have not been "properly weeded out or edited," and the tunes have not been harmonized. The basic material is at hand, but as someone has said, our folk music is "unsifted, unprocessed, unpackaged," and therefore unavailable to the people.

In 1943, as president of the Mississippi Valley Historical Association, I appointed a committee on "Projects in American History and Culture." This committee later published a report challenging the historical profession to meet scores of needs. It emphasized subjects that have pertinence for our times. It underlined the historian's responsibility to this generation. It pointed out the need for interpretation. It called attention to the fact that we have few important books dealing comprehensively with a single period of American history – books of the kind Henry Adams wrote sixty years ago. Cooperative histories we have indeed, but comprehensive works of the kind suggested we hesitate to write or we leave to a very few of our older scholars, forgetting that Bryce wrote his *Holy Roman Empire* when he was twenty-seven.

The report calls for studies of agriculture and soil erosion, conservation, science and medicine, the American city, religion and secularization, ethnic and minority groups, wit, humor, and folklore, the American mind and machines, the Great Plains, lumbering, and the American forest. It recognizes that the novelist often has done a better job than the historian – for example, in portraying the adaptation of the European immigrant to the soil, methods, machines, and ideas of the New World.

I mention this report, not for the purpose of analyzing it in detail, but simply to indicate that the historical profession is not uncritical of itself. It is probing its own service and is increasingly aware of its social responsibilities. Perhaps it has not forgotten a certain American thinker's definition of the scholar as one whose office it is to "cheer, to raise, and to guide men, by showing them facts amidst appearances."

The new interest in the American past is today showing particular vigor in folk studies and activities and in regional interpretation. Publishers are aware of a growing popular interest. They have launched such ambitious series as the American Folkways, the Rivers of America, the American Lakes, and the American Scene. Collections of folklore are reaching a wide public. Folk festivals are frequent, and their value in combating intolerance is recognized. Folk singers win large audiences, and folklore societies are springing up across the continent.

A glance at fairly recent publishers' lists also reveals a few clues as to what is happening. One notes such titles as Hutton's *Midwest at Noon*, Dorson's *Jonathan Draws the Long Bow*, Jordan's *Singin' Yankees*, Botkin's *Treasury of American Folklore*, Woods's *American Sayings*, Saxon's *Gumbo Ya-ya*, with its wealth of Louisiana folk tales, Rourke's *Roots of American Culture*, Curti's *Growth of American Thought*, Tyler's *Freedom's Ferment*, and George R. Stewart's fascinating *Names on the Land*, a study of history, folkways, and geography, with language, blood, time, and place as the principal ingredients.

One of the most active fields of all is that of regionalism, which is marked by fresh and spirited inquiry into the meaning of American culture. Let me point briefly, for a few illustrations, to my own state of Minnesota.

Under regional writing fellowships from the University of Minnesota, twenty-four authors have been at work on histories, novels, biographies, and essays. The histories have a range that includes the Dakota country, the Red River Valley, the Iron Range country, the Northwest Angle, the Minneapolis Symphony Orchestra, the white pine industry, the story of a small town that never grew up, and the Icelandic element. The essays and special studies include such themes as the Great Plains in literature, historic midwest houses, winter in the North Woods, cultural elements in the capital city of

Minnesota, and interracial relationships in Minneapolis. One biographer is studying the life of a lumber magnate and patron of art; another, the story of a midwest artist. Among the novels may be mentioned Herbert Krause's *The Threshers* and Feike Feikema's *This Is the Year.*

It is no chance circumstance that many of the books written through the regional writing fellowships have been brought out by the University of Minnesota Press. Through two decades this press, under an official policy of "cultivating its own garden, but not behind provincial walls," has given creative stimulus to an enlightened regionalism. In its broad program of publication it has made a place, and a large place, for books interpreting the Upper Midwest.

In Minnesota too, a Folk Arts Foundation, formed with a broad program of research and public education, is digging into such matters as folk ballads, folk tales, folk dances and games, proverbs (with five thousand collected during one year), place names, occupational vocabularies and symbols, even cooking, textiles, and household wares. Its president, Professor A. C. Krey, is a medievalist who is proposing a comprehensive inventory of culture, not in Renaissance Florence, but in contemporary Minnesota.

The Minnesota Historical Society is engaged in an adventure in democratic public education designed to carry the history of the North Star State to the people. It is forwarding the preparation of a series of works conceived in the spirit of dynamic history that comes up to the present and asks, even though it may not answer with blueprints, the question "What lies ahead?" One of these works is a history of the public health movement, a story of pioneering ideas, drama, tragedy, public enlightenment, and the advance of public welfare. Another is a vast study, combined with a collecting program, in the field of the history of lumber and forest products.

The University of Minnesota, alongside its International Area program, has set in motion a program of American

Studies, with the purpose of guiding "students to a broad knowledge of their own nation, in relation both to its own regions and to the world."

As I think of these and many other programs and plans which can be duplicated in other states and regions throughout the country, I have the impression that a movement is under way. What it means is that a mature people is taking stock of itself and is turning away from barren concepts of the larger community life of which it is a part.

Regionalism is not cultural separatism. It is not the doctrine of every region for itself. Its essence – and I think it is fundamentally a matter of attitude and not of subject matter – is a creative concern with the development of the region to its maximum for the cultural strength of the nation. Adding up nonentities, someone has said, is like adding a column of zeros; the result remains zero. Add up regions that lack cultural richness and strength, and you cannot achieve an impressive total in terms of national culture.

The taunt of provincialism, once so easily leveled at the champions of regionalism, is heard less often than formerly, and the reason is a widening recognition of the true nature of provincialism. Provincialism, as Helen Clapesattle has said, "sees the world in the locality's own image." It is blind to the interrelations, manifold and inextricable, of the locality with the civilization of which it is a living part. Regionalism reverses the process, to view the region in relation to the nation and the world.

An Englishman exploring "Midwest at Noon" looks for what he calls the "altogetherness" – the "something that links" up and makes the Midwest what it is, "that makes it 'tick.'" This is precisely what we need, not alone for the Midwest, but for every region in the country, so that we may be able to find out what makes America tick. Professor McDowell calls upon us to listen "not to Manhattan alone or to Minnesota alone, but to all these states, each region chanting its own chant with its own voice, and out of them all a chorus rising and blending until, with Whitman, we 'hear America singing.' "

A great novelist once remarked that "when a people becomes interested in its past life, seeks to acquire knowledge in order better to understand itself, it always experiences an awakening of new life." That kind of awakening generates spiritual self-confidence and the creative spirit.

If the phrase *folk culture* is indiscreet, none will deny that there is such a thing as "the process of creating an American cultural life." It is rooted in a common past. It is related to what someone calls a "sense of the past" as "an instrument for making the future more rich and manageable."

And so I come back to the matter of knowing ourselves – the key word of the Greek philosophers – and the society in which we live, without self-deception and with confidence as we look to the future. In such knowing, starting with community and homeland, we have the basis for knowing the universal.

Literature of the Unlettered

A WRITER in the *New Republic* not long ago hurled a bomb at the so-called "old-stock historians of immigration," and as it exploded it scattered fragments all about. One of these was the assertion that most of the "old-stock historians" have "written with an emotional remoteness that catches little of the fire curling around their footnotes."

The truth of the matter is that much writing on American immigration has been statistical and has failed to break through the crust of figures and graphs to the living realities that alone can give them significance. Much more has been filiopietistic, bathed in bias, concerned with superficial aspects of movements and forces deeply rooted in the national life – occupied with claims, alleged glory, and resentment over supposed neglect or distortion.

The manipulators of statistics have been absorbed by the current problems associated with immigration and have been little concerned with immigration and acculturation as long-range factors in the common life. The filiopietistic school, moved by a crusading zeal, has underestimated the importance of seeking out the sources upon which understanding can be built and of using them with the objective, critical concern of scholarship.

If fire curls around footnotes, both schools have failed to see the flame or smell the smoke. The figure of speech, though striking, is in fact inept, for to most readers footnotes suggest, not flame and heat, but ice and cold. In American historical writing generally, there has been a tendency to congeal the vital human content of the sources in the ice of footnotes. In the field of American immigration, however, the difficulty has been not so much a freezing of vitality in eight-point as an absence of that vitality from both text and footnotes—an unawareness of the existence of vast bodies of significant human source material or of its potential value.

Neither statistics nor emotion can offer a satisfactory substitute for history. And history can be satisfied with nothing less than an unending search for sources upon which to build its narrative and analysis.

The study of American history fortunately is not static. That is one of many qualities and values that make it fascinating and significant. New points of view, new interpretations, new approaches have from time to time changed the currents of American historical thought.

This generation happens to have witnessed an extraordinary interest in American social history. New areas have been opened by research, hundreds of trained scholars have been engaged in such research, books have been trooping from the presses, and we have seen pioneering attempts, notably that of Merle Curti in *The Growth of American Thought*, to pull the story together in a large synthesis.

Many historians have looked on with skeptical eyes and have insisted that social and cultural history lacks a fundamental frame of reference, that one cannot write the national story save upon a political or perhaps economic foundation, that our efforts at social history are fragmentary, if not inchoate.

Yet the fact remains that on wide fronts we continue to study and to write social and cultural history and that somehow it seems to make sense and does help us to understand the actualities of American life. Perhaps new concepts of cultural change will erect firmer frameworks than we have yet used: the shift from a general to a specialized society, a story that has never been told in the full sweep of its implications for modern life; or the long-range fashioning of a composite nationality; or the rise of the common man.

In any event, it has already been proved to the hilt that in many areas of social and cultural history a coherent story can be told. And sometimes the story that emerges is genuinely significant for American life today and for those who must grapple with the problem of planning for the nation's tomorrows.

One of these stories of true import is the tale being unfolded by a new school of historians of immigration and immigrant transition. Although these historians are studying an old theme, they are looking at it from what is essentially a new point of view. Two practical considerations are influencing their approach. One is national concern, centering in the tensions and problems among Americans of divergent racial and cultural backgrounds in the United States. The other is international concern, involving the relations between the United States and other nations of various racial and cultural backgrounds.

The kind of American history that provides no background, or only a superficial background, for an understanding of these national and international problems seems to me to be inadequate, even barren, and to miss a highly challenging opportunity in an age when our most urgent need is social awareness.

There are writers who feel that the United States as a "nation of nations" can offer a model for a future world nation of nations. Others suggest that if we have not succeeded in solving, or easing with measurable success, the social and cultural conflicts centering in immigrants and culture groups in one country, we may not prove precisely a model for the adjustment of conflicts in a world of differing peoples and cultures.

On the national side there are books like Louis Adamic's glorification of each racial or national group in the United States in terms of its claims and without the rigor of critical appraisal. Mr. Adamic presents a catalogic display counter—

by his own count an assortment of fifteen thousand separate facts. From this array one can of course select items that have much interest and color. But the interest is haphazard; the facts remain separate, often irrelevant, and even antiquarian.

No one would question the sincerity of the crusading author; his purposes are admirable; but he has not sounded the keynote of the nation of nations – the keynote that Walt Whitman, originator of the phrase, struck with bell-like tones. That note is to be rung, not by amassing the contributions of selected leaders, not by showering praise upon particular elements, not by heaping up counters with haphazard facts, but by coming to grips with the story of the millions of followers – the transition of the thirty millions of immigrants and their millions of descendants. In a word, the real story of nations is the story of "the people, yes."

For some years I have been suggesting approaches to this kind of history – the stocktaking of folk culture, the appraisal of cultural bridges, the use by the historian of unusual sources of information, such as the findings of the linguists who have studied the immigrant halfway house of language or the ballads and songs of those who sought the hither edge of free land; but these only hint at the wide range of possible materials and approaches.

The new immigration history is interested in the simple. It would accept, I believe, the view of John Mason Brown, who in a recent review of a popular California Norwegian immigrant play suggests that its success is "an encouraging indication of how as a people we have matured to the point of having a proper appreciation of the simple."

It is easy enough to apotheosize the simple, to extol the common man and celebrate his rise, with appropriate quotations from Lincoln. But the historian who interprets such easy phrases soon discovers that to appreciate the simple is far from being a simple matter. Folk-cultural history must use the widest variety of sources, both conventional and unconventional; there are many paths into the domain; and one's entry into it and understanding of it are facilitated by a readiness to turn to linguist, student of literature, anthropologist, scientist, expert on health and medicine, musician, critic of art, sociologist, economist, political scientist, and many another for aid in the task of seeing the story whole.

Folk-cultural history includes Old World backgrounds, the saga of migration, and the analysis of the causes and forces that set a folk movement into action. It is incomplete without the study of language, social customs, religion, press and school, intermarriage, politics in local, state, and national manifestations, social and economic institutions, folklore and folk music and folk arts, a creative literature that is sometimes buried in a foreign speech and yet strangely enough is American, daily work and play and thought as they find expression in a myriad ways, and the impact of culture upon culture in the jostling life of communities across the land.

Merely to list these objectives is to indicate that the road to the simple is highly complex.

The need of understanding the small, everyday elements in large movements was sensed by a Norwegian commentator as early as the mid-nineteenth century. Writing in 1853, he asserted that emigration proceeds "prosaically and unconsidered, like the great changes in the earth's surface, which are not studied until they appear as if they were the result of unexplained earthquakes or revolutionary changes," whereas in truth, he continued, the colossal movement of emigration is the "result of innumerable small and unappreciated causes, which exercise on human life the same disintegrating and transforming power that the chemical processes do on the earth's crust." In a word, he rejected the concept of catastrophic causation.

I have spoken of "the literature of the unlettered." Whether or not one accepts the word *literature* as used in this sense is of small importance. The fact remains that the folk were not inarticulate. They were, on the contrary, exceedingly articulate. But they have not snuggled into the bookshelves to any great extent; and meanwhile the leaders and their biographers have been definitely vocal. Any well-trained librarian can gather up an imposing shelf of their publications, works of the character of Riis's *Making of an American*, Pupin's *From Immigrant to Inventor*, Dorfman's *Thorstein Veblen and His America*, and scores of others.

These books are historically important; they have something to contribute to our understanding of national life. But when they are brought together, as they frequently are, under such placards as "Immigrant Contributions," "Out of the Melting Pot," and "I Am an American Week," something is lacking. And this is precisely what the newer historians are trying to supply: a library that catches up the life of the millions, that reveals the swirling forces that affected and gradually transformed the common life.

The pivot of the story of American immigrant contributions is the usual, not the uncommon. It is changing human life in succeeding generations, with the statistician's dots turned into Per Hansas, his lines metamorphosed into *My Antonía*, even Hyman Kaplan.

I AM not content to let my generalizations with respect to the appreciation of the simple stand without concrete illustration. Casting about for a case study, I come back to the immigrant letters which I have gathered up by the thousands and which, to my mind, illustrate the literature of the folk.

Let me open a bundle of such letters – "America letters" they were called – written in the 1860's and 1870's, sent across the seas to a home in Norway, there preserved during the intervening years, and ultimately placed in my hands.

These particular letters were written by an immigrant woman of the frontier. She came to America in 1862 and lived until 1878 in a pioneer settlement near Estherville, Iowa. That is all we should know about her if we did not possess the letters in which she recorded the experiences that to her spelled America.

The name of the letter writer does not matter. Think of her as one of hundreds of thousands, but for purposes of identification I shall call her Gro Svendsen, if only because that was in fact her name.

Gro's Old World home was in a valley called Hallingdal. She came to America as a bride, a girl of twenty-one blessed with a lively curiosity. Crossing the ocean on a sailing vessel, she made friends with the captain and crew and was given the "freedom of the ship." On Easter evening, she says, "there was dancing on the deck. We were urged to join in the merriment, but since we don't waltz and have no interest in learning, we shall have to manage to live without waltzing. Anyhow, these are not times for dancing."

Of her last glimpse of her native land, she says, "It's far in the distance like a blue mist—nothing more. I am heavy-hearted." But her thoughts were quickly distracted. A bird flew onto the deck and was killed by the captain's dog—Gro was heartbroken. "Poor little creature that sought haven with us, but instead was torn to pieces!" The dog whelped—Gro records her delight in its five puppies. Gro's mother-in-law had a baby—Gro took charge of it and held it when the captain baptized it.

A storm tosses the little vessel. Some of the passengers are in the grip of disease, die, and are buried at sea. An infant is buried one afternoon. "The ship's carpenter," writes Gro, "made the little coffin and filled it half full of sand. . . . We sang Who Knows When My Last Hour Cometh. . . . The sailors lowered the coffin. It was all strangely quiet and solemn."

Gro herself in the midst of troubles said, "We are all praying to Him, our true guide and skipper, our comfort in the hour of need. Without His help all captains, mates, sailors, and passengers are as nothing." Yet, she adds, "I think they are all of them good folk. They are most willing to answer my questions. You know that I am curious and interested in everything."

On one occasion when she was ill she called on the captain. "He gave me a drink of strong liquor to bolster me up," she writes. "I borrowed a medical book and took a look at his maps. I also looked over his library."

"Today is my husband's birthday," she wrote one May day. "He is twenty-two. Saw two whales and many grampers."

When Gro reached Quebec she was pleased to have a taste of wheat bread and a drink of fresh milk. After the long and difficult voyage she was charmed by the old Canadian city. She wrote of the sound of church bells ringing and described the spires of six Quebec churches – "shining like silver in the morning sun."

So began the journey to the interior, and there is little that fails to excite her interest and observation. She has a way of drawing sharply etched pictures – for example, of the loading onto a Great Lakes sailing vessel. "It was of utmost importance," she writes, "that the boxes and chests were strong, for I have never witnessed such rough and careless handling of goods. Because of this slipshod handling one chest was thrown into the water, the cover flew open, and the contents floated around. It held all the possessions of a very poor family. They lost everything. They had four children – no money, no clothes but those they were wearing, almost no food."

She stops at one town on the lake journey and disposes of it briefly as "sham and tinsel." She saw women "loaded down with trinkets," and remarked, "No moderation, no taste, vulgar." In Chicago the emigrants were surrounded by agents "who urged us to go here, there, everywhere. When no one paid any heed to them they became angry and ceased their prattle."

So, sometimes spending nights under the open sky, Gro and

her party made their way to St. Ansgar, Iowa. There the baby that had been born and baptized at sea died and was buried, and Gro tells the story in simple words.

She and her husband went farther west and settled near Estherville. They had not been long in America before her first child was born. At the first opportunity she sent a daguerreotype of her husband, child, and herself to her people overseas.

With her child in her arms, Gro attended an English school, "held at no great distance from here," she wrote. She had determined early that she would learn the language of her adopted country as quickly as possible. Her husband took land and became a farmer. Before long Gro herself took a position teaching school three days a week at twelve dollars a month, doing her heavier housework on the other days. Her boy grew, learned to say a few words, was smarter, she believed, than any other child in the community. "But one more thing," she wrote her father, "can you tell me how I am to get my boy vaccinated?" Later she thanked him for sending vaccine from Norway. One bottle was crushed, she said, the second damaged, the third intact.

"Life here," wrote Gro in one letter, "is altogether different from life in our mountain valley. One must readjust oneself and learn everything all over again, even to the preparation of food. We are told that the women in America have much leisure time, but I haven't yet met any woman who thought so."

A second son was born. And then, in 1864, Gro's husband marched away to the Civil War. She was left at home, she said, like a "lonely bird." The second son was baptized on the day her husband left for the war, and she insisted upon naming it Niels Olaus, the second name a form of her husband's name. By the device of the name she seems to have felt that in some mystic sense she kept him at home with her; she had a premonition that he would be killed in battle. He served in Sherman's army and returned home safely in August 1865. Gro summed up his military career in a memorable phrase: in seven thousand miles of traveling and marching, she said, "he has seen and heard and felt much." An "American soldier," she called him, and she at once had him get his picture taken in uniform in order to show the relatives abroad what an American soldier looked like.

After the war the family grew steadily larger, and its activities were faithfully and vividly reported in the letters. The oldest boy presently learned to handle oxen, hitch and unhitch them to the wagon, and, as Gro said, "do a number of things better than boys several years older than he is." Gro's interest in education was never-ending, and she constantly wrote about schools and reading. "Reading has been at a standstill this summer," she wrote in 1868. "Now, however, we have begun again, and in this district we are going to have three months of English school during the winter, with an American as a schoolteacher. The school is to be held in Erik Sando's house." She also took note of the fact that there was to be a school for several months conducted in Norwegian, with an old-country teacher in charge.

When Gro's fifth son was born, there was some difference of opinion between the father and the mother about naming him. The name, selected by Gro, was Albert Olai—the "Albert" in honor of "old Aslag," but she was unwilling to give the boy a name that would be so strange on American lips as "Aslag." When "Steffen" arrived in 1871, Gro wrote, "I thought I'd select a name that was a little more in conformity with American so that he wouldn't have to change it himself if he went out to live among the Americans."

The American tendency was also indicated when a pony on her farm was named Horace Greeley. Gro had a deep interest in names. In one letter she explained carefully the pronunciation and meaning of "Iowa." It meant, she said, the "beautiful land," and she told of its Indian derivation. She also explained how the village of Estherville got its name – in fact, she had herself, she said, entertained the American lady, Esther, for whom the village was named.

Gro liked to read and write; and in one of her letters she said that she was the "secretary" of the community – that is, she helped her neighbors to write letters. She lived so busy a life that much of her reading was done during her confinements. After the birth of her fifth child, she wrote, "I had thought of writing to you just as soon as I was strong enough, but the first two weeks after my son's birth I was in no position either to write or to read. . . . I think I must have strained my eyes by reading too much both now and in my former confinements. I have never been able to restrain myself when it came to reading. It is my greatest pleasure and I snatch every available moment for it." She subscribed to a frontier newspaper, and on several occasions wrote small contributions to it. She took a sharp interest in local government, which she found different from that at home. "The sheriff and the judge and all the rest," she wrote, "are elected in the same manner as the foreman at home."

Her children continued to attend both the English district school and the special Norwegian school, but Gro was impatient of their progress. "Had they been at home," she exclaimed, "I know well enough that they would have been much farther advanced." Her seven-year-old Ole, she reported in 1874, had the sharpest mind of all the children, and she was teaching him both English and Norwegian. Albert puzzled her, for he seemed remote and liked to ask "strange, disturbing little questions" on such subjects as creation. Another son she described in a phrase as the "actor of the family."

The first house of the family was small and ugly, Gro thought, but after the Civil War it was replaced by a much better one. A new one would have come sooner, she said, had not her husband gone to war.

She took a deep interest in the church but not in its barren controversies on theological questions. One pastor, she said, was exceptionally able and was more interested in human needs than in church controversies. When he left to become an editor, Gro expressed some doubt that his successor was a man of sufficient stature for the leadership of the church.

Of her farmer-veteran husband she always wrote proudly, and on one occasion she explained that he had held various positions of honor – constable, town trustee, and deacon in the church.

Gro's letters are filled with descriptions of the fruits of the field, the economy of a farm, American ways, methods of making butter and cheese, holidays, customs, taxes, prices, currency, names and nicknames, conditions of health and disease, land and trees and water, politics, prairie fires. "It is a strange and terrible sight to see all the fields a sea of fire," she wrote in one letter. "Quite often the scorching flames sweep everything along in their path – people, cattle, hay, fences. In dry weather, with a strong wind, the fire will race faster than the speediest horse."

She had a consuming interest in clothing and a sharp contempt for American clothes, particularly the American tendency to use cotton instead of wool and linen. "They get new clothes more often than we did at home," she wrote, "simply because the clothes don't last." When on one occasion her husband's parents presented her six boys with entire sets of new home-tailored suits, she was overjoyed.

In 1876 woe struck Gro's family – measles, the death of her daughter Sigri, and a scourge of grasshoppers that destroyed the crops. Gro, usually buoyant and dauntless, wore an air of resignation to fate. In all these happenings she saw the will of God. When the next year another girl was born, Gro named her Sigri and thought of her as a gift from God to replace the lost Sigri. Her depression continued for some time, but presently her interests revived. All six of her boys, she wrote proudly, were "going to English school every day" and were also "studying for confirmation at our pastor's." "So," she wrote, "we strive to do what we can to help them learn something useful both for life and eternity."

But she confessed discouragement as she thought of "our sacred duties as parents and the heavy responsibilities laid upon us." She lacked the means to do all she wanted to do for her children; she was discontented; and she voiced her discontent to her husband. She recorded his reply, a reply that embodied the philosophy of the immigrant pioneer: "We must try to do our best by them according to our own lights and our means and then entrust the rest to the Lord. . . ."

It was in the midst of such speculations about the duties of parents and concern over the future of her children that Gro had her tenth child. That was in 1878; she was then thirty-seven years old; she died and the stream of letters came to an end.

SIMPLE things, yes. But I wonder if these are not some of the basic elements in America's story. The books have much to say about the forces inherent in economics and politics. As one reads this sheaf of letters one quickly realizes that the most striking and notable thing about them is the hunger for education they reveal, a hunger centered by Gro upon her children. To her this was more than a cultural need; she saw it as the pathway to the larger opportunities offered by the New World.

Possibly Gro, whose name and experiences do not touch a *Nation of Nations*, might serve to sound the keynote that Mr. Adamic misses in his book. Ordeal is indeed part of her story; it is woven into her experience. But the significant thing is not ordeal. Nor is it fame or distinction. It is the sweep of life itself, the interplay of Old World heritage and American environment in a social and cultural transition that marked the lives of everyday people.

Gro was not unusual in education or in experience. If she

was in any respect untypical, it was by virtue of the grace and vividness and precision with which she put her thoughts and experiences down in black and white. If her writing is literature, it is part of the folk literature of America, the literature of the unlettered. Her letters are only one small segment of the masses of letters that I have collected in the valleys to which they were sent.

I have often regretted that I found the letters of Gro Svendsen too late for them to come under the eye of the novelist who wrote *Giants in the Earth*, but perhaps we do not need a Rölvaag to interpret Gro and millions of Americans like her. She is her own best interpreter.

THESE ARE AMERICAN FOLK . . .

Singing Immigrants

THANKS to the ballad collectors, we know about the singing cowboy – his troubles on the old Chisholm trail and his horror of being buried on the lone prairie, "where the rattlesnakes hiss, and the crow flies free." We have heard his grim warning that Comanche Bill "will lift off your hair on the dreary Black Hills," and we are familiar with his efforts to whoop, yell, and drive his "little dogies" from Texas to Wyoming.

So also we know of the singing French-Canadian voyageur, whose favorite chanson tells of crystal fountains, roundelays, nightingales, and a love lost all for an undelivered bunch of roses, and who, when not recalling those luckless roses, might recite, in rhythm with the strokes of his paddle, the glories of his bark canoe and of the rivers he traveled. We even know of the singing shanty boy whose ballads record lumbering in its golden age, the advance of the army of axes, the crash of falling pine, and the exploits of red-sashed lumberjacks.

The songs of cowboys, canoemen, and lumberjacks have been collected and made available to students of history and folklore. There has also been a wide interest in sailor chanteys, mountain minstrelsy, in American survivals of English and Scottish popular ballads, the songs of the Negroes, and the ballads of broad sections, notably the South.

But what of the singing immigrant? And the singing pioneer migrating to the West? The ballads of certain great popular movements, notably immigration and the American westward migration, have not attracted the attention they deserve. In both these fields the song materials are as extensive in quantity as they are diverse and rich in content.

The songs and ballads of migration present two contrasting themes: on the one side, that of hope, the promise of the West, the glory of the fresh start, romance, and triumph; on the other, that of deprivation, loneliness, futility, spiritual loss. It is the same contrast that stands out in the fiction of pioneering, with one school of writers portraying the westward movement as a glorious triumphant crusade, and another probing into its psychological aspects, picturing loss as well as gain. Both the hope and courage and the tragedy of spirit that so often accompanied pioneering are portrayed by O. E. Rölvaag in his novel, *Giants in the Earth;* and an interesting parallel from real life is presented in *A Son of the Middle Border.* Hamlin Garland's father was a Per Hansa in the flesh and his mother a Beret.

The theme of the elder Garland was that brave western marching song that catches so well the buoyancy of the early West:

> Cheer up, brothers, as we go,
> O'er the mountains, westward ho,
> Where herds of deer and buffalo
> Furnish the fare.
>
> CHORUS: Then o'er the hills in legions, boys,
> Fair freedom's star
> Points to the sunset regions, boys,
> Ha, ha, ha-ha!
>
> When we've wood and prairie land,
> Won by our toil,
> We'll reign like kings in fairy land,
> Lords of the soil!

That song, writes Hamlin Garland, was "a directing force in the lives of at least three generations of my pioneering race," and he tells us that its call continued to entice his father until, after ceaseless journeys, he found himself an old man, "snowbound on a trackless plain," his hopes largely frustrated, but still in spirit "the tiller of broad acres, the speculator hoping for a boom."

But the mother of the son of the Middle Border preferred a plaintive, questioning ballad in the form of a dialogue between husband and wife. The husband is ready to migrate:

Away to Wisconsin a journey I'll go,
For to double my fortune as other men do,
While here I must labor each day in the field
And the winter consumes all the summer doth yield.

But the wife does not agree:

Dear husband, I've noticed with a sorrowful heart
That you long have neglected your plow and your cart,
Your horses, sheep, cattle at random do run,
And your new Sunday jacket goes every day on.
Oh, stay on your farm and you'll suffer no loss,
For the stone that keeps rolling will gather no moss.

The husband is not convinced, however. He pleads with his wife to go, and holds out alluring prospects:

While you some fair lady and who knows but I
May be some rich governor long 'fore I die.

But the wife reminds him of realities and suggests the immense amount of labor that awaits them, and the heavy expense,

Your horses, sheep, cattle will all be to buy,
You will hardly get settled before you must die.

When the husband again promises riches and tempts his wife by adding, "We will feast on fat venison one half of the year," she advances an argument he cannot meet,

Oh, husband, remember those lands of delight
Are surrounded by Indians who murder by night.
Your house will be plundered and burnt to the ground
While your wife and your children lie mangled around.

The husband then gives in:

> Oh, wife, you've convinced me, I'll argue no more,
> I never once thought of your dying before,
> I love my dear children although they are small,
> And you, my dear wife, I love greatest of all.

And so they both join in a final refrain,

> We'll stay on the farm and we'll suffer no loss
> For the stone that keeps rolling will gather no moss.

Such ballads the elder Garland did not like, and we can readily understand why. The men of the westward movement preferred the faith of robust, optimistic songs, with challenges to the venturesome:

> Come, all you young men, who have a mind for to range,
> Into the western country, your station for to change;
> For seeking some new pleasure we'll all together go,
> And we'll settle on the banks of the pleasant Ohio.

This Ohio ballad tells of good lands, a veritable Garden of Eden, rivers full of fish, lofty sugar trees, and bountiful wild game. It discounts the Indian menace and closes with an appeal to fair maidens:

> Come all you fair maidens wherever you be,
> Come, join in with us, and rewarded you shall be;
> Girls, if you'll card, knit, and spin, we'll plough,
> reap, and sow,
> And we'll settle on the banks of the pleasant Ohio.
> Girls, if you'll card, knit, and spin, we'll plough,
> reap, and sow,
> And we'll fold you in our arms while the stormy wind
> doth blow.

Not less persuasive or insistent in its claims for an Eden was the early booster ballad, "El-a-noy":

'Way down upon the Wabash,
Sich land was never known;
If Adam had passed over it,
The soil he'd surely own;
He'd think it was the garden
He'd played in when a boy,

And straight pronounce it Eden,
In the State of El-a-noy.

CHORUS: Then move your family westward,
Good health you will enjoy,
And rise to wealth and honor
In the state of El-a-noy.

'Twas here the Queen of Sheba came,
With Solomon of old,
With an ass load of spices,
Pomegranates and fine gold;
And when she saw this lovely land,
Her heart was filled with joy,
Straightway she said, "I'd like to be
A Queen in El-a-noy."

She's bounded by the Wabash,
The Ohio and the Lakes,
She's crawfish in the swampy lands,
The milk-sick and the shakes;
But these are slight diversions
And take not from the joy
Of living in this garden land,
The State of El-a-noy.

At the end of the ballad is a tribute to the remarkable virtues of the people of Chicago, possibly introduced, Carl Sandburg suggests, by "some joker who felt challenged by the preceding verses":

Her men are all like Abelard,
Her women like Heloise;
All honest virtuous people,
For they live in El-a-noy.

Sometimes the praise of a region turns satirical, as in "Dakota Land":

We've reached the land of desert sweet,
Where nothing grows for man to eat.

Oh! Dakota land, sweet Dakota land,
As on thy fiery soil I stand,
I look across the plains
And wonder why it never rains
Till Gabriel blows his trumpet sound
And says the rain's just gone around.

Or in the ballad tribute to a county in the state of Nebraska:

Hurrah for Lane County, the land of the free,
The home of the grasshopper, bed-bug and flea,
I'll holler its praises, and sing of its fame,
While starving to death on a government claim.

How happy I am as I crawl into bed,
The rattle-snakes rattling a tune at my head,
While the gay little centipede, so void of all fear,
Crawls over my neck and into my ear.
And the gay little bed-bug so cheerful and bright,
He keeps me a-going two-thirds of the night.

Perhaps the choicest of the booster ballads is "Michigania," in which the people of New England were cordially invited to move out to the West:

Come all ye Yankee farmers who wish to change your lot,
Who've spunk enough to travel beyond your native spot,

And leave behind the village where Pa and Ma do
stay,
Come follow me, and settle in Michigania, –
Yea, yea, yea, in Michigania.

Then there's old Varmount, well, what d'ye think
of that?
To be sure, the gals are handsome, and the cattle very
fat:
But who among the mountains, 'mid clouds and snow,
would stay;
When he can buy a prairie in Michigania? –
Yea, yea, yea, in Michigania.

There is the land of Blue Laws, where deacons cut
your hair,
For fear your locks and tenets will not exactly
square,
Where beer that works on Sunday a penalty must pay,
While all is Scripture measure in Michigania, –
Yea, yea, yea, in Michigania.

Then there's the State of New York, where some are
very rich;
Themselves and a few others have dug a mighty
ditch,
To render it more easy for us to find the way,
And sail upon the waters to Michigania, –
Yea, yea, yea, in Michigania.

The ballad passes in review the claims of Ohio, Indiana, and Illinois, grants that these states are fine indeed, but concludes that they fall far below Michigania. It proceeds to chant the praises of particular Michigan localities and issues directions after the fashion of a guidebook:

If you had rather go to a place called Washtenaw,
You'll find the Huron lands the best you ever saw;

The ships sail to Ann Arbor right through La Plaisance Bay,
And touch at Ypsilanti in Michigania, –
Yea, yea, yea, in Michigania.

And at the end it reiterates its friendly, if somewhat selective, invitation to the East:

Then come, ye Yankee farmers, who've mettle hearts like me,
And elbow grease in plenty, to bow the forest tree,
Come, take a quarter section, and I'll be bound you'll say,
This country takes the rag off, this Michigania,
Yea, yea, yea, this Michigania.

It may be added that the lumberjacks, singing "Michigan - I - O," were somewhat less enthusiastic than the settlers who chanted Michigania. The shanty boys, in ballads of a type familiar among both railroad workers and cowboys, sang,

The grub the dogs would laugh at. Our beds were on the snow.
We'll see our wives and sweethearts, and tell them not to go
To that God-forsaken country called Michigan - I - O.

A ballad from pioneer times called "The Beauty of the West" celebrates the attractions of the North Star State. It tells of an Ohioan who sets out for the West in search of the Promised Land:

When first I left old Buckeye
Location for to find,
I heard of a distant country
In language most divine,
A land of milk and honey
And water of the best,
They called it Minnesota,
The Beauty of the West.

And when I came to Galena
I didn't like the town.
The streets they were too narrow,
And winding was the ground.
I stepped up to my tavern
And wrote upon my chest
"I'm bound for Minnesota,
The Beauty of the West."

He goes on to tell of boarding a steamer, the *Northern Belle*, which ascended the Mississippi and in due time landed him at Winona. "And when I got recruited," he sings, "A'rambling I did go, I wandered the state all over, I trailed it through and through." In the course of his wanderings he came to have a warm admiration for the girls of Minnesota, and he closes with a tribute to them:

The Gopher girls are cunning,
The Gopher girls are shy.
I'll marry me a Gopher girl
Or a bachelor I'll die.
I'll wear a stand-up collar,
Support a handsome wife,
And live in Minnesota
The balance of my life.

Another version of this ballad is called "The Lily of the West." It too tells of a traveler in search of pleasant lands in the West:

In Eighteen hundred and fifty-four, I left my native shore,
My worthy friends and native home, never to see them more.

The singer is emphatic in his advice:

Come all ye noble emigrants that are inclined to roam

Into this Western Country, to seek you out a home,
If you will be advised by me, I'll tell you what's
the best,
Come settle in Minnesota, the Lily of the West.

Oh, Michigan is not the place, nor Illinois the same,
The soil and climate can't compare in raising of the
Grain,
For here our noble Farmers raise abundance of the
best,
In this plentiful Minnesota, the Lily of the West.

WHILE native Americans were singing of the beauties and lilies of the West, the magic of the inland empire was making itself felt in every part of northern Europe. There was in process a new discovery of America brought home to the consciousness of the humblest farmer and laborer. This accompanied a mass migration, a phenomenon which was recorded and is reflected in sources of great variety.

The official statistics and government documents have been much used, not to say abused, by students, often without seeming awareness of the truth that immigrants were people. Impressive as the statistics are, they do not open doors to understanding the human interest and significance of the migration of millions of human beings to the New World from the Old. It is time for us to read the letters and narratives of the immigrant himself – to understand the impact of America upon European minds and of immigrants upon American life. Nor, if we would get at the inner history of the immigrant, should we neglect the ballads and songs and poems of the movement in which he figured. How rich such sources are may be suggested by some selections from the ballads and songs of the migration chiefly from one northern country, Norway.

To go or not to go was the question the European mulled over as he looked westward. His perplexity is mirrored in dialogue ballads not unlike those sung by Hamlin Garland's mother. Sometimes these songs were touched with satire hinting at an origin in the camp of the enemies of emigration. In a Norwegian ballad of 1844, for example, the first singer voices his discontent:

When pointed icicles cling to eaves
And snow goes whirling above the leaves,
When through my kitchen the cold winds blow,
To the Mississippi I fain would go.

And for a half-dozen stanzas he tells of empty granaries, stony meadows, and early frosts, and sighs for the delights of America, where

The grass springs up, turning into hay,
Your crop you cut in a single day,
Enough to last all the winter through –
America is the land for you!

But a second singer takes up the song, points out that there are two sides to everything on this earth, insists that

An Eden means more than lovely woods,
And more than stores filled with earthly goods,

and suggests that there is such a thing as unhappiness amid abundance. Will American prosperity last? he inquires:

The land you seek with a hopeful heart –
Its smiling Fortune may soon depart
And famine stalk through the countryside.
Alas, your Eden may not abide.

The singing debater then snaps his fingers at the rigors of Norse winters, explains that with the mountainsides covered with birch there is no difficulty about getting wood for the home fires. He says,

I find no reason why I should roam,
I make my climate in this, my home.

In a similar dialogue from 1846, one singer launches a song debate by declaring,

> I'll not stay on in this northern valley,
> I'll journey west to America,
> My strength and will I shall have to rally
> And go where best I can make my way.

Cheap land, light taxes, a chance to make a living with his hands: these are the things about America that most appeal to him. He warms to his theme as he criticizes the conditions in his own country:

> Of precious freedom they like to prattle,
> How we the people control the purse!
> But bureaucrats treat us like cattle,
> They fatten – we bear the poor man's curse.

Finally he is answered by a philosophical comrade, who explains that the indictment is sound in part, but that things are getting better, and then asks, somewhat plaintively,

> If in Wisconsin old worries languish,
> If fortune rolls all my debts away,
> What's the good, if my mind's in anguish?
> If longing gnaws me each bitter day?

As such debates went forward, many a song was written sternly adjuring people to remain at home. One from the 1860's asks the emigrant if he expects to find in America the same sun, the same summer, the same music in the streams:

> Nay, you will not find it so,
> This, your fate, you've bidden:
> Sun shut out by clouds below,
> Stars by black night hidden;
> Speech and custom of your past
> From your life you sever,
> Exiled you will be at last,
> Down the years forever.

And another used more than twenty stanzas to drive home this solemn warning:

> You little know what it is you're doing,
> You face a grim disillusionment.

Others took up the challenge, however:

> I'm moving west, come with me, you,
> Don't sit at home and wait;
> Come, let us bid this toil adieu,
> This grinding work we hate.
> For some, I know, it wins rich gains,
> The Philistine, of course,
> But we get nothing for our pains,
> Save only grim remorse.

Pilgrim ballads promptly answered the singers who gloomily foretold disillusionment and an end to sun and summer. Sometimes, as in a Swedish "America ballad" from the 1850's, the songs were marked by a gay irony that did not mask the essential truth underlying them:

> Brothers, we have far to go,
> O'er the salty waters,
> There we'll find America –
> Far across the ocean.
> Isn't that impossible?
> Ah, but it is wonderful!
> Pity that America
> Is so far away!
>
> Trees that strike their roots in earth
> Sweet they are as sugar,
> Country full of maidens –
> Lovely dolls they are, Sir.
>
> Chicks and ducks come raining down,
> Steaming hot and tender,

Fly upon your table,
Knives and forks in place, Sir.

The shining sun goes never down,
Everyone's your friend there,
Drinks your health in wine, Sir,
Takes you out to dine, Sir.
  Isn't that impossible?
  Ah, but it is wonderful!
  Pity that America
  Is so far away!

There was no stopping the movement. The people went, in ever-increasing thousands, until the poet Wergeland could sing, in plaintive tone,

Now with horror we recall
Scourge of Black Death reaping.
Over valley hangs a pall,
Through it fevers sweeping.
Gone the folk, the hearth is cold,
Desolate the farms of old.

But the victims of the America fever did not abandon hearth and home without singing farewells to friends and familiar things:

Farewell, valley that I cherish,
Farewell, church and trees and home,
Farewell parson, farewell parish,
Farewell kith and kin, my own,
Lovely gardens, walks of beauty, –
Would to God this were undone! –
Home, you stay me in my duty,
Calling, "Leave me not, my son!"

From the deep woods of Wisconsin in the 1840's came this goodbye, with its bitter undertone:

Blessed land, farewell forever,
Stern thy ways, severe thy hand,
Bread denied to fair endeavor,
Still I honor Motherland.
All things vanish – care and sorrow
Pass, their marks engraved on me,
Yet my soul fronts each tomorrow
Glad, refreshed with thought of thee.

And the emigrant woman, Kari, found it hard to leave her old spinning wheel:

Goodbye, my old comrade,
As now I must leave you,
My heart, it is breaking,
My going will grieve you.
No longer at night,
By the glow of the fire,
Shall we sit and gossip,
And know heart's desire.

These things all about us
Had roots in my heart,
Ah, now it is bleeding
And torn as we part.
But if I must choose
From these home things I cherish,
Ah, give me my cradle
To have till I perish.

In the ballads one can follow the emigrants to the waiting vessel and see them go aboard amid a "confusion of speech, song, laughter, weeping, and music."

The flapping sails swell with the breeze,
The ship glides out upon the seas,
Its pennons proudly flying.
Dim eyes the fading woodlands seek,

As valleys and the highest peak
Sink down, dissolving, dying.

Farewell, the final word leaps forth,
Storms shout it, sweeping from the North,
The call by waves is tendered
Offshore, in lapping melody,
They chant it like a threnody,
From mystic dreams remembered.

There are ballads celebrating the emigrant brigs, proud vessels that bore such names as the *Valhalla*, the *Achilles*, the *Preciosa*, and the *Superb*. Across the sea they went to New York or Quebec, then to the West Indies, then back by way of England, to start the triangle again.

While emigrants sailed out to the West, many Norwegians somehow managed to resist the lure, but not without singing explanations of why they stayed at home. One Norseman refused to join a party of prospective gold hunters who bought a vessel and sailed from western Norway for California by way of South America – sailed, be it noted, only after the entire party had joined in two songs, one of hope and anticipation, one of farewell to snow-capped mountains and to the beauty and music of native waterfalls. The stay-at-home did not deny that California was a land of glory:

O El Dorado! Lovely, golden name!
It rings upon the ears like ducats clinking!
Search all the world, no country, to my thinking,
Will yield such peace, such happiness, such fame.
Ah, there the very trees bear fruit of gold,
And golden doubloons fill the mouths of fishes,
The ears of corn are golden, too, I'm told,
One gathers golden flowers, if one wishes.

He appreciated the ease of getting supplies for one's table in the Far West, where, he sang,

The fields yield crops without a touch of rake,
Don't doubt my word, you know I'd never lie, son.
Suppose you'd like to eat a juicy steak –
That's easy, hurl your lasso at a bison.

But there were disadvantages, and these the singer carefully points out:

It's true you're more than apt to lose your life,
The Redskins, they will scalp you if they catch you,
And if they don't a Yankee's sure to snatch you
And neatly carve you with his bowie knife.

And the song maker at the end gives his final judgment:

So let the West retain its precious gold,
In this, my hut, contentment casts no shadow,
In peace and song I find a joy untold,
This haven is my lasting El Dorado.

Others remained behind in a long wait, among them Wergeland's Sigrid, an anticipation of Solveig in Ibsen's *Peer Gynt*:

Here mid these bleak walls,
Where yet I see him everywhere,
Here will I live,
Here will I cherish my love,
Here will I pledge each day
My faith to my beloved.

Here will I wait for him
Till I am old and wrinkled:
For he will come.
The wild winds carried him away,
The winds will bring him back.

Yet others, also remaining behind, flung taunts at the emigrants in such songs as this,

O many a fool sailed across the sea
To Yankeeland to seek for riches,
But back he came full of misery,
With nary a shilling in his breeches.
For go you East, Sir, or go you West,
Your northland home still will be the best.
There is my pride
And there with my bride
In peace I want to live forever.

Meanwhile, fools or not, the emigrants sailed out into what Jonas Lie called the "wilderness of waters," pausing even in mid-ocean to sing of hope mingled with nostalgia. The nostalgic note is sounded over and over again in songs and ballads, and it reminds one of the forlorn Beret in *Giants in the Earth*. Sometimes the songs tell of strength from pain, as in an "Evening Prayer on the Atlantic":

The night has fallen, and breezes of evening
Hurry our ship toward its westerly goal,
But the ties that bind me to home and to homeland
Fire my courage and strengthen my soul.

A Swedish emigrant ballad from the 1850's found no similar consolation as it told of the breaking of home ties:

We sold our home and then we started
On our journey far,
Like birds that fly away
Under summer's waning star.
Oh, they'll come flying back
When the spring is in the air,
But we shall never see again
Our native land so fair.

The nostalgia lessened with time, and then the songs told of experiences in America – hardships, suffering, and frustration, yes, but also achievement, rewards, and success. A ballad from the 1870's reviews the whole story, opening with the traditional "Come, ye Norsemen from mountain and valley," and rehearsing difficulties of language, land selection, and adjustment to a new life. It was no easy thing for the immigrant to learn English:

> The new speech, it was tough to acquire,
> And we often got into a mess.
> When a Yankee your name would inquire,
> You'd solemnly answer him, "Yes."

And in the matter of choosing land there was much to learn:

> We had come from a national quarry
> And of land claims we didn't know beans,
> So the Yankee would settle the prairie,
> While we clung to the woods and the streams.

But the general tone of this homely ballad is one of satisfaction as it tells of friendly neighbors, good farms, schools, churches, and a gradual adaptation to the new life:

> So now as old settlers they hail us –
> Things have gone, on the whole, very well.
> No longer do troubles assail us –
> And our story we're happy to tell.

An interesting aspect of the emigrant ballads is the faithfulness with which they reflect special trends and episodes: for example, the adventures of immigrants who sought fortunes in the gold mines of the West, the reactions of participants in Norway's labor movement of the 1850's, and the story of the paternalistic colony established by the violinist, Ole Bull, in Pennsylvania in the early 1850's.

The idealistic Ole Bull stunned his countrymen when he bought, or thought he bought, a hundred and twenty thousand acres of land in Potter County, Pennsylvania, and projected the colony of New Norway, centered about the town of Oleana. He invited settlers and busied himself with a dozen magnificent schemes. Naturally there was a burst of songs and ballads about this marvelous development. Jubilant songs they were.

Come, hail the Music Master,
Hurrah for Ole Bull!
To cheats he's brought disaster,
Their cup of woe is full.
New Norway he is founding,
A gift to every man,
So come, your shouts resounding,
With freedom in the van.

Another ballad praised Ole Bull as a friend of the working class:

Good men of Norway, strong of arm,
If fortune's barbs have torn you,
Behold a friend whose heart is warm,
A man who will not scorn you.
Better he than gold or fame!
Ole Bull – yes, that's his name!

He knows that here are grief and pain,
Your burdens he would lighten.
Freedom, bread – these you will gain –
Your future he will brighten.
Better he than gold or fame!
You know him – Ole Bull's his name!

Alas, Oleana proved a bubble. The violinist had fallen into the hands of land speculators; cheats had brought disaster to him, not he to them; the colonists knew nothing but disillusionment; and the whole grand scheme went to pieces. Precisely at the climax, in 1853, the rollicking ballad of "Oleana," by Ditmar Meidell, appeared. It was a satirical song, with

Land-of-Cockaigne stanzas, that was sung for two generations on both sides of the Atlantic.*

I'm off to Oleana, I'm turning from my doorway,
No chains for me, I'll say goodbye to slavery in
  Norway.
  Ole – Ole – Ole – oh! Oleana!
  Ole – Ole – Ole – oh! Oleana!

They give you land for nothing in jolly Oleana,
And grain comes leaping from the ground in floods
  of golden manna.

The grain it does the threshing, it pours into the sack,
  Sir,
And so you take a quiet nap a-stretching on your
  back, Sir.

The crops they are gigantic, potatoes are immense, Sir,
You make a quart of whisky from each one without
  expense, Sir.

And ale as strong and sweet as the best you've
  ever tasted,
It's running in the foamy creek, where most of it is
  wasted.

The salmon they are playing, and leaping in the
  brook, Sir,
They hop into the kettle, put the cover on and cook,
  Sir.

And little roasted piggies, with manners quite demure,
  Sir,

*For a fuller account of Oleana, with music, see Theodore C. Blegen and Martin B. Ruud, *Norwegian Emigrant Songs and Ballads* (Minneapolis, 1936), 187–98. My verse translation, here presented in full, is reprinted from *Norwegian-American Studies and Records*, 14:117–21; and I have also published it in *Common Ground*, 5:73–77 (Autumn 1944).

They ask you, Will you have some ham? And then
you say, Why, sure, Sir.

The cows are most obliging, their milk they put in
pails, Sir,
They make your cheese and butter with a skill that
never fails, Sir.

The bull he is the master, his calves he likes to boss,
Sir,
He beats them when they loaf about, he's never at
a loss, Sir.

The calves are very helpful, themselves they skin
and kill, Sir,
They turn into a tasty roast before you drink your
fill, Sir.

The hens lay eggs colossal, so big and round and
fine, Sir,
The roosters act like eight-day clocks, they always
tell the time, Sir.

And cakes come raining down, Sir, with cholera
frosting coated,
They're nice and rich and sweet, good Lord, you eat
them till you're bloated.

And all night long the sun shines, it always keeps
a'glowing,
It gives you eyes just like a cat's, to see where you
are going.

The moon is also beaming, it's always full,
I vow, Sir,
A bottle for a telescope, I'm looking at it now, Sir.

Two dollars for carousing they give each day, and
more, Sir,

For if you're good and lazy, they will even give
you four, Sir.

Support your wife and kids? Why, the county pays
for that, Sir,
You'd slap officials down and out if they should leave
you flat, Sir.

And if you've any bastards, you're freed of their
support, Sir,
As you can guess since I am spinning verses for your
sport, Sir.

You walk about in velvet, with silver buttons bright,
Sir,
You puff away at meerschaum pipes, your women
pack them tight, Sir.

The dear old ladies struggle, and sweat for us, and
labor,
And if they're cross, they spank themselves, they
do it as a favor.

And so we play the fiddle, and all of us are glad, Sir,
We dance a merry polka, boys, and that is not so bad,
Sir.

I'm off to Oleana, to lead a life of pleasure,
A beggar here, a count out there, with riches in
full measure.

I'm coming, Oleana, I've left my native doorway,
I've made my choice, I've said goodbye to slavery
in Norway.
Ole – Ole – Ole – oh! Oleana!
Ole – Ole – Ole – oh! Oleana!

There were some well-known poets among the makers of the ballads and songs of immigration and westward migration, but for the most part they are of undistinguished origin, humble products of a folk movement. For that very reason they have the tang of things earthy. They are close to the soil, to elemental things, to the human heart; and with the earthy tang goes an unmistakable authenticity.

Of their historical interest these illustrations can leave one in no doubt. The domain of the songs and ballads is that of social and economic history and of folk literature, one in which the historian interpreting a great human movement can make common cause with students of literature, language, folklore, music, and other fundamental manifestations of the human spirit.

The America Book

AS WE look back to 1837, across a gulf of a century, we seem to see "through a glass, darkly." Schoolbook memories stir our minds, however, and we discern a few outlines and forms: Andrew Jackson, gaunt and stern-eyed, emerging from the White House to make way for Martin Van Buren; the collapse of banks and business in a financial panic; and across the waters a girl of eighteen ascending the throne of England, opening an era that was to bear her name. But all this is far in the past – cold print and quaint pictures, remote from modern life.

Can we bring the pictures to life, dispel the dimness, and know the men and women of a hundred years ago, who tasted joy, knew sorrow, worked, played, died?

If we think of the *people*, the mists may lift a little. And our vision will gain clearness if we remember the flow of life from that day to this – our lives projected from those of our parents, theirs from our grandparents. Only a few stages, and we are back to the world of a century ago. A single life may bind ten decades together. In 1937 newspapers told of a woman, living then, who was a child in 1837. Call 1837 remote if you will, but one human heart continued to beat through all that incredible space of a century.

But if we really would pierce the mists of time, we must remember that the life of a hundred years ago left its imprints in records and its living influence upon its posterity. We are challenged to know the records and to understand the influence, to use the second sight of history.

That second sight enables us to reconstruct a few scenes in one story from a hundred years ago. The first scene is neither

White House nor palace, but a little sailing vessel in the middle of the Atlantic. Its name was the *Aegir*, its captain, Christian K. Behrens, and on board were eighty-four Norwegian emigrants. They were almost all farmers who had sold their farms in western Norway, packed their chests and trunks, and assembled at old Bergen, from which, on April 7, 1837, they set sail for New York and the New World, intending to go to a wonderful place called "Illinois" far out in the West, where some of their pioneering countrymen had already settled.

There were rumblings of economic and social discontent in the old country. Ever since Cleng Peerson and the sloopfolk had gone to America in the 1820's, rumors and reports of the marvels of life in the United States had been spreading. Now, in the 1830's, the unrest exploded into decision and departure. Whole shiploads of people set out for the New World.

The emigrants on the *Aegir* were not sailors, and many of them promptly got seasick. But they soon grew accustomed to the salt air and the pitching of the vessel, and they had a merry time on board. A contemporary newspaper account of their voyage tells of their experiences after the seasickness was over:

"With its passing, all anxiety seemed to disappear. Farmers who had never before seen the ocean saw that it was calm, lost all fear of its terrors, and were confident that the ship was sailing on toward milder regions. The fiddle was brought out, and every evening sailors and young people danced to it with lusty abandon until the captain was forced to ask them to give it up, since the ballroom floor (the deck) was being seriously damaged by the huge nails in the soles of the dancing slippers of the young gallants and their ladies; unless they were willing to dance in their stocking feet."

On May 8 an English ship, the *Barelto*, crashed into the *Aegir* broadside, and for a time it looked as if the emigrant vessel would go down. But the damage was soon repaired, and it sailed on. And on May 17, the terrors of the collision forgotten, all the emigrants celebrated the Norwegian national holiday. At dawn there was a salvo of cannon. Everybody wore his best clothes, and in the morning a play was performed. Both the title and the text are unknown to us, but we are told that the play was about the land the emigrants had left and also about "the hopes that smiled to them from the shore whither they were sailing." At noon there was a banquet, and toasts were drunk to the Seventeenth of May, to the Fatherland, to Liberty, and to the King and his son. And then a song, composed for the occasion, was sung, the earliest of the known Norwegian emigrant ballads:

Beyond the surge of the stormy deep,
The mists hide Norway's rocky shore,
But longings rise, their tryst to keep
With magic forests known of yore,
Where whistling spruce and glaciers' boom
Are harmonies to Norway's son.

Though destiny, as Leif and Björn,
Call northern son to alien West,
Yet will his heart in mem'ry turn
To native mountains loved the best.
As longs the heart of a lone son
To his loved home once more to come.

This mid-Atlantic song of 1837 was composed by the young, talented, and trusted leader of the emigrant group, Ole Rynning. Born in the miraculous year of 1809 which gave Lincoln to the world, by what strange destiny was he now aboard the *Aegir* journeying toward the state of Lincoln?

Rynning had abandoned the paths then customarily followed by young Norwegians of birth and education. His father, Jens Rynning, was a prominent clergyman of the Norwegian state church, minister for more than thirty years in the parish of Snaasen; and young Rynning, given every educational advantage – private tutors and training in the national university – had the road to success in church or state open to him. Yet for some reason he turned his back on all that and threw in his lot with humble farmers who dared the venture of the New World.

He doubtless had special personal motives, but the records make it clear that Rynning, democratic by instinct and critical of the state church of which his father was a typical member, had other and higher motives too. Deeply in sympathy with the farming and laboring classes of Norway and keenly aware of their problems, he saw emigration and America as the solution and was determined to join and to help a movement that was in league with the future. "Nothing," said one of his friends, "could shake his belief that America would become a place of refuge for the masses of people in Europe who toiled under the burdens of poverty."

This man's fiber is revealed in the second scene of our story – out in the Illinois country, in the Beaver Creek settlement, some seventy miles south of Chicago. The *Aegir* had duly arrived at New York on June 9, just two months and two days after it sailed out of Bergen harbor. The immigrants had spent a week in New York, then gone by steamer on the Hudson to Albany, continued by boat on the Erie Canal to Buffalo, and there caught a vessel that took them to Detroit. After a wait of five days there, they found places on a crowded boat that carried them down to Chicago, then an infant city just emerging from village status.

Here a hard blow fell upon the party. All this time their intention had been to proceed to Cleng Peerson's colony in the Fox River Valley, but scarcely had they reached Chicago when they heard unfavorable reports about the Fox River country. On no account must they go there.

As they gave up their cherished plans, discouragement settled upon many of the immigrants. Fox River had been the goal they had crossed half a world to reach; and here they were in a strange country, their plans defeated. But, wrote one of them, in this situation the "greatness of Ole Rynning's spirit was revealed." He comforted those in despair, counseled those in doubt, calmed everyone with his own composure and courage. The upshot of it all was that, after a committee had gone down to investigate the Beaver Creek region, oxen and wagons were bought, and most of the group, led by Rynning, went to that place.

So the immigrants settled in the Illinois country, building log houses, grappling with hardships, and meeting the sacrifices of a first year of pioneering in a strange land.

Throughout this winter of 1837–38 Rynning was thinking about the problems and needs of his countrymen in Norway. "A great and good idea," wrote his friend Ansten Nattestad, "formed the central point of all his thinking. He hoped to be able to provide the poor, oppressed Norwegian workman a happier home on this side of the sea, and to realize this wish he shunned no sacrifice, endured the greatest exertions, and was patient through misunderstandings, disappointments, and loss."

An interesting thing happened that winter in Beaver Creek, and Nattestad, who was there with Rynning, gives us the setting. He explains that Rynning was contented with little "and was remarkably patient under the greatest sufferings." And, he continues, "I well remember one time when he came home from a long exploring expedition. Frost had set in during his absence. The ice on the swamps and the crusts of snow cut his boots. He finally reached the colony, but his feet were frozen and lacerated. They presented a terrible sight, and we all thought he would be a cripple for life."

It was while in this condition, crippled and confined to his bed, that Ole Rynning wrote the manuscript of his book, a *True Account of America for the Information and Help of Peasant and Commoner*. He called in his neighbors as he finished each chapter so that he might read it aloud to them and profit by their criticisms. The man rose above personal misfortune and local circumstance, took a broad and fair-minded view of America and its conditions, and addressed himself to his fellow men of the Old World. In his preface, signed on February 13, 1838, he stated that his purpose was "to answer every question that I myself raised, to make clear every point in regard to which I observed that people were in ignorance, and to refute the false reports which came to my ears, partly before my departure from Norway and partly after my arrival here."

Before looking into that book, we must picture a third scene in our story. This time the hero is Ansten Nattestad, for in the spring of 1838, taking Rynning's manuscript with him, he set out for Norway, going down the Mississippi to New Orleans and sailing by way of Liverpool. He then crossed the North Sea to Norway, published Rynning's book at Christiania late in 1838, and found himself looked upon as a sort of Marco Polo. Some people traveled as far as a hundred and forty miles to see him and talk with him about the United States.

Rynning's book was read with great interest in many parts of Norway. "The America Book," people called it. "Many who were scarcely able to read," said one immigrant, "began in earnest to practice in the America-book." A second edition came out in 1839, and it was soon reprinted in Sweden, so that in a sense it became the America Book for the Scandinavian North. There can be no doubt that this compact, informative little volume, crammed with shrewd observation and sound sense, played an influential role in the development of early Norwegian migration to America. The America Book assures Rynning a secure place among American immigrant leaders.

In thirteen short and concise chapters, each headed by a definite question or group of questions, Rynning takes up such topics as the climate, soil, and products of America; the cost of land and provisions; the nature of the American government; religious conditions in the New World; the problems of language and education; the story of the earlier pioneers from Norway; and general prospects for immigrants. With quiet common sense he disposes of absurd rumors and silly assertions that had been given currency in Norway by enemies of emigration. He praises the freedom and equality of America, but denounces the slavery system of the South. And he closes with a chapter of advice about all the details of the journey to America: vessels, routes, food and supplies, medicines, and the like.

Unhappily, a fourteenth chapter in Rynning's manuscript, though written, was never printed. It was a chapter criticizing the Norwegian state church ministers for intolerance and for inactivity in advancing the welfare of the people in economic and educational matters. This chapter was read by a state church minister who did not like it and therefore threw it out. Today we honor the courage of Rynning in writing the chapter and regard the minister who excised it as a narrow-minded zealot.

That Rynning had foresight is clear when we read his prediction of the Civil War, written at his Beaver Creek cabin twenty-three years before that war came. After a vigorous description of the slavery system, Rynning wrote, "The northern states try in every Congress to get the slave trade abolished in the southern states; but as the latter always oppose these efforts, and appeal to their right to settle their internal affairs themselves, there will in all likelihood come either a separation between the northern and southern states, or else bloody civil disputes."

In another chapter Rynning assures his Norwegian countrymen that America is not a land of heathens. "Every one can believe as he wishes," he writes, "and worship God in the manner which he believes to be right, but he must not persecute any one for holding another faith." After describing the nature of the American national government, he adds, "For the comfort of the faint-hearted I can, therefore, declare with truth that in America, as in Norway, there are laws, government, and authorities. But everything is designed to maintain the natural freedom and equality of men."

He has a word to say in yet another chapter about the status of women in America. "Women are respected and honored far more than is the case among the common people in Norway," he writes, and then adds, somewhat slyly, "So far as I know, only two or three Norwegian girls have been married to Americans, and I do not believe that they have made particularly good matches. But there are many Norwegian bachelors who would prefer to marry Norwegian girls if they could." He mentions two classes who must not come to America. These are drunkards, "who will be detested, and will soon perish miserably," and "those who neither can work nor have sufficient money to carry on a business."

Several Norwegians who emigrated to America in 1839 brought guns or rifles with them. They had read this passage in Rynning: "If a settler is furnished with a good rifle and knows how to use it, he does not have to buy meat during the first two years. A good rifle costs from fifteen to twenty dollars. The chief wild animals are deer, prairie chickens, turkeys, ducks, and wild geese."

Rynning did not want immigrants to starve during the voyage. He advised them to include among their provisions pork, dried meat, salted meat, dried herring, smoked herring, dried fish, butter, cheese, primost, milk, beer, flour, peas, cereals, potatoes, rye rusks, coffee, tea, and sugar. There is much specific information about prices and wages and a variety of other subjects, precisely the kind of information needed by prospective immigrants, information of a sort that warranted Professor Edward Channing's characterization of the book as "the work of a keen observer." Rynning's account did in fact present a true picture of American conditions to the common people of Norway, and it is not surprising that its circle of influence widened.

Ansten Nattestad, the immigrant Marco Polo, prepared to lead a shipload of emigrants to the United States. "I remained in Numedal throughout the winter and until the following spring," he wrote. "The report of my return spread like wildfire through the land, and an incredible number of people came to me to hear news from America." With what authority could not the man speak who had himself made the long journey and with his own eyes viewed the wonderland of the West! One Norwegian who saw Nattestad wrote, "Ministers and bailiffs tried to frighten us with terrible tales about the dreadful sea monsters, and about man-eating wild animals in the new world; but when Ansten Nattestad had said Yes and Amen to Rynning's Account, all fears and doubts were removed."

Nattestad's "Amen" was made the more hearty when in 1839 he published a second book, this one made up from the simple diary that his brother Ole Nattestad had kept on his journey to America in 1837. This diary, recording the everyday details of emigration, gives a favorable picture of the New World but reminds emigrants that "one must first taste the bitter before he can drink the sweet."

The final scene in this immigrant drama has its setting at Beaver Creek. Ole Rynning regained his health and the use of his feet and once more took up his work among the colonists. But the misfortune of winter was as nothing in comparison with the disaster of spring and summer. Not Utopia, not happiness and golden prosperity, but wet lands, the deadly attack of malaria, sickness, despair, and for many a miserable death: these were the fate of the colonists. We have glimpses of the leader, Ole Rynning, comforting the sorrowing, helping those in distress, clinging to his belief in America.

Then came a quick ending. The university-trained scholar worked for a month that summer of 1838 on the Illinois

Canal, spade in hand, blistered, exposed to the elements. The dread malaria attacked him, and close on its heels came typhoid. In September, still under thirty years of age, he died.

The circumstances of his burial are reported to us by the founder of St. Olaf College, B. J. Muus, himself a nephew of Rynning, and he had the tale from the lips of a resident of Beaver Creek who knew Rynning. Only one person in the colony was well when Rynning died. This man went "out on the prairie and chopped down an oak and made a sort of coffin of it. His brother helped him to get the dead body into the coffin and then they hauled it out on the prairie and buried it." The grave went unmarked.

Many of the other colonists died, and the Beaver Creek settlement broke up, some of the survivors fleeing to the Fox River settlement. The last of the settlers to leave was one Mons Aadland, who in 1840 managed to exchange his farm for a small herd of cattle and removed to Wisconsin. Few of the settlers had been able to sell their land, however. They simply abandoned it. "Only the empty log houses remained," we are told, "like silent witnesses to the terrors of the scourge, and afforded a dismal sight to the lonely wanderer who ventured within these domains."

The scenes fade away, and the story seems to end in stark tragedy, like a Greek drama. But that is only in the seeming, for Ole Rynning's voice was not stilled when the log coffin was lowered into prairie soil. His book was an "articulate audible voice" to a generation of his own people, and it sounds across the decades to our ears. Tragic was the fate of the immigrants who sailed so blithely on the *Aegir*, but the Emersonian compensation of gain for loss went with the tragedy. The courage and patience and sacrifice of Rynning and his fellow pioneers were a contribution to America. They are a part of our heritage, caught up in the flow of life, and we may look back to 1837 with a sense of realities in an unbroken unity of past and present.

Immigrant Marthas

THOUGH much is said in general terms about the role of women in the making of America, historians have tended to leave to novelists the important task of exploiting this theme in detail. Even in the history of the westward movement little place has been given to the achievements and influence of women, though Arthur M. Schlesinger has said that "no proper conception of the subjugation of the wilderness by the forces of civilization can be gained without an appreciation of the part that the women pioneers played."

The preoccupation of American historians with political development and their comparative neglect, until recently, of the domain of social history account in part for the "pall of silence" they have permitted to rest over the role of women in the American epic. Or perhaps there has been a scarcity of contemporary documents yielding the information necessary for a realistic handling of the subject.

The three documents herewith published date respectively from 1847, 1850, and 1866. They are translations of letters written by three Norwegian immigrant women in America to relatives in Norway. I found the originals during the winter of 1928–29 while I was engaged in a search for materials in Norway bearing on American history. They constitute a small contribution to the understanding of the part of immigrant women in the conquest of the wilderness and in the building of the mid-continental domain. They are simple documents, written with no art save that which the simplicity of truth stamps upon them. For that very reason, however, they possess a peculiar value as authentic records of the experiences of pioneer women.

Jannicke Sæhle, who tells of her emigration from Norway in 1847, emerges from the record as a sprightly girl, cheerful, brave, with a sense of humor, undaunted by the experience of making her own way in the New World thousands of miles away from her old home. She evinces keen enjoyment of the American scene and proves herself alert and adaptable. She journeys to America as a maid, or caretaker, for an emigrant family, and is paid by receiving the products of three acres of land for a period of three years. In Wisconsin she leaves a log cabin at Koshkonong Prairie and makes her way to Madison, where she receives employment at wages of one dollar a week, with prospects of rising to a dollar and a quarter and eventually to the munificent figure of a dollar and a half.

The experience of Henrietta Jessen, an emigrant of 1849, is much harder than that of Jannicke Sæhle. She comes to America as a wife and mother. Her heart is torn by homesickness, but she comforts herself with thoughts of the future. Her husband is taken seriously ill, and for seven weeks, while nursing him and caring for him, she does not lay off her clothes for sleep. She is sustained by faith in God, by her own courage, and by her hopes for her children. She chronicles in simple language the friendliness and helpfulness of other immigrants to her in her trials. She does not neglect to discuss the prospects for Norwegians planning to come to America, and she offers sound advice. From her letter one gets a clearly etched portrait of a brave woman, worthy of the best traditions of the women of the American frontier.

Over the grave of Guri Endreson stands a monument erected by the state of Minnesota in commemoration of her heroism at the time of the Sioux Massacre in 1862. The story of what she did after an attacking party of Indians had slaughtered her husband and one son, wounded another son, and carried off two of her daughters as captives has been told many times and is familiar to thousands of people. They know how she aided two severely wounded men from a settler's cabin to an ox-drawn wagon, after dressing their wounds and attending to their wants; then started with them, her small daughter, and her wounded son for Forest City, about thirty miles distant; guarded the party through an all-night vigil; and doggedly pushed on the next day until the haven of safety was reached.

Though much has been published about these details in the saga of this frontier heroine, her own story as told to her people in Norway has not been known. Many have regarded her as one of those inarticulate spirits who have left a legacy of courage expressed in action alone. Guri Endreson did write her story—but she waited four years, and then set it down in the form of a letter to her relatives dwelling thousands of miles away in a lonely district of western Norway. The letter was treasured and preserved in the family circle.

A few discrepancies between Guri Endreson's own narrative and the well-known tale of her deeds will be apparent, and the reader will be struck by her omissions. Her story, it must be remembered, is written in the language of simplicity and sorrow and comes from a woman who would perhaps naturally understate or avoid mention of her own services to other people. But the letter supplies something that has been lacking from the familiar tale: a picture of a very human woman, with no inkling that she is a heroine, sustained in her sorrow by a pious faith in God, taking up the tasks of life again, retaining ownership of her land with a view to resumption of farming, and looking with courage to the future.

For those who like to interpret human actions in terms of heroism, the spectacle of Guri Endreson four years after her harrowing Sioux War experience, making two hundred and thirty pounds of butter from the summer product of her cows, writing encouragingly about America to her daughter in Norway, and holding aloft the promise of her faith, is not less impressive than that of the same woman helping others in the

August days of 1862, when she was carrying the burden of fresh agony. Her letter is of interest not only for the light it sheds upon the character of Guri Endreson but also for its picture of the resumption of normal conditions in the area that had been visited by the horrors of the Sioux Massacre.

It should be noted that the surname of the Endresons was Rosseland. Lars Endreson Rosseland was the full name of Guri's husband. She signs her own name simply as "Guri Olsdatter."

Jannicke Sæhle to Johannes Sæhle, September 28, 1847

KOSHKONONG PRAIRIE, September 28, 1847

Dear Brother:

It seems to me that in my last letter to you, written from my former home in the Old World, I hoped that from my new home in the New World I should be able to write to you with even greater happiness and contentment, and God has fulfilled this wish. As I wrote you, we did not leave our dear native land until April 24, as we had to remain eight days at Holmen in Sandvigen waiting for a number of passengers who had not yet arrived.

We sailed in the morning at seven o'clock, with fair wind and weather, and we had lost sight of the shores of our dear fatherland by half-past three, when the pilot left us. I remained on deck until six o'clock in the evening; as the wind was sharp and cold I was not able to stay there any longer, but had to go down to the hold, where general vomiting had been going on for a long time. And after five minutes my turn came, also, to contribute my share to the Atlantic Ocean.

Still, what can I say? Not in all eternity can I sufficiently thank God, for the America journey was not for me what it was for many others. It seems now like a faint dream to me and as if through God's providential care I had been carried in protecting arms, for I was sick only four days, and even on these I went on deck now and then. I was not afraid, but slept just as peacefully as I had in the little room that I so recently had left behind. My traveling companions were just as lucky as I, but a number of passengers had to keep to their beds nearly the whole journey, for the weather was stormy almost the entire voyage and besides, it was so cold that there were few days when we could remain on deck for the whole day. But the wind had a good effect on conditions in the hold, which was well aired, and warmer weather would have been less desirable. So, as we went steadily forward we hoped for the best, and our hopes were not disappointed.

By the fourteenth of May we had already reached the Banks, where the captain and the skipper caught nine great cod, and for dinner on the Seventeenth of May we ate fish, though it was such a stormy day that we had to steady our plates with our hands, and not infrequently we were jerked backwards with our plates in our hands.

In naming the skipper I can greet you from an old friend of our younger days, John Johannessen, who used to be in the service of Captain Fischer and once worked in his little fishing vessel. He is now much more alert as a seaman and looks much better than in the old days, but he is plagued by a long-standing malaria which he cannot get rid of, despite all the medicines which he is said to have used. His wife is dead. He has one married and three unmarried daughters. This was his fourth trip to this country – and this one the fastest.

As the wind continued favorable, the general opinion was that we would reach Staten Island, one mile from New York, by Whitsunday; but late in the evening before Whitsunday there came a calm, and a thick fog covered everything, so that it was necessary to keep up a constant ringing and shooting in case other sailing vessels should be in the vicinity. Later the fog lifted and we saw several vessels, and in the afternoon, about four o'clock, the captain saw a sailboat that resembled a pilot's vessel, and when he looked at it through his glass, it turned out to be so, to our delight, for the captain had not expected to get a pilot so late in the day. It was not long before the man was on board, and the next day near dinner time we anchored on American ground. The foggy weather continued and we were able to see only the delightful island, with its many lighthouses, pretty forts, and buildings, which stood out majestically among the charming stretches of woods.

After the good old doctor had come on board and we had all had the good fortune of being able to walk smartly past him, he gave his permission for the vessel to proceed immediately in to New York, where we arrived in the evening at five o'clock. The next day we made ready to go up to the town on the following day to look about, but as we had the children with us and that day was very warm, we did not get very far. The skipper accompanied us as a guide who knew the place and as an interpreter.

First we came to a large and beautiful park for pedestrians, outside of which were a great number of fruit dealers, and pleasant carriages for hire. We immediately took possession of one of these and had ourselves driven for a mile through the streets, for which we paid six pennies each, about the same as six Norwegian skillings. The next day we went to the museum, which we thoroughly enjoyed. Here we saw animals and birds, from the largest to the smallest, and many things, some of which I understood, some of which I didn't, portraits of all the generals that there have been in America, and finally an old man with a richly braided uniform who stood on a pedestal. After we had looked about us at this place, we were informed that a drama was being played, and when we reached the theater there was a representation of Napoleon's funeral, which was very beautiful to see. This came to an end at half-past five. A play was to be presented again from seven to ten, but we were already satisfied. We paid about thirty skillings.

On May 20 we left our good ship *Juno*, with its brave crew, who said goodbye to us with a three-times-repeated hurrah.

The captain accompanied us on board a steamer which was to carry us to Albany. He took us about to see things. It was like a complete house four stories high, and very elegantly furnished, with beautiful rugs everywhere. He now parted from us with the best wishes. Captain Bendixen treated us more like relatives than like passengers. He was very entertaining and was courteous in every respect.

The later journey was good beyond expectation. Things went merrily on the railroads. Once in a while the passengers, when we neared some of the noteworthy sights that we rushed past on the trip, would stick their heads out of the windows so that they might see everything, but one after the other of them had the misfortune to see his straw hat go flying away with the wind caused by the speed of the train.

On the third of June, after we had passed several cities which for lack of space I cannot tell about, we reached Milwaukee, where we remained three days. We left Milwaukee on the seventh and came to Koshkonong on the ninth. Torjersen, after having made the acquaintance here of a worthy family named Homstad, from Namsen, who settled here last year and found this land the best after long travels, has now bought a little farm of forty acres of land, with a fairly livable log house and a wheat field of four and a half acres. This has brought him forty-five barrels of winter wheat, in addition to potatoes, beans, peas, more than a hundred heads of cabbage, cucumbers, onions in tremendous amounts, and many other kinds [of vegetables]. For this farm he paid $250, and with the farm followed respectfully four pigs.

After having lived here and having been in good health the whole time, I left on the sixteenth of August for Madison, the capital of Wisconsin, which is situated twenty-two miles from here. There I have worked at a hotel for five weeks, doing washing and ironing; and I enjoy the best treatment, though I cannot speak with the people. I have food and drink in abundance. A breakfast here consists of chicken, mutton, beef, or pork, warm or cold wheat bread, butter, white cheese, eggs, or small pancakes, the best coffee, tea, cream, and sugar. For dinner the best courses are served. Supper is eaten at six o'clock, with warm biscuits, and several kinds of cold wheat bread, cold meats, bacon, cakes, preserved apples, plums, and berries, which are eaten with cream, and tea and coffee – and my greatest regret here is to see the superabundance of food, much of which has to be thrown to the chickens and the swine, when I think of my dear ones in Bergen, who like so many others must at this time lack the necessaries of life.

I have received a dollar a week for the first five weeks, and hereafter shall have $1.25, and if I can stand it through the whole winter I shall get a dollar and a half a week, and I shall not have to do the washing, for I did not think I was strong enough for this work. Mrs. Morison has also asked me to remain in her service as long as she, or I, live, as she is going to leave the tavern next year and live a more quiet life with her husband and daughter, and there I also could live more peacefully and have a room by myself, and I really believe that so far as she is concerned I could enter upon this arrangement, provided such a decision is God's will for me.

I am well and so far I have not regretted my journey to this country. I have now been with the Torjersens for four days and have written to Bergen and to you, and tomorrow I shall journey up to the Morisons', where I find myself very well satisfied. I have had the honor of sitting at their daughter's marriage dinner, and I ironed her beautiful bridal gown. She was in truth a lovable bride, beautiful, and good as an angel, and she has often delighted me with her lovely singing and her playing on the piano. She was married on the sixteenth of September and left on the seventeenth for Boston with her husband to visit her parents-in-law.

And now, my dear Johannes, I must say farewell for this time. God bless you. Do not forget, I shall give you Torjersen's address, so that you may write me here. I greet you affectionately. Do not forget to thank God, on my behalf, who has guided me so well. I cannot thank Him enough myself.

Jannicke

[WRITTEN IN THE MARGIN:]

I have now received from Torjersen for my services, three acres of land for cultivation for three years, and it is now planted with winter wheat – if God will give me something to harvest.

Henrietta Jessen to Eleonore and "Dorea" Williamsin, February 20, 1850

MILWAUKEE, February 20, 1850

My dear Sisters Dorea and Norea:

Fate has indeed separated me from my native land and all that was dear to me there, but it is not denied me to pour forth my feelings upon this paper. My dear sisters, it was a bitter cup for me to drink, to leave a dear mother and sisters and to part forever in this life, though living. Only the thought of the coming world was my consolation; there I shall see you all. Of the emigrants from Arendal, I think, probably none went on board with a heavier heart than I, and thanks be to the Lord who gave me strength to carry out this step, which I hope will be for my own and my children's best in the future. So I hope that time will heal the wound, but up to the present I cannot deny that homesickness gnaws at me hard. When I think, however, that there will be a better livelihood for us here than in poor Norway, I reconcile myself to it and thank God, who protected me and mine over the ocean's waves and led us to a fruitful land, where God's blessings are daily before our eyes.

When you have received these lines, dear No and Do, I must ask you to write my dear mother as quickly as possible and to tell her that I have had the joy of receiving her letter by the post. That was the greatest day of happiness I have had since I came to America. Greet Mother and Ma and Georgia and say that they must not expect any letter from me before midsummer. Tell Mother that I have not received the letter she sent by the brig *Juno.*

Since we came to America neither my children nor I have been sick abed a day, for which God is to be thanked, who strengthens my body and my poor soul. I have not had so pleasant a winter as I might have had. My husband fell ill in the middle of September and had to keep to his bed until eight days before Christmas. Then he began to sit up a little and now he is up most of the day, but he is so weak that he cannot think of beginning to work for two months and perhaps not then. The doctor calls the sickness dysentery. Yes, my poor Peder has suffered much in this sickness. The doctor gave up all hope of his life and we only waited for God's hour, but at twelve o'clock one night his pulse changed and the doctor said that now it was possible that he would overcome the sickness, but he said that it would be very stubborn and [the recovery] slow.

That sickness I can never forget. Think, in one terrible day and night my husband lost eight pots of blood, that was the night before he was near death, and I was alone with him and my children. But afterward there were a few of the Norwegians who were so kind as to help me for a time watching over him, the one relieving the other. For seven weeks I was not out of my clothes.

From these lines you will see that I have experienced a little in America; but now that the worst is over, I thank the almighty Father from my innermost heart, who has cared for us and met our daily needs. We have lacked nothing. Good food and drink we have had daily. I believe I may say that even if I had been in my own native town I would hardly have received the help I have had here and I receive two dollars a week (that is, in goods). I will not speak of my own kind family, what they would have done for me, but I mean the public. There are four Norwegian families quite near where we live who have been very sympathetic with me in my misfortune and have proved their faith by their works; they have given me both money and articles for the house. Among these four families there is a man named Samuel Gabrielsen, who has been like a rare good brother to me. I will not say how much that kind man has given us, for he has told me that I should not tell anyone. "I give to you now because I know that it will be a help to you, but I do not give to be praised." He knows my brother-in-law well; in fact, Gabrielsen says that Williamsin is the best man he knows in the world and all the Norwegians whom I talk with say the same.

There are a large number of Norwegians here from the vicinity of Farsund, most of them seamen. It is the sailors who are paid best in America and all the sailors get rich. Here an ordinary seaman gets from eighteen to twenty-five dollars a month. Clerks have gone without work here this winter and carpenters and shoemakers are the artisans that are best paid. Glass workers and tailors are not able to make a living for their families. This is easy to understand when you know that you can get window panes of any size and at small cost, and it does not take much intelligence to put in a pane.

My dear sisters, when I last wrote to Farsund it was farthest from my thoughts that I ever should be separated so far from my native land and my home. How often I think of you and of your innocent angels, whom I never have seen and never shall in this life; but in my thoughts I seem to see your innocent little ones. From Mother's letter I learn that all is well with my dear ones in Farsund, and this gives me much happiness. I hope that you all, with God's help, will be strong and in good health when these lines reach you.

Your butter tub, Norea, I have used daily since I came to America, but it has not held butter since I left my native land. It would not be well if I should lack needed articles in a foreign country where I have neither mother nor sisters to comfort me in dark times such as this winter when my dear Peder is sick, and I suppose I have often wished that I were surrounded by my dear ones. I suppose it is a little strange to receive a dress in Norway and not to thank [the giver] for it before one comes to America, but better late than never. I will therefore, dear Dorea and your husband, thank you both for the dress that you gave me last summer for my Georgine S. She still has it in good condition and when it can no longer be used it will be put away as a remembrance of Uncle Perneman and Aunt Dorea in Norway. The greatest pleasure I have is talking with the children about their grandmother and aunts and uncles in Norway; that is our daily talk, and what pleases me so specially is that from the smallest to the largest they answer me with a happy smile as soon as I begin to talk about home in Norway, about grandmother and aunts.

Seval greets "Aunty" Norea, but he says he cannot remember aunty. He received the blue socks from Aunt Norea, and he is so glad to look at them when I unlock the chest, then he is quick to ask if he may see his little socks. I shall not praise my own child, but I surely believe that if I live he will give me happy days, he is so tender and understanding for me. And Søren is an unusual little fellow for his age, he has kept us supplied with wood this winter and works like a little horse. George is a little rascal; Georgine is large for her age; everybody asks if they are twins.

Tell Mother that I long since looked up Christiane Lydeman. She is well off and greets Aunt. I am often with Christiane, she is kind and pleasant to me.

The winter here in America is just as long as in Norway and much colder, but the nights are not so long. At Christmas time we had light until five o'clock in the afternoon. Ask Margaret to tell Peder Mekelsen that I advise him to go to New York and from there by canal boat to Buffalo and then by steamboat here to Milwaukee. Nels Klaapene, the sail maker, lives here in the vicinity; his wife's name is Ingebaar.

I am writing with a pen and the paper says stop. And now in conclusion I ask God's blessing upon you all. God guard you from all evil in your peaceful homes. A thousand greetings to you, Norea, with your husband and children, and you, Dorea, with your husband and children, from me, my husband, and my children.

Your devoted sister,

Henrietta Jessen

[POSTSCRIPT:]

Greet my dear Mother a thousand times, M. and her children, and Mrs. Hal and Mrs. Ramlu, with their husbands and children. Goodbye, goodbye, all my dear ones. God bless you.

Henrietta

Guri Endreson to Relatives, December 2, 1866

HARRISON P.O., MONONGALIA CO.,*
MINNESOTA, December 2, 1866

Dear Daughter and your husband and children,
and my beloved Mother:

I have received your letter of April fourteenth, this year, and I send you herewith my heartiest thanks for it, for it gives me great happiness to hear from you and to know that you are alive, well, and in general thriving. I must also report briefly to you how things have been going with me recently, though I must ask you to forgive me for not having told you earlier about my fate. I do not seem to have been able to do so much as to write to you, because during the time when the savages raged so fearfully here I was not able to think about anything except being murdered, with my whole

* The northern half of the present Kandiyohi County constituted Monongalia County from 1858 to 1870.

family, by these terrible heathen. But God be praised, I escaped with my life, unharmed by them, and my four daughters also came through the danger unscathed.

Guri and Britha were carried off by the wild Indians, but they got a chance the next day to make their escape; when the savages gave them permission to go home to get some food, these young girls made use of the opportunity to flee and thus they got away alive, and on the third day after they had been taken, some Americans came along who found them on a large plain or prairie and brought them to people. I myself wandered aimlessly around on my land with my youngest daughter and I had to look on while they shot my precious husband dead, and in my sight my dear son Ole was shot through the shoulder. But he got well again from this wound and lived a little more than a year and then was taken sick and died. We also found my oldest son Endre shot dead, but I did not see the firing of this death shot. For two days and nights I hovered about here with my little daughter, between fear and hope and almost crazy, before I found my wounded son and a couple of other persons, unhurt, who helped us to get away to a place of greater security.*

To be an eyewitness to these things and to see many others wounded and killed was almost too much for a poor woman; but, God be thanked, I kept my life and my sanity, though all my movable property was torn away and stolen. But this

* Solomon R. Foot, one of the two men whose heroic rescue is attributed to Guri Endreson, tells the story himself in great detail in Lawson, Tew, and Nelson, *History of Kandiyohi County* (St. Paul, 1905), 106–10. He, like his comrade, Oscar Erickson, had been badly wounded. Of Mrs. Endreson he writes: "She washed our bodies, bandaged our wounds and gave us every possible comfort. Fortunately my wagon stood so near the cabin that the Indians had not ventured to take it. She drew this as near the door as possible, put into it bedding, blankets and other things we might need. She assisted us into it, propped us up in a half reclining position, placed my gun by my side, hitched the young unbroken oxen to it and started." At night "Mother Endreson supplied all our wants and again bathed our wounds" and she "spent a sleepless night watching over us, ever on the lookout for the savage foe." In view of this evidence, Guri Endreson's statement that she found two persons, unhurt, who helped her to escape, seems inexplicable.

would have been nothing if only I could have had my loved husband and children – but what shall I say? God permitted it to happen thus, and I had to accept my heavy fate and thank Him for having spared my life and those of some of my dear children.

I must also let you know that my daughter Gjærtru has land, which they received from the government under a law that has been passed, called in our language "the Homestead law," and for a quarter section of land they have to pay sixteen dollars, and after they have lived there five years they receive a deed and complete possession of the property and can sell it if they want to or keep it if they want to. She lives about twenty-four American miles from here and is doing well. My daughter Guri is away in house service for an American about a hundred miles from here; she has been there working for the same man for four years; she is in good health and is doing well; I visited her recently, but for a long time I knew nothing about her, whether she was alive or not.

My other two daughters, Britha and Anna, are at home with me, are in health, and are thriving here. I must also remark that it was four years on the twenty-first of last August since I had to flee from my dear home, and since that time I have not been on my land, as it is only a sad sight because at the spot where I had a happy home, there are now only ruins and remains left as reminders of the terrible Indians. Still I moved up here to the neighborhood again this summer. A number of families have moved back here again so that we hope after a while to make conditions pleasant once more. Yet the atrocities of the Indians are and will be fresh in memory; they have now been driven beyond the boundaries of the state and we hope that they never will be allowed to come here again. I am now staying at the home of Sjur Anderson, two and a half miles from my home.

I must also tell you how much I had before I was ruined

in this way. I had seventeen head of cattle, eight sheep, eight pigs, and a number of chickens; now I have six head of cattle, four sheep, one pig; five of my cattle stayed on my land until February 1863, and lived on some hay and stacks of wheat on the land; and I received compensation from the government for my cattle and other movable property that I lost. Of the six cattle that I now have three are milk cows and of these I have sold butter, the summer's product, a little over two hundred and thirty pounds; I sold this last month and got sixty-six dollars for it. In general I may say that one or another has advised me to sell my land, but I would rather keep it for a time yet, in the hope that some of my people might come and use it; it is difficult to get such good land again, and if you, my dear daughter, would come here, you could buy it and use it and then it would not be necessary to let it fall into the hands of strangers.

And now in closing I must send my very warm greetings to my unforgetable dear mother, my dearest daughter and her husband and children, and in general to all my relatives, acquaintances, and friends. And may the Lord by his grace bend, direct, and govern our hearts so that we sometime with gladness may assemble with God in the eternal mansions where there will be no more partings, no sorrows, no more trials, but everlasting joy and gladness, and contentment in beholding God's face. If this be the goal for all our endeavors through the sorrows and cares of this life, then through his grace we may hope for a blessed life hereafter, for Jesus sake.

Always your devoted

Guri Olsdatter

Write to me soon.

Pioneer Folkways

GENEROUS hospitality was characteristic of the Norwegian-American frontier homes. There were people who liked to be complimented for their "genuine old Norwegian hospitality," but the spirit was essentially that of the American frontier. The frontier rule was that no one should be turned away unfed and unwarmed, and this rule was followed by immigrants and native Americans alike.

Even a home temporarily deserted might be occupied by strangers upon occasion. Sören Bache tells of coming in 1839 to a house where he and his companion hoped to secure lodging. They entered it, found no one at home, and made themselves comfortable. Presently the American housewife returned. She was surprised to find strangers in her house, but welcomed them as guests, explaining that she was not frightened, for she knew "there had been no Indians in the vicinity that year." Even the Indians, however, would stalk into a frontier home in the almost certain expectation that they would be given food.

Usually the Norwegians had their own social nuclei, for friends and relatives tended to settle in compact groups, often with the pleasant bond of dialect among them. Even on the prairie complete isolation was rare. There might be house-to-house visits among the women, who sometimes walked miles with small children trudging along with them. Organized activities usually waited upon the founding of a church, but the arrival of a visiting minister on his periodic rounds meant the assembling of scattered people. Even if the traveling parson arrived on a weekday, the news of his coming spread rapidly, and the people flocked to some central cabin for a religious service.

Visitors were doubly welcome because ordinarily they brought news of the outside world from which many of the immigrants felt permanently cut off. The arrival of a Norwegian newcomer occasioned calls from people throughout the community who hoped for news of friends and relatives in the old country; and the receipt of letters from the older settlements or from Norway was similarly an inducement to community visiting.

But the visitor *par excellence* was the minister. All homes were open to him, and he was besieged with invitations. Mrs. Koren, in a charming diary of the 1850's which is one of the treasures of the social historian, describes the "royal progress" of her husband and herself into Iowa to the Washington Prairie community where they spent their first American winter. In Dodgeville, Wisconsin, the Korens expected to stay at a tavern, "but a Norwegian blacksmith asked us if we would not accompany him home." They were crowded into a little "cramped and suffocating" *stue*, or room, where presently the workman's wife arrived, "amazed to find company."

On another occasion, in Iowa, they were ushered into "quite a large living room with a big stove in the center of it" and were greeted by their hosts, who "were overjoyed to have the minister they had been waiting for so long, actually in their midst." They "offered us the best the house could afford and were on the whole so friendly that we soon felt very much at home." The loft in which the Korens were given a bed also accommodated a mother and three children recently arrived from Norway. The next evening the hosts served cream porridge to the distinguished guests.

Not long afterward Mrs. Koren was meeting her parishioners in the crowded room of the largest house of the community in which her husband had just held his first service. Invited to a dinner, she found that her hostess eagerly wished her to remain not merely for the meal but overnight. She was treated to homemade wild grape wine and *fattigmand* and then sat down to a table "loaded down with fried pork, spare-ribs, sausages, bread and butter, cake, and excellent coffee."

Always the pastor's wife found herself regarded with friendly curiosity. One woman hoped that Mrs. Koren would allow her to drive her around in the community on some day when the minister was away. "It would be very nice if I could show off the minister's wife to them," she said.

If the minister's family was always welcome in the pioneer homes, it followed that the parsonage was a social center, a permanent open house. "Helene had no sooner cleared the table for one group when she would have to set it again," wrote Mrs. Koren on a winter day in 1854, "so that the entire day the house has been full of the delicious fragrance of fried pork."

Once, making a Sunday call, Mrs. Koren found a family in the midst of its devotions: a man "in his rocking chair reading out loud from the Bible," a young wife with a child in her lap, a grandmother and greataunt, "grey hair tucked up under their caps," seated on stools, and an old man lying on his bed.

Occasionally such visiting within the parish was supplemented by the social pleasure of synodical meetings, to which wives accompanied the pastors. At one, held in Janesville in the autumn of 1854, Mrs. Koren recorded an invitation after dinner to Pastor Unonius' for "coffee in the evening." Once a meal was served in the open, with the "starry sky as a ceiling," and the ministers joined heartily in singing old familiar songs.

Scenes on the Dakota prairies in a later period are reminiscent of those on the Iowa and Wisconsin frontiers of the 1850's. Mrs. Realf Ottesen Brandt, crossing the prairie with her pastor husband, finally came to the one-room home of Mons Steensland. There the ministerial family was cordially greeted; and in the one room that night slept the farmer and his wife, a number of children, Pastor and Mrs. Brandt, and the driver. In the Dakota community the parsonage was the largest house and so it "served . . . as a community center for the activities of the congregation." The choir met in the living room, the confirmation class in the kitchen, and bazaars and festivals were held in "the larger unfinished room upstairs."

The hospitality of established settlers to newcomers was boundless. Lars Larson in Rochester, New York, kept open house for the immigrant throngs moving westward, sometimes entertaining fifty or more people at one time. Even Heg converted his Muskego barn into an immigrant receiving house and won fame in Norway and in America for his unfailing generosity. Of Lars Davidson Reque of the Koshkonong settlement in southern Wisconsin, R. B. Anderson writes, "He has done a great deal for newcomers from Norway. His house in Deerfield has been a sort of objective point for them. He has taken them into his home, fed them free of charge, taught them valuable things regarding American affairs, and sent them forth with hope and cheer to begin life in the 'new world.'"

On September 19, 1853, a number of Norwegians living in the Boston region carried picnic baskets to a lake called Fresh Pond. This place, wrote one of the campers, "had something so Norwegian about it that involuntarily we were reminded of our dear fatherland." Here they sang and made speeches, and one of the group composed a special song for the occasion. The practical outcome of the picnic was that they "decided to form a society for the purpose of helping Norwegian newcomers who did not know the language or the customs" of America.

More characteristic than such secular celebrations were the festivals of the church, scrupulously observed, though perhaps lacking some of the solemnity that clothed them in the old country. "In preaching to his various congregations," writes Mrs. Brandt, "my husband observed and made good use of all the church festivals during the year: first, second, and third day of Christmas, Maundy Thursday, Good Friday, first, second, and third day of Easter, Pentecost, prayer day, Thanksgiving, and so forth. Services were held in sod houses and in schoolhouses when they were available." The adoption of American holidays came gradually, though Thanksgiving was observed in the 1850's by the Norwegians in Wisconsin, long before President Lincoln's historic call for a national day of thanks.

The immigrants had not been long in America before they felt the contagion of the American Fourth of July. In 1846 Sören Bache participated in a July 4 celebration marked by a parade, speeches, a public dinner at noon, music and orations at a near-by grove in the afternoon, and a torchlight parade in the evening. Laurence M. Larson tells of the typical July 4 celebration in an Iowa community in the years after the Civil War: the "roar of something that was called artillery" in the morning; the rumble of farmers' wagons coming into town; the procession to a grove, where there was a program culminating in an oration; and then, later in the day, amusements, dancing, and a display of fireworks.

In the 1870's, when Larson was a boy, Norwegians were occasionally represented among the speakers of the day. "Nothing so far in my life had impressed me like this gorgeous day in Forest City," Larson wrote many years later. "The crowding and jostling on the rickety sidewalks, the noise and din to which there was no lull, the blare of the band and the overpowering rhythm of the martial airs, the pageantry, the flags, and the bunting – all of these had a subtle power of fascination, even when they confused and almost distracted me."

As the Norwegian Americans developed their own community life, they began to plan and manage their own Fourth of July celebrations, sometimes including a sermon alongside the usual patriotic address, and singing both "America" and the national anthem of Norway.

There seems to be little evidence of an interest in the Norwegian national holiday in the early Norwegian colonies of the West. By the 1860's Seventeenth of May celebrations were being held in some communities where there were many Norwegian immigrants, but widespread observance of the holiday did not develop until somewhat later. Its vogue in America was influenced by the rise of the custom in Norway, which in turn was closely connected with Norwegian political currents of the 1860's. *Syttende Mai* became ultimately a recognized social institution among the Norwegian Americans – a part of their folkways – and many organizations gave it a large place in their activities.

Christmas among the early immigrants was celebrated, as in Norway, for the entire Twelfth-night period. There was an attempt to reproduce the traditional Norwegian Christmas, but inevitably there were American innovations; and as the settlers adjusted themselves to the American tempo, the celebration tended to be distinctly less protracted than it had been in the old country. In the early years Christmas was primarily a family occasion, though neighbors might drop in as guests. There seem to have been at first few presents, seldom a Christmas tree, no hanging of stockings, and no talk of Santa Claus, but in time American customs were widely adopted and merged with the Norwegian.

An authentic picture of Christmas customs on the frontier is given by a daughter of pioneers, Aaste Wilson: "They practiced the old customs from Norway. They invited one another to Christmas celebrations, and then they had home-brewed ale, made from malt or molasses or sugar cane. There were some who had whiskey, too, but money was scarce and they couldn't have much of anything. . . . Nearly everybody slaughtered for Christmas so that they could have meat and sausages. Then they had potatoes and flat bread and doughnuts and sauce made from dried apples. And most of them had cream porridge.

"We youngsters liked to stay and listen to the old folks

and thought it good fun when they told about old things from Norway. They would talk about all kinds of things and even tell stories of trolls and ghosts. . . . Sometimes they would sing ballads and *stev* [a reciting of impromptu rhymes]. I heard father occasionally sing 'Sons of Norway, the age-old kingdom'. . . . It was the women especially who sang *stev*, and sometimes they would have *stev* competitions."

Before Christmas came, "everybody was terribly busy," for "then people had to whitewash their log houses and bake and slaughter." The children "longed desperately for Christmas to come"; it was a wonderful event to them "even if the houses were small and low." Then on Christmas Eve there was a great dinner, with cream porridge as the chief dish. There were songs before and after the meal, and there was a table prayer when "we held each others' hands and gave thanks for the food. Father said they always did that at home in Sauherad."

Laurence M. Larson reports that December 24 – Little Christmas Day, as it was called – was essentially secular, a day for the children, whereas Christmas Day proper and the second and third Christmas days were church days, observed with special services, including an offering to the minister. Larson recalls that both the house and the children were scrubbed vigorously in preparation for the great day.

The Yule meal was the Christmas Eve dinner, introduced by a hymn, the reading of the Christmas story, and a grace by one of the children. Then came a feast on rice pudding, bread, apples, and candies. "To have so many good things at the same meal was a real experience."

Lulla Preus remembers that in the Preus parsonage at Painted Creek the custom of using a Christmas tree was observed, with candles, paper ornaments, gilded nuts, and the like. There were dancing, singing, and playing around the tree, then a banquet to which *fattigmand* and *julekake* added the crowning touch. In the Veblen home in Wisconsin there was a special cake for each child, with his name inscribed in frosting. Each youngster (including a lad named Thorstein) was given a large, hand-dipped candle, and all the candles were lighted simultaneously "so that the sudden outburst of brightness would be a symbol of the Star of Bethlehem." In many communities the fine old custom of putting out a sheaf of grain for the birds was carefully observed.

Alongside the familiar hymns of the immigrants, sung both in church and in home, was a wealth of folk song kept alive through use on many occasions. Some of the songs were rollicking and lusty, some plaintive and melancholy. There were cradle songs like "Bissam, bissam baadne," and love songs like "Oh, Ole, Ole, I loved you so dearly" or "Astri! My Astri!" – a charming ballad reminiscent of the English "Drink to Me Only with Thine Eyes." There were shepherd's calls that seemed to carry echoes within echoes, and there was a sad lament for "My Tulla," a favorite sheep traded to the wolf for a "bloody spot on my finger." At a frontier party, nearly everybody both could and would join heartily in singing to a lively tune the ancient song "Oh, Carry Water and Carry Wood":

Oh, carry water and carry wood,
And drive the timber o'er the line, Sir.
Oh, drive and carry whate'er you would,
I'll take my sweetheart every time, Sir.
With cheeks so red and with eyes so blue,
The lovely maidens they thrill me through.
For me alone
Give me my own,
And life will be a merry rhyme, Sir.

On father's farm there's a curious pine
With boughs that always sway and sigh, Sir;
And so a wife must this year be mine,
Or I a bachelor will die, Sir.

So drive and carry whate'er you would,
I'll drive my own good wife with me, Sir;
She is so kind and she is so good,
No other girl I'll ever see, Sir.
With cheeks so red and with eyes so blue,
The lovely maidens they thrill me through.
For me alone
Give me my own,
And life will be a merry rhyme, Sir.

It was no chance circumstance, but a natural development, that Auber Forestier and R. B. Anderson in the early 1880's brought out a *Norway Music Album* which made available for home use the old Norwegian folk songs, spring dances, and hallings, with English translations of the original texts.

The immigrants were familiar with the traditional lore of legend, superstition, riddles, and proverbs that came out of the long Norwegian past. For the most part, however, they were emancipated from belief in the ancient superstitions, as were the people of Norway in an age of rapid change in the national economy. Yet the superstitious beliefs, transmitted from one generation to another, were told and retold because they were entertaining, and witchcraft and trolls figured in the immigrant lore.

There was little creation of new episode, however, in the realm of superhuman phenomena. Einar Haugen collected from Dane County, Wisconsin, one pioneer tale of a log-cabin household of some eight or nine persons who "lived and slept in the same room." The grandfather was sick, and one day near midnight the family heard an unseen power pick up the stove handle and drop it on the stove three times. This signified, according to the grandmother, that the sick man would die within three days, and – so goes the story – he did.

Professor Haugen has also rescued the tale of a pioneer who believed that a neighbor woman employed witchcraft in producing better butter and getting higher prices for it than he did. In his efforts to counteract her special power he employed a traditional Norwegian remedy. He attempted to seal a curious fungus into a gun barrel, but in the process of forging, the barrel exploded – and the pioneer later said that the witch was on her way to the scene when the explosion occurred!

Riddles well worn with use were always popular, such as "What is it that goes all day long but doesn't move from the spot?" – a clock; and "What tree grows with its root up and its top down?" – an icicle. And the old proverbs of Norway, many of them peculiarly applicable to the conditions of pioneer life, were transplanted to the immigrant West: "Little pitchers have big ears"; "When the need is greatest, help is nearest"; "He knows best how the shoe pinches who has it on"; and – a four-word condensation of the thought embodied in the saying about never crossing a bridge until you come to it – "That day, that sorrow."

Marriage was generally regarded as a sacrament of the church, and few immigrant couples felt that their union had been properly celebrated until the church had set its official stamp of approval upon it, even if the traditional religious ceremony postdated the actual marriage in common law. In frontier settlements where ministers appeared only on rare occasions, it was no uncustomary thing for the marriage to be performed by a lay preacher or perhaps a justice of the peace; but whether such formalities had been observed or not, church sanction was likely to be requested and accorded later.

When a clergyman arrived, couples came from many parts of the countryside to be married. Sometimes they were a trifle hazy about the precise legal requirements, as in the case of a young man who appeared with his bride before the Reverend Nils Brandt. When asked to produce his marriage license, he solemnly handed the minister his first citizenship papers.

Weddings were sometimes sedate, even severe, affairs, unattended by special celebrations; but usually, and especially after the earlier difficulties of pioneering had been overcome, they occasioned much celebration and merrymaking, with everybody clad in his best clothes. At many parties there was a generous consumption of whisky. Often there were dances lasting far into the night. An interesting account of a frontier wedding in the Wisconsin Spring Prairie community tells of the bridegroom's playing host in serving whisky to the guests, followed by an elaborate wedding supper and – after the minister had conveniently departed – a dance which continued until daylight. The dancing was interrupted by the traditional frontier charivari, and about midnight there was a "grand meal of lutefisk and smoked meats."

A hasty remarriage by a widow or widower was looked upon with grave disapproval by most of the immigrants. When the pioneer minister C. L. Clausen, whose first wife died in November 1847, remarried in February, Bache felt moved to make a severe entry in his diary: "People, especially Clausen's most loyal supporters, have lost some of their wholehearted enthusiasm for him as a result of this precipitous remarriage." He took note of the fact that the ceremony was performed, not by the Norwegian minister Dietrichson, but by an American clergyman. The implication seemed to be that Dietrichson would have nothing to do with the affair.

There was also grave suspicion of the wisdom, if not the morality, of marriage outside the Norwegian fold. There were instances of intermarriage between Norwegians and Americans or people of other stock in the earlier frontier period, and with the passing years the practice became common, but the feeling of doubt about such a departure from a straight Norwegian alliance lingered long. It was particularly acute if a Protestant-Catholic union was involved. The theme ultimately appeared in fiction, for Rölvaag describes the marriage of the Norwegian Lutheran Peder Victorious to the Irish Catholic Susie, and he brings the traditional folkways into a clear focus by probing the troubled attitude of Peder's mother, Beret.

Notwithstanding a considerable amount of indulgence in liquor among the early Norwegian immigrants and the retention of many time-flavored amusements and festivities from the old country, there was a deeply rooted Puritan spirit among them, particularly among those who shared the Haugean religious viewpoint. This spirit expressed itself not only in the movement for temperance reform but also in a severe disapproval of dancing, the theater, card playing, display in dress, and other practices and customs that for one reason or another were considered worldly and sinful. Alongside this Puritanism ran a more tolerant attitude which sprang from traditional ways in the old country that had not been bent by the Haugean philosophy.

Marcus L. Hansen believes that the immigrant Puritanism became progressively more pervasive with time. He contends that church discipline tended to become "more and more strict," and he writes, "One after the other, social pleasures that were brought from the Old World fell under the ban. Temperance and Sunday observance were early enforced. Then card playing and dancing were prohibited. Simplicity in dress and manner of living were praised as virtues. The children of the immigrants were the subject of much concern." Ultimately, he says, the immigrant churches adopted "much of the New England atmosphere."

That there was a pervasive Puritanism among the Norwegian immigrants is beyond all doubt, but its roots are deeper than Professor Hansen's essay suggests. The temperance movement among the immigrants certainly drew much strength, if not its original inspiration, from American sources; but in general the Norwegian-American Puritanism was independent of New England, or American, Puritanism. It was brought to the West from Norway by the immigrants themselves, particularly by those who accepted and followed the teachings of Hauge, Eielsen, and other apostles of pietism. The spirit was rooted in a sincere protest against the "worldly" practices that were associated in the popular mind with rationalism. It represented an alliance of godliness with a profound distrust of human pleasures that tempted people away from the straight and narrow path.

The noted preacher, Elling Eielsen, had scarcely landed in New York in 1839 before he sounded a warning against the dangers of freedom and declared that human beings could "stand little of the cup of joy." He scanned the American metropolis for signs of drinking, dancing, and amusements, and soon he was thundering among the immigrants against dancing and drinking as the principal causes of ungodliness among them. He exemplified a Puritanism that was carried across the ocean from Norway and that out-Puritaned the Puritanism of the New Englanders.

That this general interpretation is historically sound is suggested not only by ample evidence from the history of the Norwegian Americans but also by the similarity of Swedish-American Puritanism. The Swedish immigrants also had a deep strain of Puritanism that was firmly rooted in the pietistic movements of their mother country.

Death was such a frequent visitor in the early immigrant communities, especially during cholera or other epidemics, that it was not always possible to observe the customary solemnities of the church in the matter of funerals. Rölvaag does not allow the body of Per Hansa, recovered months after his death, to be laid to rest until the minister finally arrived in the community. Ordinarily, however, funeral services would be held in the absence of the minister, and when he next visited the settlement "he would chant and cast earth upon the grave and deliver a sermon."

Aaste Wilson pictures the frontier immigrant burial customs in stark detail. "For funerals," she writes, "people always had to be invited." There were always two meals, "one before they went to the graveyard, the other after they came back." Simple black homemade coffins were used, with nails driven halfway into the covers. The service opened with a hymn: "Who knows how near me is my death."

Aaste's father, a layman, usually had charge of the services in the Wisconsin settlement where he lived: "He would give a talk in remembrance of the departed one and give thanks for him." Thereupon the people walked past the coffin for a last look, "and immediately afterward we heard the sad sound of the hammering of the nails on the coffin lid." Then Aaste's father would say, "The day is passing and time is advancing, and the dead must go to his grave and final resting place." The coffin was carried out of the church while the people sang, "Though I must now depart, depart not Thou from me."

The coffin was put in a wagon, driven to the graveyard, and the mourners walked behind it. Men took turns in digging the grave. When it was ready they placed their spades crosswise on it and sang: "Now the grave is a comfort to me, for Thy hand shall cover me." Then all said the Lord's Prayer, and that was the end. "It was simple but dignified and there was a Christian spirit and a deep sincerity in it all," writes Aaste Wilson. "They did it as well as they could."

In early years many settlers had family burial plots on their own land, but usually the immigrant cemeteries were in or near the churchyards. When Ole Svendsen's wife Gro died, he wrote a description of her grave in an Iowa cemetery and sent it to his wife's parents in Norway. "I want to tell you about Gro's grave," he said. "It has been decorated with a white marble stone on which are engraved the date and place of her birth as well as of her death, how many of her family survived her, and a verse from David's Psalms. . . . I myself have planted a tree on the grave to keep weeds from spreading over it. Her friends have planted flowers and it has been enclosed with a very nice railing."

The majority of the immigrants seem to have accepted the hazards they met on the ocean crossing and in the western settlements with a fair degree of stoicism, but not a few were terror-ridden, haunted by the fear of disaster in the wilds of an unknown country. Most poignant were the anxiety for sick children and the anguish over their loss. Rölvaag pictures a woman who went mad when her small child died and was left behind in an unmarked grave on the prairie. Fear and sorrow, combined with the monotony of the prairie and a deep nostalgia, threw a pall of melancholy over many pioneer mothers and unbalanced some. Per Hansa's wife fell into a trauma after the birth of her son Peder. She was tortured by many things, not least the grim power of the prairie to thwart her ambitious husband. Finally, half maddened, she concealed herself in an immigrant chest, a self-chosen coffin that seemed holy ground to her in the strange prairie land.

The episode is fiction, but Rölvaag knew prairie life and human beings, and his portrayal of the psychological turmoil in the spirit of Beret is an authentic study of one aspect of the emotional history of immigration.

In no realm do folkways express themselves more revealingly than in family life and the ways of children, and this realm is of particular significance for an understanding of immigrant transition. That it has been so largely neglected by American social historians is partly due to the inadequacy of the historical records of child life and the difficulties of exploring the activities and thoughts of youngsters in a bygone age. The setting is the home, however, and letters and diaries make it possible to get some pictures of the intimacies of home life.

One does not read much or long in these sources without realizing the profound truth that people were people in the pioneer era. Some immigrant children had a pitifully bleak life, but many knew good homes, childish joys, normal happiness. Parents, like parents the world over, took great pride in their offspring. They wrote eagerly to their relatives across the ocean of little triumphs in the family circle. They were concerned about bringing up their children in accordance with the familiar precepts of the church. They transmitted to their children the folklore they themselves had learned in childhood, and the second generation knew about trolls, woodland and mountain pixies, and traditional fairies.

Immigrant parents liked to report that their children could use and understand the speech of the old country, but they were no less proud to mention that they also were mastering the language of the new. Sometimes, like Beret, they feared a potential alienation of the second from the first generation and refused to have anything but their native tongue used in the home.

Contemporary pictures of frontier family life are etched in such charmingly subjective sources as Mrs. Koren's diary and the family letters of Olaus Duus, a frontier pastor.

Mrs. Koren was a lady of fastidious tastes, and sometimes she was dismayed by the number of children she found in small houses, especially when they were noisy and dirty. Once, however, in a "tiny log house," she found a flock of children who were "so clean and tidy it was a pleasure to look at them." She thought it unusual "to see children who were not all smeared with the everlasting molasses that they are constantly eating." Some youngsters, she observed, were carried papoose-fashion by their mothers. One day Anne Aarthun called "with no less than five children, the oldest nine, the youngest not yet a year." They brought "life enough into the house for one day and they raced up and down the attic stairs." Later they "went out and drove with my sled and horse and took care of the chickens." The "terrible uproar," Mrs. Koren said, "has certainly kept my fingers moving steadily all afternoon."

But Mrs. Koren, like all women on the frontier, found children a great comfort in the fight against loneliness. "Yes, now it is different to be home alone," she wrote after the birth of her first child.

Olaus Duus drew word pictures of family scenes in the

1850's that retain a startling vividness across the years. His idol was his boy Olaf: "You should see him now as he sits eating prairie chicken and brown chicken broth on his mother's lap, with a piece of chicken in his hand. We can't give him any of our venison or any pork because he frightened us the other day by choking himself until he was quite blue in the face. . . . He is large for his age and quite a man."

Duus returned from a drive on a bitter winter day: "The horse dashes along, urged both by my whip and by the comfortable assurance of oats and corn, and presently the equipage is out in the drive, while Wife and Little Boy stand at the window with beaming faces. Little Boy is all excitement. He stamps with his feet on the kitchen bench and claps with his hands on the window panes; he wants to get his hands on both Papa and Kitty [the horse], and Mamma has to hold him with both hands lest he make too hasty an acquaintanceship with the floor."

The father sent a lock of the boy's hair to Norway. He reported that the boy liked to trot all over the house and to bring "Papa shoes, handkerchiefs, whip – whatever I ask for." Olaf was never quiet except when asleep. "You should see him when he comes stamping along in his long bodiced dress, with his little neck bare, his hair standing up in a cockscomb, red roses in his cheeks, with large and almost black eyes." Duus built a fence around his house and garden since Olaf and the pigs could never become reconciled. When the pigs were impudent Olaf liked to seize them by the snout and bite their ears.

Olaf sent his thanks for a toy wagon he had received from Norway. The boy was often in the garden. "He races around with a straw hat on and a short little frock, with bare feet and legs, his father's driving whip in his hand," rushing after the goose with shouts of "Get up! Get up!" The father thought Olaf a singularly pious boy, for the "minute he sees me take down the Book, he crawls up on the sofa and folds his hands."

One moment Olaf was "romping and shouting so that we

could hardly hear ourselves think," the next he was fast asleep. The boy learned to talk and the father recorded his words, some English, some Norwegian. In time a second son and a daughter were added to the family circle. A gift box came from Norway and was unpacked amid great excitement, Olaf "blowing large blasts with his harmonica." Duus's two boys played in the ash pile and emerged looking like Espen Askelad in the fairy tale. Another time they played "Confirmation," and Olaf solemnly asked the Bishop [his young brother], "Will you please read me the fourth article?"

Amid such scenes an immigrant family arrived from Quebec. The father and mother had been crowded and pushed; all three of their children had had measles during the trip; despite "wind and weather" the parents had to hold them in their arms night and day. One child died and was buried by Pastor Duus. He tried to comfort the mother. She said, "Oh, if only the child could have been spared the tortures of the journey." A few days later the second of their children, a boy of ten and a half, died; and the third, a younger boy, grew steadily weaker.

Growing children found many ways of amusing themselves in frontier times. They went sledding, skiing, and tobogganing in winter, swimming, fishing, trapping, hunting, and flower-picking in summer. One of the Heg boys at Muskego was a hero to the community when he shot a swan. Youngsters tried to tame wild animals: foxes, woodchucks, possums, coons, coyotes, wolves, even skunks. A household animal was usually assigned to each child – an artful way, perhaps, of insuring a more cheerful care of the animals.

On some frontiers neighbors lived very far apart, and families were obliged to be socially self-sufficient for considerable periods of time. But families were large. Birth control was unknown, and ordinarily there were annual additions to the family. The number of children frequently ranged from half a dozen to a dozen or more. Professor Larson tells of a neighbor who could never remember offhand how many children he had, though by calling the roll he generally managed to list them all. Such large families meant that each farm was a little community in itself.

Rölvaag in *Peder Victorious* gives a vivid account of recess time in a Norwegian school, when hot rivalries had full swing and the teacher frequently had to intervene. There were also interracial rivalries. Hamlin Garland, recalling the district school he attended as a boy, writes, "Here I came in contact with the Norwegian boys from the colony to the north, and a bitter feud arose (or existed) between the 'Yankees,' as they called us, and the 'Norskies,' as we called them." Garland remembers that sometimes the feud broke into open war, when "showers of sticks and stones filled the air, and our hearts burned with the heat of savage conflict." It was usually at parting that diplomatic relations were broken. The boys might walk pleasantly together for a half a mile, when they "suddenly split into hostile ranks, and warred with true tribal frenzy as long as we could find a stone or a clod to serve as missile." Garland recalls no "personal animosity" in this feud; to him it was Pict fighting Angle.

Such rivalries among the boys sometimes had parallels in the relations between adult Norwegian Americans and other groups. Larson, for example, has told the story of a riot in an Iowa community where the Norwegian element seemed to be getting control of a local political convention. Fence rails and neck yokes were the weapons in a fight between a gang of malcontents, largely Irish, and a crowd of Norwegians. Larson pays tribute to the fighting qualities of the Irish, but they were finally driven from the field by their opponents, who outnumbered them. "Clan sentiment," Professor Larson asserts, was definitely present in the 1870's, but he points out that "racial antagonism could not long endure the wearing force of daily contact, and soon it disappeared altogether."

In the summer the immigrant children often went on berrying expeditions, and in the autumn parties went nutting in the woodlands – unless they chanced to live on the treeless plains. Lulla Preus recalled excursions to pick flowers, plums, grapes, walnuts, hickory nuts, and hazelnuts; and Larson remembered the attraction of prairie flowers, especially the violet, which he called "night and day." Rosinweed was the frontier boy's chewing gum.

There were also indoor amusements. Lulla Preus spoke of the invariable readiness of her mother "to entertain the young people. Either she played the piano for us, told us stories, or taught us any number of games which she could take part in, too, and thus give them added life." She remembered twilight scenes when her father would tell stories or sing. "There seemed to be no end to the hymns and little songs which my parents knew."

There appear to have been relatively few competitive sports. Wrestling was popular among boys, however, and both boys and girls took part in spelling matches. In some games old counting-out rhymes were used, not unlike "eenie, meenie, minie, mo."

The immigrant frontier boy, according to Larson, was looked upon as sufficiently developed at fourteen to do the work of a man; and many a farmer found the road to prosperity cleared for him by the manpower of his own family as his many boys reached the age when they could share in the rough work of the fields. Sometime between fourteen and sixteen, confirmation was solemnized. When this event took place, "in some respects a person was considered as having attained his majority." One reminiscent writer says that confirmation "for us settlers' children was the day when boys or girls had to begin supporting themselves." If this was its practical significance, it must be remembered that it was primarily a religious landmark. Larson's minister insisted that he be confirmed as he neared his sixteenth year, and his parents acquiesced, though the son seemed not to be impressed with the necessity of the rite and his parents were sadly aware of the state of his mind. He cannily realized how stereotyped the ceremony often was, and how seemingly futile the hammering of required answers into the heads of some of the country dolts.

"Dost thou renounce the devil and all his works?" the minister asked a terrified youngster who had no idea of the meaning of the strange word *renounce*. "No," he answered in swift relief, to the horror of the congregation. The clergyman rephrased the question, avoiding the word *renounce* and putting the matter so that it called for a negative answer; but the boy, now aware that his original "No" was wrong, blurted out "Yes."

The sacrament was, of course, a solemn occasion, prepared for by a period of "reading for the minister"; and the confirmands, as well as the proud parents, were dressed in their best when the fateful day of public examination and vows arrived. Sometimes guests visited the homes of the young confirmed people after services were over, and occasionally there were confirmation gifts.

A little recognized role of pioneer immigrant children was that of mitigating the nostalgia of the pioneer mothers. So common and so deeply rooted was this immigrant nostalgia that it was a part of the folkways of the people.

But there was a never-ending round of tasks and activities to occupy the women: loom and spinning wheel to be run, meals to be cooked, the sick to be cared for. There was child-bearing year after year, and the incessant demands of infants and children of varying ages. Time, and not least the unrelenting work that packed its passing hours, did indeed heal their wounds. The initial ordeals of pioneering were met, and for many there came the better days that had beckoned them. Events crowded upon the homes and upon the communities of which the homes were a part. Time and interest were poured into church and social relationships.

There was the eternal march of the seasons, each posing its particular problems and challenges. Children passed from infancy to their teens, girls shared in the work of the house as boys went out to share in the work of the field, and presently the second generation came of age. Some of the pioneer mothers did not survive their ordeals to win final rewards, but many had the satisfaction of seeing their children solidly established on prosperous farms or in the near-by towns, sometimes making places of trust and service for themselves in the life of community and state.

The hunger for schooling and education that marked the spirit of the pioneers was a significant phase of the frontier folkways. The immigrants saw education as the path to the larger opportunities that America offered. The hunger was that of parents ambitious for the welfare of their children, and it communicated itself to those children. It became a common thing for the younger generation to go to school and to push on to academies, colleges, and universities, and they began to make careers in the professions.

So in a thousand ways the transition to American life, working across the years and generations, made good the hope that gave confidence to the immigrants: the hope of a brighter tomorrow.

Halfway House

WHY do the novels of immigrant pioneering so largely center about ordeals? About grimness, frustration, despair?

I suspect that writers of fiction, notably of fiction purporting to be realistic, are persuaded that readers will not be gripped by recitals presenting anything less harrowing than dramatic ordeals. Possibly they are right in their view. There is no denying that ordeal is part of the total story. The men and women who came from the Old World knew hardship and made sacrifices, from the initial cutting of home ties to the fight with the wilderness. Their saga includes long voyages across the Atlantic in small sailing vessels, with human strength tried by storm, crowding, disease, and hunger. On the American side it tells of people who went to frontiers, lived amid primitive conditions, knew poverty, were struck by epidemics, faced Indian outbreaks, prairie blizzards and fires, and other frontier hazards. But these things were not all of life.

Perhaps the interpreters of the past do the natural thing in emphasizing such ordeals. The manner in which they were met is, of course, a part of the American pioneer heritage. In any event, the ordeals have become so conventional a part of our literary tradition that, to quote James Gray, a "pattern, fixed and unalterable" has developed which most novelists-of-the-soil follow. Their stories reach a climax as the "desperately struggling family" is toppled into a "new chasm of despair" from the "modest little plateau of hope to which its members had resolutely climbed." "The crop had looked fair and full of promise. But just before it could be harvested, thereby ensuring a trousseau for the daughter, a liberal education for the son, as well as an assortment of major operations and new cream separators for mother, some great natural catastrophe" sweeps the "whole bright prospect away in one malign stroke." Any practiced reader can readily foretell the approach of one of these disasters – whether it be "drought or dust storm, plague of grasshoppers or blizzard."

Notwithstanding the predictability of their pattern, these novels continue to appear in an unending stream. Feike Feikema's *Golden Bowl* is a recent successful novel which follows pretty much the traditional plot. A classic American story of the ordeal of pioneering is Rölvaag's *Giants in the Earth*, but, despite the play of ordeal in it, this is no conventional story.

Rölvaag understood that there is a bigger story than *Giants in the Earth*. Historically considered, his entire production – from the immigrant letters, which reflected his own experience as a newcomer to America, to his final novel, *Their Fathers' God*, which concerned itself with the problems of the second generation – assumes increasing significance with the passing years, and the reason is plain. For in the sweep of his entire work, with deeper insight and greater power than almost any other writer, he recorded and interpreted the American transition of the immigrants who made their way to the Western World. That, rather than ordeal, was the theme of his writing. That is the clue to its dynamic quality.

In my own interpretation of the immigrant in American history, the keynote is not ordeal, but transition. Immigrant pioneering was not a fixed mode of life. Its characteristic was change. Nothing was fixed. There was a constant interplay of two creative forces – the Old World heritage and the American environment. And in my opinion, we shall not achieve what Louis Adamic calls "Common Ground" until we understand this interplay not in terms of dramatic ordeals but in terms of the everyday life of people. For the experience is general. It has not been limited to a single element or group of elements, it has been common to all; it has to do with millions of people, and its outcome is modern America. What novel, apart from the Rölvaagian trilogy, gives us in broad sweep this story of the common life?

The immigrant, no matter what country he sailed from, disembarked in a land of different culture. The chests and bundles under which he staggered at the ports of landing were filled with tangible evidences of his own culture: tools, clothing, furniture, food. Just as surely as the farming implements he brought could not be used effectively on American soil or the clothes he wore were not suitable to American temperatures, so too he would find the less material parts of his Old World culture, those packed away in the immigrant chests of thought and tradition, no longer adequate to his needs.

Culture is dynamic. As Professor James G. Leyburn points out, "So closely related are the ideas, the behavior, and the material goods of a group, that each of them has an inner logic in terms of the other." A single material change can alter the culture of a people, so that habits, behavior, and perhaps even moral standards are changed. The invention of the automobile, for example, brought far-reaching changes in American life—all the way from curb-service hamburgers to trailer towns, new courtship customs, and hitchhikers. The automobile was a material change, yet it affected not only our material goods, but also our ideas and behavior.

Americans, at first fiercely loyal to the horse, had time to adjust themselves to the "horseless carriage" and other changes wrought by technology. But what of the immigrants who were plunged directly from one kind of environment, of possessions, ideas, and behavior, into another? Let us look, for example, at the Norwegian immigrants. When great numbers of them reached the Middle West in the 1850's, the McCormick reaper was beginning to come into general use. They not only did not know how to handle the machine; they had no name for it. "Threshing crews" too were outside their vocabulary and experience. A study of their changing language patterns suggests that about fifty per cent of American agriculture was new to these immigrants. They expected, of course, to learn how to use new tools and grow different crops in America, but did they realize that old rituals, customs, and celebrations connected with the Norwegian harvest would have little or no place in a foreign field?

Harder, perhaps, to bear, was the belief that their moral standards were threatened. Young girls going out unchaperoned, children flouting parental authority, laborers spending their wages lavishly instead of sewing them up in the mattress with traditional thrift, lack of Old World respect for the clergyman – such behavior was unnerving to many. Weddings had been celebrated as great festive occasions in the old country. Here, as one immigrant declared, the boys and girls "run off and get married without anyone's knowing it, maybe not even themselves."

Sometimes the shock was on the other side. The early German immigrant puzzled over the fact that the Americans thought he was desecrating the Sabbath by going to hear music in a beer garden. New England eyebrows were raised when European immigrants "bundled" – though it was at that time a respectable mode of courtship in the cold houses of some European countries, and the institution was not wholly unfamiliar to Americans.

How did the immigrant move from one set of ideas, one environment, one kind of possessions, to another? Did he keep his balance in the process? A new language, new surroundings, food, clothing, ways of working, social life – what bridges, if any, spanned the gap between old and new?

Did the immigrant dress himself into American life? A Norwegian immigrant letter in the 1850's from Springfield, Illinois, comments with caustic wit on the arrival of "thirty pieces of Norwegian beef, enveloped in homespun and sacking." If their appearance was ludicrous to their own countrymen, how much more so to the Americans! It was only a matter of time before the immigrant found himself torn between thrift and vanity. To the young it was a short-lived conflict. As one bachelor, asking for an "unspoiled Norwegian girl," wrote home to Norway: "The first Sunday after their arrival [the Norwegian servant girls] still wear their usual old Norwegian clothes; the next Sunday, it's a new dress; the third, a hat, a parasol, a silk shawl, new clothes from top to toe."

Not all made the transition so easily. Frequently the immigrant viewed American clothes with horror, for they did not conform to the Norwegian sense of thrift and modesty. A Norwegian New Yorker told of women dressed in velvets and silks, promenading on Broadway, yet whose table linen was hardly presentable and whose husbands rarely had a meal at home. Another noted that "American women do look like angels; it may well be that the resemblance is heightened by all this daubing, for after all, in all these blessed years, who has ever seen any except painted angels?"

Gradually the transition was made, however. Family photographs in immigrant albums show how soon the wedding costumes were discarded for American wedding regalia, though not until the end of the century did wedding veils become the rule. Norwegian apparel and jewelry – the embroidered folk costumes and filigree brooches – were put away in immigrant chests, to become treasures for the third generation. And they were not forgotten. One Norwegian American, long after wedding veils had taken the place of the Old World costume, recalled that "the women never tired of describing" their mother's "beautiful wedding dress of green and white striped delaine with garlands of roses."

Less obvious than the red barns of the Middle West – the Scandinavians did not follow the color scheme of New England's white structures – the immigrant from Northern Europe kept other symbols of the color and life he had known and loved in another country. Even today, in certain parts of Wisconsin, *rosemaling*—wood painting in lively colors—carries on the traditional art and design of the Scandinavian folk.

In food as in clothing, the immigrants had to adjust themselves to new ways. The excessive eating of pork, particularly among the pioneers, troubled the immigrant palate and stomach alike. A minister's wife on the frontier complained that alive, the pigs invaded both church and cabin, and slaughtered, they appeared on the pioneer's table three times a day. But others welcomed the new foods they learned to cook in America. An anonymous Norwegian wrote home to Norway in 1851 to tell of a "wonderful dish . . . which is called *Pai*." He did not quite know what this marvelous concoction was, but one thing he knew: "it glides easily down your throat." And when the immigrants reached a stage of minor affluence, cake became such a favorite, according to one immigrant, that whereas a woman in Norway won renown who could spin the most yarn or weave the most cloth in a day, the Norwegian-American woman was the most famous who could bake the best cake.

But all Norwegian dishes were not crowded out by the newer American foods. In the drama of a California Norwegian family, the Norwegian meat ball comes into its own—a delightful tale not only of a mental bank account but also of immigrant transition. Today there are other lingering signs of the immigrant bridge to American life. There are Scandinavian towns in Minnesota which observe "afternoon coffee" as an established social institution. Vernon County, Wisconsin, is said to import each year some twenty-five tons of lutefisk. "Smörgasbord"—without debating whether its inspiration is Swedish or Norwegian—is a familiar course of American dining, from church suppers to New York restaurants, though Webster, in the conservative fashion of dictionaries, has not yet caught up with the full flavor of the word.

Marcus L. Hansen has said that the future student of American literature, if he conceives of it in "more than a parochial sense, must be master of at least ten or a dozen languages." Among the Norwegian Americans alone one could gather up a bookshelf of over a hundred novels, written from the 1870's to Rölvaag's time, nearly all of which are still imprisoned in the language of the immigrant and virtually unknown to the American public. Many deal with the problems of pioneering and immigrant adjustment. Most of them are of purely historical interest now, but a few are literary achievements of value. Printed in small editions, they were often serialized in Norwegian-American newspapers.

The immigrant press was a much used bridge of transition. Hungry for news from the old country and barred by language from reading the local accounts of foreign and American news, many a pioneer immigrant would perhaps have subscribed to his old home newspaper if he could have afforded it. But, besides the high subscription price, he would have had to pay a ghastly price, some thirty or forty dollars, in postage a year. So he started papers of his own, giving much space to clippings selected from the papers of the old country. Many Americans looked on the immigrants' foreign language press with suspicion, as an alien, propagandist tie with another world. Actually, as both historians and sociologists have demonstrated, these newspapers aided and eased the process of adjustment to the New World.

As time wore on and news from home seemed more remote and less precious, the columns of foreign news shortened. Hansen has said that the process of Americanization can almost be measured by the gradual lengthening of the columns devoted in the immigrant press to American news and immigrant activities in the United States. In the years before 1914, he asserts, "probably the class of ordinary American citizens best read in international affairs were not the residents of

Boston or New York, but the older generation of immigrant farmers in the Middle West."

From the publication of the first Norwegian newspaper in a Wisconsin community in 1847 to this day, the Norwegian element has never been without newspapers of its own. It has, in fact, had more than four hundred different newspapers during the past century. Whatever its shortcomings, that press was a basic social and cultural immigrant institution. As it gradually broke away from its purely Old World reporting, it became a forum for debate on problems of American politics and government, a magazine carrying stories and poetry and essays into homes, an Americanizer of the immigrant, a widener of cultural horizons. And it enlarged the interest of the immigrants in American politics.

This political interest is part of the pioneer saga. Many reasons have been advanced to explain its unusual vitality, among them the fact that large numbers of the immigrant settlers became landowners; that they were quick to become American citizens; and that they had a background of democratic tradition. But a more fundamental factor was the circumstance that in large farming areas the Norwegian pioneer settlers had to manage their own community affairs, manipulate American institutions, and often conduct district and town meetings before they could speak the language of the country. They brought with them a knowledge of local self-government, and in the West, owing to circumstance, they themselves often had to organize and carry on their own local government. So the "ballot was as necessary a tool in their life as the ax, the spade, the hoe, the plow, and the harrow."

Against such backgrounds of practice and of experiment in the American laboratory of community government, the immigrants participated in state and national government and presently were producing governors and congressmen. It is not so much the emerging leadership that is historically important, however, as the more fundamental fact that the immigrants played a part in the functioning of the democracy with which they had merged.

Another form of American democracy, which most Norwegian immigrants accepted with gratitude but which puzzled and even frightened others, was the public school. I have spoken of the shock experienced by the newcomer who saw behavior and ideas in America which he could not understand and which seemed contrary to his conceptions of family life and society. In horror a pastor of the 1850's wrote to a Norwegian paper: "Such a thing as discipline in the school, or respect for the teacher, is rarely seen in the West. . . . I have tried several times to send . . . my own children . . . to these district schools, but the experiences I had each time were such that I doubt that I shall send them . . . any more. My daughter, then six years old, came home from school the first day . . . with this curious observation: 'Just think, Papa, the schoolma'am calls us "Ladies and gentlemen"!' What wild pedagogical ideas lie in this one remark!"

Another parent, likewise disturbed by the lack of authority in the schools, suggested an ironical remedy. He admitted that if the Yankees insisted on children being "brought up in freedom," then of course the immigrant children "must be free." But, he added, when the schoolma'am is through scolding them in English, if they misbehave at home you still have the privilege of thrashing them "in Norwegian."

The immigrants recognized that schools on the remote frontiers could hardly be expected to offer adequate facilities or highly trained instructors. Some bewailed the fact that these primitive frontier schools gave only a smattering of such elementary subjects as geography, reading, arithmetic, and history, but observers could not help admiring the democratic urge to education in the pioneer communities. Twenty-four Norwegian children were described as being "as studiously at work as I ever saw" in the attic of a Minnesota log cabin which housed two families below. "Myrtle and prairie wild flowers adorned the walls," and the teacher's desk – a flour barrel – was graced with a bouquet.

The quarrel of the orthodox church leaders with the American school system was not primarily one of discipline or instruction. One of the obstacles to Norwegian transition to American education was the reluctance of the church to accept a school system that omitted religious instruction. And when you have a controversy involving a people's religious beliefs and interest in its children's welfare, you can expect that the clash of traditions will not easily be resolved.

For nearly thirty years, beginning in the 1850's, debate was waged in the immigrant settlements over the question of public versus parochial education. This debate reveals much of the immigrant's emotional approach to new standards and ways of living. Attacked on one side as "religionless" and "heathen," the public school was defended on the other as the means through which immigrant children could become "true Americans, one nation, together with all other Americans." From the common school, said one defender, "a wave of progress will roll over our prairies and will bury all bigotry, intolerance and superstition, ten thousand fathoms deep."

The Norwegian immigrant recognized the fact that, of its very nature, a public school could not offer sectarian teaching. But some felt that the public school worked in opposition to the kingdom of God. Gradually, however, the transition was made. The average Norwegian immigrant quietly accepted the public schools through all the years that church leaders were denouncing them as heathen. Meanwhile the parochial schools gradually dwindled. The average Norwegian found them inexpedient on the grounds of cost and efficiency, but the chief reason for rejecting them was a belief in the soundness of the democratic idea of primary education available, at public cost, to all. When states began to enact compulsory attendance laws, Norwegians accepted them cheerfully. The public schools themselves improved vastly in quality. The space had been bridged.

In 1911 Professor Rölvaag wrote: "We have become strangers – strangers to the people we forsook and strangers to the people we came to. . . . The people we forsook, we remain apart from, and the people we came to, we also remain apart from. We have thus ceased to be an integral part of a larger whole; we have become something by ourselves, something torn off, without any organic connection either here or there." Nearly two decades later he wrote again: "The giving up of one language and the acquiring of a new requires a spiritual adjustment which forever will be beyond the power of the average man, because it requires a remaking of the soul. He cannot give up the old because that would mean death to him, and he cannot master the new – the process is simply beyond his power."

This plight, between two worlds and cut off from effective communication with either, has been called by some the "tragedy of the immigrant." It may have been a tragedy, but if so, I suspect that it was not so great a one as might at first be thought. The struggle of the immigrant was a struggle for adjustment by large groups of people; and by its very nature it implied contacts at innumerable points with the new American world into which they were projected. The immigrants did not remain wholly apart from the people they came to; they were not wholly torn off from those they forsook. What happened can be interpreted by historian, novelist, and sociologist, but in some ways most effectively by the linguist.

The immigrant neither gave up his old language nor, though he learned some English, did he wholly master the new, but he was nevertheless not helpless or greatly frustrated. What he did was to create, by gradual and normal processes of change, adaptation, and growth, something like an intermediate language which combined both languages, broke the shock of his New World plunge, and on the whole served his needs effectively. While residing in this linguistic halfway house, he enjoyed the security of a fairly solid, though temporary, foundation of what may be described as a European-American way of life. It was not exactly European nor was it wholly American, but it had contact with both and was colored by both. It possessed many inner bonds – of custom, speech, social life, institutions, the propinquity that was the reward of group settlement, and, perhaps above all, the bond of mutual sharing in processes of change.

The immigrants from Norway were from the first aware of the need of learning English. Their language, like the tools and clothes and food they brought to America, was based on a "self-contained and hand-labor economy." As I mentioned earlier, half of the American agricultural words had no equivalent in the Norwegian language. The immigrant farmer, like the immigrant laborer, needed to understand and use words which fitted the new jobs he performed. He could not go to a store or trade, and his children could not go to school, without running into the problem of language. The wife at home might manage very well for a time with the Old World tongue, but it was not long before the children brought home strange words she wanted to understand, and when she opened the mail-order catalogue there were things she wanted to possess and know how to name.

The immigrant took the English language into his system, not in a mighty gulp, but bite by bite. He adjusted himself idea by idea. The adaptation of Norwegian to American started very early among the immigrants. But it was not a direct shift from Norwegian to English. A keenly observant Norwegian traveler who visited a Norwegian-Wisconsin settlement in 1847 has left us an early analysis of immigrant language transition. He noticed how the immigrants did "not bother about keeping the two languages separate," so that they might "speak Norwegian to their own countrymen and English to others"; instead they eliminated "one word after the other from their Norwegian" and substituted "English words in such a way that," he felt, Norwegian would "soon be forgotten." By this process "the immigrant's vocabulary was . . . being constantly atrophied at one end and renewed at the other."

This early traveler had a sharp ear for the changes he heard in the Norwegian immigrants' speech. For instance he noted that the immigrant farmer called what lay beyond his garden, *fila*. This, he explained, was the English word *field* used with the "genuine Norwegian feminine article 'a.'" From just such absorbed English words grew the linguistic halfway house of Norwegian-American. As old words went out, new words came in. His old language, shaped to fit the economy and culture of the Old World, was reshaped to fit the New. The language process followed the reorientation of the immigrant mind.

Professor Einar Haugen, after intensive research in the field, has given a brilliant analysis of Norwegian-American. He finds it consists of three separate aspects. First are the words which the immigrant retained with little or no change. *Light*, *wall*, and *head* are among them. Next come the Norwegian words which acquired a shifted meaning in America; finally there are the new English terms. Abstract ideas did not quickly change to English words, nor did the immigrant's vocabulary for home and family life, for bodily sensations, emotions, and thoughts. "His entire family life from courtship to offspring was a private concern, into which American influence was slow to penetrate." "Home and church were the social institutions which the immigrant brought with him, just as surely as the parts of his body and the stirrings of his mind, and his language reflects the extent to which he maintained them intact against the inroads of American influence."

But American influence was rapid in other spheres. Quickly Norwegian-American acquired such words as *drugstore*, *saloon*, *sheriff*, *running for office*, *Wild West show*, or *ball bearing*. The immigrant kept his own word for blanket—*kvitidl*—when he spoke of the homemade variety, the kind he had known in Norway, but he *bought* a "blanket." He might have kept the Norwegian terms for rivers and creeks, but nothing in the Middle West with its placid slow-flowing streams reminded him of the rushing torrents of his native land. So he adopted New World terms for the changed streams.

For the social historian, it is not so much the technical aspects of the linguistic process that challenge attention as the procession of words and the transition in outlook they reveal. Professor Haugen feels that it is possible to follow a parallel "development of language and social circumstance in practically every phase of life." For example, the terms of family relationship in Norway were more complicated than in American families. The greater significance of the family clan in Norway explains the difference. Thus as the immigrant began discarding such terms as *farfar* and *morfar*, *farbror* and *morbror*, to distinguish maternal and paternal kinsmen, for the neutral terms of *bestefar* and *onkel*—grandfather and uncle—he was making a step into American family life, though still using a purely Norwegian vocabulary.

Norwegian-American is now primarily a matter of historical interest, yet the reconstruction of its development has been called as "exciting as the geologist's study of layers in the earth's surface." There are still some so-called "fossil specimens" whose language dates back to the language of the first generation of Norwegian settlers, persons who speak excellent English as well as a relatively unsullied Norwegian dialect. But their Norwegian is a "holiday luxury, a speech for special occasions," not the Norwegian-American of the descendants of the majority, whom they accuse of "undue mixing" of speech.

As Norwegian-American turned more and more into pure American, only the shell remained Norwegian; the heart became American. Yet no one searching through a Minnesota or Dakota telephone directory today can overlook one result of the Americanization of Norwegian. Thumbing down the pages of Johnsons, Olsons, and Nelsons, even an intimate acquaintance is frequently at a loss to locate a friend in the columns of similar surnames. This duplication is in part a result of Norwegian-American, and I mention it to show that the transition has left its mark on even the most utilitarian of books. Such surnames as Olson, Johnson, and the like, derived from the first name of the immigrant's father, were used in part because they were easy for Americans to pronounce and spell, whereas the genuine surnames were often completely baffling to Americans. This was one way in which the immigrant fitted himself into a new world and a new language.

The immigrant unconsciously made use of the flexibilities of language to aid him in achieving a "unified cultural personality." The strange language that he created within a shell of Norwegian seems upon superficial retrospect to be linguistic confusion, but in reality it betokens a struggle of large numbers of people toward some kind of intellectual, or cultural, unity.

There are two sides to immigrant pioneering. One is that of the land taker, the conquest of the frontier, the transformation of a wilderness. That story is big both in its sweep from ocean to ocean and in its significance for American tradition, character, and practice. The other side is primarily social and cultural and has to do with frontiers of mind and spirit. The two, taken together, when viewed as dynamic processes of transition and growth, constitute one of the significant themes in the social history of America. It is a theme we need to understand if we would understand the history of the American people. And it is clear that the road to understanding is multidisciplinary, with historians, linguists, students of literature and folklore, and yet others joining hands in the search for truth.

. . . AND THIS IS AN AMERICAN REGION

The Fashionable Tour

FROM the days of trail blazer and trader to those of lumberman, farmer, and town builder, rivers have been of great importance to the Northwest; and one in particular captured the imagination of the pioneers – the Mississippi. It was the path of explorer and voyageur, the line of steamboat pageantry, the route of incoming settlers, the link of frontier with civilization. To all it was dignified by the term "the river," and it is still "the river" – great in its sweep from Itasca to the sea, great in its span of the nation's history, great too in its role in American life.

The very magnitude of "the river," geographically, historically, and in many-sided interest, perhaps explains why no historian has yet succeeded in writing the book of the Mississippi – a magnum opus that tells the story in its full range and interprets it in all its varied aspects. One must turn to Mark Twain, to the poets and singers, to the narratives of old steamboat men, and to a hundred other sources to understand the meaning of the Mississippi and to know the glamor of the *War Eagle*, the *Northern Belle*, *Time and Tide*, and other steamboats that churned its waters.

The historians are doing their part, however, for they are piecing together this chapter and that in the story, hunting out and preserving the old records, and gradually building up materials for a broad history of the Mississippi.

That history should include some account of the beginnings of the Northwest tourist trade, which has become, we are told, a major industry. It was the Mississippi and its steamboats that inaugurated the trade and spread the fame of Minnesota as a vacation land, promising to the enterprising tourist the adventure of a journey to a remote frontier coupled with the enjoyment of picturesque scenery and of good fishing and hunting.

Giacomo Beltrami, a passenger on the *Virginia* when that first steamboat on the upper river made its maiden journey in 1823, may perhaps be called the first modern tourist of Minnesota. The mercurial Italian was bent on a voyage of exploration, but he traveled up the Mississippi as a tourist who compared the wonders of its towering bluffs and wooded hillsides with the scenery of the Rhine.

Beltrami recorded the astonishment of the Indians when they viewed the boat on which he was traveling. "I know not what impression the first sight of the Phoenician vessels might make on the inhabitants of the coast of Greece; or the Triremi of the Romans on the wild natives of Iberia, Gaul, or Britain," he wrote, "but I am sure it could not be stronger than that which I saw on the countenances of these savages at the arrival of our steam-boat." Some "thought it a monster vomiting fire, others the dwelling of the Manitous, but all approached it with reverence or fear."

To another traveler goes the distinction of calling attention to the vacation possibilities of an upper Mississippi journey and also of giving it a slogan-like name. George Catlin, the well-known artist of American Indian life, made a trip by steamboat up the Mississippi from St. Louis to Fort Snelling and the Falls of St. Anthony in 1835. "The majestic river from the Balize to the Fall of St. Anthony, I have just passed over; with a high-wrought mind filled with amazement and wonder," he wrote.

"All that can be seen on the Mississippi below St. Louis, or for several hundred miles above it, gives no hint or clue to the magnificence of the scenes which are continually opening to the eye of the traveller, and riveting him to the deck of the steamer, through sunshine, lightning or rain, from the mouth of the Ouisconsin to the Fall of St. Anthony."

After describing the scenery above Prairie du Chien, he said, "I leave it for the world to come and gaze upon for themselves." He proposed a "Fashionable Tour"—a trip "by steamer to Rock Island, Galena, Dubuque, Prairie du Chien, Lake Pepin, St. Peters, Fall of St. Anthony," and he expressed the opinion that "This Tour would comprehend but a small part of the great 'Far West'; but it will furnish to the traveller a fair sample, and being a part of it which is now made so easily accessible to the world, and the only part of it to which *ladies* can have access, I would recommend to all who have time and inclination to devote to the enjoyment of so splendid a Tour, to wait not, but make it while the subject is new, and capable of producing the greatest degree of pleasure."

One wonders why the modern boosters of Minnesota and the Northwest have not built a monument to George Catlin.

The idea of a Fashionable Tour up the Mississippi quickly spread. Each year saw increasing numbers of sight-seers who took Catlin's advice. Most of them in the earlier years were men, but there were a few women who were willing to hazard the dangers of a journey to the outposts of America.

One of these, a vivacious lady of eighty years, was none other than Elizabeth Schuyler Hamilton, the widow of Alexander Hamilton. She had gone west to visit her son William in Wisconsin in the summer of 1837 and decided "to ascend the Mississippi to the St. Peter's." She journeyed to Fort Snelling on the new steamboat *Burlington*, saw the Falls of St. Anthony and Minnehaha, and, as befitted a queen of fashion, was accorded a royal reception by the officers of the fort. "A carpet had been spread," wrote a friend of Mrs. Hamilton, "an armchair [was] ready to receive her, the troops were under arms, we passed between two double rows of soldiers, and a very fine band was playing."

The Fashionable Tour was stamped with the approval of this distinguished lady, who was delighted with the Minnesota country and her experiences. The next year, in 1838, Captain

Frederick Marryat, the author of *Mr. Midshipman Easy*, traveled up the river, saw the sights, witnessed a game of lacrosse, which curiously he said was "somewhat similar to the game of golf in Scotland," and studied "the Indians in their primitive state." His *Diary in America*, published in England in 1839, recorded the entire experience—and his was but one of many narratives putting before the world the story of travel on the upper Mississippi.

Something more was needed, however, to establish the popularity of the Fashionable Tour. The impetus came from the motion pictures of our grandfathers, the panoramas, great unwinding rolls of painted canvas which artists exhibited in America and Europe to the accompaniment of lectures. As early as 1839 John Rowson Smith and John Risley presented a panorama of the upper valley. About a decade later John Banvard showed to the world a vast panorama of the Mississippi. His canvas, with its many scenes, was three miles long, but unhappily it portrayed only the river below St. Louis.

By 1849, however, three more Mississippi panoramas were giving the public a demonstration of the potential delights of the Fashionable Tour. Henry Lewis had spent the summer of 1848 making a leisurely tour of the river between St. Louis and Fort Snelling, and the next year he began to exhibit his famous panorama, a canvas twelve hundred yards long and twelve feet high. Leon Pomarede and S. B. Stockwell, both associates of Lewis, soon had competing panoramas on display, and by the end of the 1850's there were eight or ten panoramas of the upper Mississippi touring the show halls of the nation.

The panoramists tried to picture in faithful detail not only the river but also the life alongside it: the native Indians and their villages and the American towns and cities. In their attempts at realistic effects they used ingenious devices. Pomarede, for example, somehow managed to make real smoke and steam roll from the steamboats in his pictures. And yet the artists felt the inadequacy of their efforts. Lewis wrote in his diary one day, "As I looked I felt how hopeless art was to convay the *soul* of such a scene as this and as the poet wishes for the pencil of the artist so did I for the power of descript[i]on to tell of the thousand thoughts fast crowding each other from my mind."

Crowds of people went to see these travel movies of the 1840's and 1850's and thus toured the great river vicariously. The throngs that wished to view Banvard's panorama were so great when it was displayed in Boston and New York that railroads ran special excursions to accommodate them. In these two cities alone more than four hundred thousand people saw the exhibition. "The river comes to me instead of my going to the river," wrote Longfellow. Whittier, after seeing a panorama, sang of the "new Canaan of our Israel," and Thoreau, who not only viewed a panorama but also made the tour itself, envisaged a coming heroic age in which simple and obscure men, the real heroes of history, would build the foundations of new castles in the West and throw bridges across a "Rhine stream of a different kind."

Risley's canvas, unwound before audiences in Oslo in 1852, touched the imagination of the Norwegian poet Vinje, who came away from the exhibition convinced that America was destined to conquer the world. Banvard had a run of twenty months in London, with admissions exceeding six hundred thousand.

Meanwhile, people were coming singly, in honeymoon couples, in small groups, and sometimes in parties of hundreds to make the tour portrayed in the panoramas. Sometimes they chartered boats to carry them up the river and back, and often the steamboat companies, with an eye to increasing business, organized excursions of their own, advertising their plans far in advance through newspaper announcements and offering low rates.

Such excursions were conducted from places as far away

as New Orleans and Pittsburgh. Ordinarily the fare from St. Louis to St. Paul was $12.00. From Galena it was $6.00, though rate wars brought it at times as low as $1.00. The tours were made expeditiously. In 1850, for example, the *Dr. Franklin* left Galena on Thursday, spent one day in St. Paul, and was back at Galena on Tuesday. The round trip from St. Louis normally took eight or nine days, but might be made in six or seven on speedy boats.

The idea of excursion boats reserved for patrons of the Fashionable Tour captured the fancy of travelers, and by the late 1830's such outings were not uncommon on the upper Mississippi. The tourists could view the scenery, see Indians at first hand, and enjoy their vacations without the hubbub and the annoyances encountered on vessels heavily loaded with freight for the frontier forts or fur-trading stations.

As the fame of the upper Mississippi Valley spread, travelers from the far South and the East increased in number. By the middle 1840's tourists from New York, Washington, Pittsburgh, and Cincinnati, as well as from New Orleans, St. Louis, and Galena were making the trip. One of the tourists was Nathaniel Fish Moore, president of Columbia College. In the summer of 1845, weary of faculty meetings, he made his way to Fort Snelling by way of Buffalo, Detroit, and Chicago, recording in his diary the discomforts of travel by railroad, stagecoach, and steamboat. On the far frontier Moore saw the falls later celebrated by Longfellow under the name Minnehaha and pronounced them a "perfect gem."

The time came when one could go all the way from the East to the Mississippi by rail. The Fashionable Tour was thus brought more easily within the range of possibility for thousands of people. When the Rock Island Railroad was completed from Chicago to the Mississippi River in 1854, a special celebration was arranged which included a voyage in chartered steamboats up the river from Rock Island to St. Paul. Twelve hundred persons in a flotilla of seven steamboats made the tour commemorating this union of steel and water. The party included ex-President Millard Fillmore, the historian George Bancroft, Professor Benjamin Silliman of Yale, and a regiment of journalists. Charles A. Dana of the *New York Tribune*, Samuel Bowles of the *Springfield Republican*, Thurlow Weed of the *Albany Evening Journal*, and Epes Sargent of the *Boston Transcript* were among the writers whose detailed reports advertised Minnesota not only to prospective settlers but also to those interested in an unusual kind of pleasure jaunt.

The journey upstream was enlivened by music, dancing, popular lectures, mock trials, and promenades from boat to boat. Four of the steamboats, for example, were lashed together as they plowed their way up through Lake Pepin. At the river towns there were gala receptions, with addresses of welcome by local citizens and responses by the visiting dignitaries. Everyone talked about the marvels of the Mississippi scenery and the coming greatness of the West, and everyone accepted the view of Catherine Sedgwick that the "fashionable tour will be in the track" of this excursion.

St. Paul was out in force to welcome the visitors, to listen to the praises of Fillmore and Bancroft, and to provide vehicles for a trip to the Falls of St. Anthony and Minnehaha. Dana, writing to the *New York Tribune*, described the infant town of St. Paul. There were, he wrote, "Brick dwellings and stone warehouses, a brick capitol with stout, white pillars, a county court-house, a jail, several churches, a market, school-houses, a billiard-room, a ten-pin alley, dry goods' stores, groceries, confectioners and ice-creamers, a numerous array of those establishments to which the Maine law is especially hostile, and a glorious, boundless country behind."

There were a few discordant notes in the general hymn of praise, however. One journalist wrote:

"As the Upper Mississippi must now become a route for fashionable Summer travel, it is only proper to say that those who resort here must not yet expect to find all the conveniences and comforts which abound on our North River steamers. Everything is very plain; the staterooms are imperfectly furnished, but the berths are roomy; the table is abundant, but butter-knives and sugar-tongs are not among its luxuries."

In due time these and many other luxuries appeared. Companies, competing sharply for traffic, vied with one another in bettering accommodations, providing well-furnished staterooms, improving steamboat architecture, serving good food, rigging up bars where, as Mark Twain says, "everybody drank, and everybody treated everybody else," employing bands and orchestras, and in other ways adding to the attractions of the Fashionable Tour. And when large and luxurious river boats docked at the St. Paul levee, their captains liked to invite local citizens on board to see the wonders of the ships and to join in "grand balls," as was done, for example, when in 1857 the *Henry Clay* brought up an excursion party from St. Louis.

The captains and pilots, the envied monarchs of the river, took unbounded pride in their boats. One pilot in after years recalled the *Grey Eagle* as "long, lean, and as graceful as a grey-hound" – the "sweetest thing in the way of a steamboat that a man ever looked at." Steamboats, he believed, had souls; and his idea of heaven was the *Grey Eagle* plying "celestial waters, carrying angels on their daily visits, with their harps," Daniel Harris, captain, and himself the pilot.

The general picture of beautiful boats, luxury, and gala entertainment must not close one's eyes to another side of river traffic: the vast throngs, on most of the boats, of immigrants who crowded the lower decks while the tourists occupied cabins and balconies on top of the decks. Coming in ever-increasing swarms, the immigrants accounted for great profits to the steamboat companies, and, with the expansion of freighting, they help to explain why, in the 1850's, the number of steamboat arrivals at St. Paul sometimes ran to more than a thousand in a single season.

Bound for the Promised Land, the immigrants faced, as Dr. William J. Petersen says, the hazards of "runners, black-legs, and gamblers, explosions, tornadoes, and devastating fires, snags and sandbars, poor food and wretched accommodations, sickness, suffering, and death." When cholera and other diseases broke out on board ship, they were likely to spread with appalling rapidity. On one occasion a traveler complained because the towel in the washroom was filthy. "Wal now," said the purser, "I reckon there's fifty passengers on board this boat, and they've all used that towel, and you're the first on 'em that's complained of it."

What did the people who made the Fashionable Tour in early days see? For most, the magnificence of the scenery made up for torment by mosquitoes and the inconvenience of crowded quarters. Indeed, many were so delighted that they accepted philosophically the hazards of explosions and collisions. The scenery held them spellbound upon the decks of the steamboats through the days and often far into the nights. Said one traveler:

"I had taken my impressions of the Mississippi scenery from the descriptions of the river below St. Louis, where the banks are generally depressed and monotonous. But nothing can surpass the grandeur of the Upper Mississippi. Is it then strange that I was fascinated while floating through these Western paradises, over which the moon shed her soft, shadowy light, and where the notes of the whippo[or]will rose and died far away, as I had heard them in my boyhood's home?"

Another tourist wrote:

"We came . . . on the Steamer Yankee, and a delightful trip we had. The scenery of the Upper Mississippi, for wilderness, beauty and grandeur, is unequaled and perfectly indescribable.

"We had grand moonlight scenes on this glorious river, that were perfectly enchanting. It seemed as though I could gaze all night; that my eyes would never tire or be satisfied, in beholding the beauty and grandeur of its ever-varying banks and lofty hills."

And Fredrika Bremer, the kindly and observant visitor to America from Sweden, wrote, "I have . . . seen the scenery on the upper Mississippi, its high bluffs crowned with autumn-golden oaks, and rocks like ruined walls and towers, ruins from the times when the Megatherium and mastodons walked the earth, – and how I did enjoy it!"

Sometimes a traveler, vexed by the slow progress of his boat, annoyed by its unscheduled stops on sandbars, or wearied alike by travel and by travelers, failed to join the usual chorus. Ida Pfeiffer, an Austrian lady of wealth, had sober second thoughts. "This is a grand thing to think of at first," she wrote, "but after a few days one gets tired of the perpetual monotony of the scenery." Even she relented, however, when her boat entered Lake Pepin, for the sight of it, she said, "almost made me amends for my long and tedious voyage up the river."

George T. Borrett, an English visitor, made the journey during a period of extremely low water. He chronicles his impressions with solemn detail:

"A broad expanse of extremely shallow water; a number of oddly-shaped marshy-looking islands, a tortuous channel in and out amongst them, very difficult of navigation, and intersected by frequent sandbanks, on the top of which the keel of our boat grated at every other bend in the stream, with a dull sound that brought home to the passengers the uncomfortable apprehension of the possibility of sticking fast on one of these banks and seeing much more of the Mississippi than we had bargained for; a low vegetation on most of these islands, very much like that which may be seen on any of the alluvial deposits on the Thames; a range of steep bluffs on either bank rising abruptly from the water's edge, sparsely wooded and bare alternately, but bold in outline and precipitous. Such was my first impression of the Mississippi scenery, and such it is now, for there was little or no variety."

The Father of Waters appeared to him "very much in the light of an impostor." "I think it extremely doubtful," he said, "whether, in his then state of aqueous insolvency, proud little Father Thames himself would have owned him even for a poor relation."

Borrett's boat was crowded, the accommodations were inadequate, and he found the company intolerable. Ida Pfeiffer shared his scornful attitude toward the fellow passengers and was especially indignant at the impudence of two young ladies who patted her on the shoulder and genially called her "grandma." She also thought the manners displayed at the dinner table were somewhat less than perfect, particularly the strange custom of certain people of pelting "each other with the gnawed cobs of Indian corn." In the evening, she says, the ladies took possession of the ten available rocking chairs, "placed them in a circle, threw themselves back in them, many even held their hands over their heads, stuck their feet far out, and then away they went full swing."

Let us draw the distressed Ida away from this shocking spectacle and introduce her to a fellow sufferer, Anthony Trollope, the English novelist, who made the Fashionable Tour in Civil War days. The author of *Barchester Towers* had many melancholy reflections to record. "Nine-tenths of the travellers," he exclaimed, "carry children with them. . . . I must protest that American babies are an unhappy race." The parents seemed to Trollope as untalkative as their babies were discontented and dyspeptic. "I found no aptitude, no wish for conversation," he said; "nay, even a disinclination to converse." And poor Trollope's cabin was too hot. This circumstance led him to generalize about the effects upon Americans of their taste for living in the "atmosphere of a hot oven." To that taste he attributed their thin faces, pale skins, unenergetic temperament, and early old age.

When Catlin made his tour in 1835, there was only a lonely frontier outpost at the junction of the Minnesota and Mississippi rivers and a rough trading post close by to signalize white civilization at the northern terminus of the Fashionable Tour. The characteristic note of the region was Indian life. Catlin, like Marryat a few years later, was entertained by a Sioux game of lacrosse and by a variety of Indian dances. From Fort Snelling south into Iowa, the wilderness was broken only by an occasional Indian village or trader's post.

Charles Lanman in 1846 felt that at St. Peter's, at the mouth of the Minnesota River, he was "on the extreme verge of the civilized world, and that all beyond, to the ordinary traveller," was "mysterious wilderness."

In 1852 Mrs. Elizabeth Ellet thought it "curious to see the primitive undergrowth of the woods, and even trees, left" in portions of St. Paul "not yet improved by buildings." In walking from her hotel to the home of Governor Ramsey, she "passed through quite a little forest . . . and saw a bear's cub at play – an incident in keeping with the scene." She was attracted by the "curious blending of savage and civilized life. . . . The lodges of the Dakotas had vanished from the opposite shore . . . but their canoes yet glided over the waters of the Mississippi, and we met them whenever we stepped outside the door."

Mrs. Ellet found "excellent quarters" in the Rice Hotel in St. Paul. St. Anthony, she reported, "has but recently emerged from a wilderness into the dignity of a village."

"In the summer months the town is much resorted to by visitors, especially from the southwestern States. These have come in such numbers that no accommodations could be found for them, and they were obliged to return with but a glance at the curiosities they had come to view. Now the state of things is more favorable to the lovers of fine scenery; an excellent hotel—the St. Charles—having recently passed into the proprietorship of Mr. J. C. Clark, and under his excellent management, already obtained a reputation as one of the best in the northwestern country."

Mrs. Ellet boarded one of Willoughby and Powers' stagecoaches for what was called the "grand tour." It consisted of a drive from St. Paul to St. Anthony, then out to Lakes Harriet and Calhoun, "thence to the Minnehaha Falls and Fort Snelling, and by the Spring Cave to St. Paul, arriving in time for the visitors, if in haste, to return with the boat down the river." Shortly before Mrs. Ellet's arrival, the beauties of the Lake Minnetonka region began to be appreciated, and during her stay in St. Paul she took advantage of an opportunity to visit what in due time was to become one of the most popular summer resorts in the Northwest. Frontenac, White Bear, the St. Croix country, and many other places became widely known as ideal for tourists and vacation seekers.

The early pioneers were not so absorbed with the task of building cities, towns, and farms that they closed their eyes to the recreational attractions of Minnesota. They were, in fact, belligerent boosters. Every newspaper was a tourist bureau, but James M. Goodhue, the editor of the *Minnesota Pioneer*, was perhaps the leading promoter of them all. He intoxicated himself with his own superlatives. In 1852 he invited the world, and more especially the people of the South, to make the Fashionable Tour, to breathe the marvelous air of Minnesota and be healed of earthly ailments. In true Goodhuean style, he asked:

"Who that is idle would be caged up between walls of burning brick and mortar, in dog-days, down the river, if at less daily expense, he could be hurried along through the valley of the Mississippi, its shores studded with towns, and farms, flying by islands, prairies, woodlands, bluffs—an ever varied scene of beauty, away up into the land of the wild

Dakota, and of cascades and pine forests, and cooling breezes? —Why it is an exhilarating luxury, compared with which, all the fashion and tinsel and parade of your Newports and Saratogas, are utterly insipid."

He pictured the miserable life of a southern planter and of his "debilitated wife and pale children, almost gasping for breath." "What is such a life to him and those he loves, but death prolonged?" he asked.

"A month in Minnesota, in dog-days, is worth a whole year anywhere else; and, we confidently look to see the time, when all families of leisure down South, from the Gulf of Mexico along up, will make their regular summer hegira to our Territory; and when hundreds of the opulent from those regions, will build delightful cottages on the borders of our ten thousand lakes and ornament their grounds with all that is tasteful in shrubbery and horticulture, for a summer retreat."

In this, as in many other fields, Goodhue the booster was Goodhue the prophet. Even before the Civil War large numbers of people from the South flocked to Minnesota as a summer resort, and the habit was resumed not long after Appomattox. Folk from East and West joined in exploiting the vacation and tourist attractions of Minnesota. The day of the Fashionable Tour on the upper Mississippi passed when steamboating declined in the face of railroad competition. Local excursions continued to be popular, but the gala period of the steamboats and the great excursions was over. The fame of Minnesota as a summer resort had been established, however, and the railroads made the lakes and rivers of the North Country even more accessible than they had been when sleek and picturesque vessels graced the river in its golden age.

Word Hunters

ON A spring day in 1834, the steamboat *Warrior* puffed its way to the landing at old Fort Snelling, and two young Connecticut Yankees, Samuel William Pond and his brother Gideon Hollister Pond, stepped ashore.

They were laymen who had been converted in a New England revival three years earlier and were now seeking a field for missionary work among the Sioux, or Dakota, Indians of the Northwest. They were without experience as missionaries, had no official backing, lacked even a government permit to enter the Indian country, and did not know the language of the people whose conversion and civilization they wished to promote. Yet they were not without qualifications for the work they proposed to do. They had enjoyed an excellent elementary schooling, had worked on farms, knew how to use their hands, and had practical good sense, simplicity of taste and habit, active and inquiring minds, persistence, and quiet courage.

Both men, we are told, "were over six feet tall, stalwart and sinewy, alert and genial." The Sioux named them "Red Eagle" and "Grizzly Bear."

The Ponds harbored a pious zeal for their mission, coupled with a firm belief that God had prepared the way for them. "I have a friend who sticketh closer than a brother," wrote Gideon a few days after his arrival. He summed up his first impressions in these words, "Through the protection and mercy of God I have arrived at one of the most beautiful places I ever saw."

The brothers were given an abrupt initiation into their

labors. Major Bliss of Fort Snelling held a hearing to determine whether or not to exclude them from the Indian country as unauthorized visitors. He plied Samuel with questions and suddenly asked him to explain the plans the two brothers had formulated. Samuel answered simply that they "had no plan except to do what seemed most for the benefit of the Indian." The major then told him that the Sioux at the village of Kaposia not far from the fort "wanted plowing done and had a plow and oxen" but did not know how to use them, whereupon Samuel promptly offered to give them a practical demonstration.

The offer was accepted. The Indians themselves conveyed a plow in a canoe from Fort Snelling to their village, and Samuel drove down a yoke of oxen. He then spent a week's time teaching plowing to Big Thunder, the father of Chief Little Crow, and Big Iron – the missionary driving the oxen, the two Indians alternately holding the implement. Samuel had the insight of a good teacher. "I could have ploughed as well, perhaps better, without their aid," he wrote later, "but I promised to help them only on condition that they would help themselves."

Gideon, meanwhile, was having a similar experience, for he worked with a plow among the Sioux living near Lake Calhoun. Not least among many notable contributions of the Pond brothers was the willing help they gave the red man in meeting the transition to the white man's mode of life. They grasped the need of understanding the Indian mind; they saw that the natives must learn through doing.

Major Lawrence Taliaferro, the noted Indian agent, had sponsored a Sioux agricultural village under Chief Cloud Man on the southeast side of Lake Calhoun. Upon his suggestion, the Ponds decided to establish their first mission station at that place. They built a two-room cabin of peeled logs with a bark roof. Gideon described it as "a good snug little house"; it "seemed like a palace" to Samuel. "That hut," wrote Gideon later, "was the home of the first citizen settlers of Hennepin County, perhaps of Minnesota, the first school room, the first house for divine worship, and the first mission station among the Dakota Indians."

Major Taliaferro was highly pleased with the thought that the two Yankees, thus stationed, would fall in with his idea of teaching the Indians the arts of civilization – how to plow, how to plant corn and potatoes, how to cultivate mother earth. They did indeed give notable assistance to the major, but they made his civilizing scheme secondary to the conversion of the Indians to Christianity. This was their first and central purpose.

Meanwhile, a tour of investigation in Minnesota made for the American Board of Commissioners for Foreign Missions at Boston by Dr. Thomas S. Williamson in 1834 was bearing fruit. Other missionaries appeared on the scene. In 1835 the Ponds helped Jedediah Stevens to establish a mission station at Lake Harriet a mile south of their cabin. Gideon joined Dr. Williamson at Lac qui Parle in 1836 and remained there three years, aiding the doctor in translating the Bible, while Samuel, not content with his layman's status, returned to Connecticut, was ordained in 1837, and received an appointment as a regular missionary from the American Board. Both brothers returned to Lake Harriet in 1839.

During these years the Ponds, while meeting other demands and performing other duties, were engaged in a thrilling hunt, and their success in bagging game gives them a secure place in history. "The language was the game I went to hunt," wrote Samuel, telling of a Sioux hunting party he had joined, "and I was as eager in the pursuit of that as the Indians were in pursuit of deer."

The mastery of the Sioux tongue was essential to the Ponds' missionary purpose, but it had not yet been reduced to written form, and to this task the brothers addressed themselves with industry and shrewd intelligence. As early as the winter of 1833, when Samuel, then at Galena, first proposed to Gideon a plan to work among the Sioux, he remarked, "From them we could learn the language which is spoken by a vast number of Indians, from the Mississippi to the Pacific." In his own narrative he tells of his first triumph in the campaign to acquire the Dakota language. This occurred at Prairie du Chien on the way northward to the Minnesota country. He was told by a white man how to ask in Dakota what a thing is called. Seeing a Sioux standing near a heap of iron, he walked up to him, pointed to the iron, and inquired of him the Dakota word for it. The Indian "promptly replied *maza* and then dipped a little water in his hand from the river and said *mini*—then took up a handful of sand and said *wiyaka*."

This episode greatly pleased Pond. Telling of it later, he said that "no other acquisition ever afforded me so much pleasure as it did then to be able to say in Dakota, What do you call this? We had a key now to the Dakota names of visible objects, and it did not rust in our hands for want of use."

By 1839 Samuel Pond had a dictionary collection of three thousand words and had completed a small manuscript grammar. He and his brother, pioneering in the field, adapted the English alphabet for use in writing Dakota. In order to express a number of strange Dakota consonant sounds, they took certain English letters that were not needed in Dakota and gave them "new names and powers." In their alphabet "no two letters could be used to denote the same sound so there was but one way of spelling any given word."

That this "Pond alphabet" was workable was proved not only by the fact that a native Sioux, using it, quickly learned to write his own language, but also by the circumstance that it was adopted generally and formed the basis of a great *Grammar and Dictionary of the Dakota Language*, published in 1852 under the patronage of the Minnesota Historical Society by the Smithsonian Institution. This work was officially edited by Stephen R. Riggs, who had been tutored in Dakota by Samuel Pond, but it was in a sense an outcome of the collecting begun by the Ponds in 1834. It embodied much of their material and must be considered a climax to their Dakota studies.

Word hunting and recording, however, represent only one aspect of the achievement of the Pond brothers in reference to the Dakota language. Samuel was responsible for a Dakota spelling book issued in 1836, the first work printed in that language. In 1839 he and Gideon brought out a translation of the *History of Joseph*, from the story in Genesis, and Gideon collaborated with Dr. Riggs in a *Dakota First Reading Book*. Samuel prepared a *Second Dakota Reading Book* in 1842, a *Dakota Catechism* two years later, and various other works; and in the early 1850's Gideon actually edited a monthly newspaper or illustrated journal, the *Dakota Tawaxitku Kin*, or *Dakota Friend*, most of which was written in Dakota. This unusual venture had as its purpose the promotion of mutual understanding and good will between red men and white.

So a veritable Dakota library was created by the pioneer missionaries among the Sioux. The Ponds, who according to Dr. Folwell "knew and spoke Dakota better than any other white men," deserve recognition as the pioneer recorders of that language, which they found an oral and left a written language. In performing this fascinating task they both became linguists. They learned not only Dakota but Hebrew, Greek, Latin, and French, and Samuel also acquired German.

The Ponds were recorders not only of the Dakota language but also of Sioux life and customs. With characteristic missionary patience and fidelity they recorded their experiences and observations in letters and other manuscripts that are today a rich storehouse of dependable information. Samuel's elaborate account of the Sioux as they were in 1834 is perhaps the most detailed and informing description we have of that nation before it lost its vast hunting grounds.

And in his poems he has left a lasting record of the legends of Winona and of the Falls of St. Anthony and also of his own impressions of the beauty and natural charm of Lakes Harriet and Calhoun and of Minnesota, which stirred his imagination:

> As with a wild delight I view
> Nature, unmarred by hand of man.

There were scenes of barbarism in this primitive Minnesota, however. In 1839, the year when Samuel took charge of the Lake Harriet mission, these friendly shores became a "dark and bloody ground." The killing of a Sioux hunter at Lake Harriet in the summer of that year caused the ancient Chippewa-Sioux feud to flare into open war, with bloody battles at Stillwater and Rum River. For a month the Sioux celebrated their triumphs in their Calhoun village with dances under the seventy poles on which they flaunted scalps torn from the bleeding heads of their enemies. The brave agricultural experiment of Taliaferro had run its course; the village was exposed to Chippewa attack on the edge of the Sioux country; and so the Sioux warriors, their wild dances ended and their crops garnered, prudently removed to the Minnesota River near Bloomington.

Thither the Ponds, after some time spent at Fort Snelling and elsewhere, followed them; and there Gideon built a sturdy cabin of tamarack logs in the winter of 1842–43. From that cabin he went to St. Paul to be a member of Minnesota's first territorial legislature in 1849. The present brick house replaced the cabin in 1856, but Gideon, who had been ordained as a Presbyterian minister in 1848, remained at Bloomington until his death in 1878, serving in his later years the incoming white settlers. Samuel in 1847 removed to the village of Chief Shakopee to launch a mission and school there, laboring in the midst of a turbulent band until the Sioux removal in the 1850's. Then, declining to follow these "lawless, reckless sons of Belial," as he called them, he ministered to the pioneer settlers until 1866, when he retired. But he lived on until 1891.

The Pond brothers fixed in written form the language of the mighty nation of the Sioux. They recorded the native life that flourished in the Minnesota region a hundred years ago. They taught agriculture and the arts of civilization to the Indians and tried to promote better understanding between the white and red races. They persisted courageously in their efforts to Christianize the Indians in the face of a general tendency of the Sioux to reject the white man's religion. They served as ministers to congregations of pioneer settlers. They left a legacy of character marked by simplicity, honor, and good sense.

Samuel and Gideon Pond contributed something to the cultural texture of western frontier society. For what they were and for what they did they richly deserve to be remembered and honored by Minnesota and America.

Attic Inventory

ONE evening in April 1854 an Indiana man hammered a final nail into the lid of a box and declared his packing finished. At midnight he and his wife and children would board a packet for Minnesota Territory. The long and hard job of getting ready was done. Before setting out for the wharf, he stopped to write a few lines in his diary.

The Hoosier said that Minnesota was a land for which he felt a "buoyant hope of future Happiness." It was not easy for him to leave his home community of Wabash, however, and he told why: "Have seen this country a wilderness and witnessed its gradual rise & progress, was here when it was organized for Judicial purposes attended its first election. Saw this town . . . before the Stakes were driven to indicate the corners."

And then this line: "In short I have seen the day of small things here and it gives me pleasure to remember them."

Small things—and growth, beginnings—and change; a panorama of events in which one has played a part. Yes, it is pleasant to remember—to remember the "day of small things" in the perspective of years. Not the man from Wabash alone, but many pioneers of the Northwest had that feeling about the communities they had left, and many folk have it about the communities where they have lived through the years. The American saga is a saga of change from the "day of small things." And the heart of the saga is in the old diaries that record the everyday experiences of people who had a "buoyant hope of future Happiness."

I have seen motion pictures of the covered-wagon people, but the best picture I know is that given in an old notebook kept by a woman who journeyed into Minnesota in 1873 in a covered wagon. There is not much glamor about it. It has not been published. It has not been turned into a Hollywood film. But somehow it is the real thing.

The woman's name was Jane Grout. She went by wagon from central Wisconsin to Luverne, Minnesota, and she passed through such places as St. Charles, Rochester, Owatonna, and Worthington. The faded diary conveys a sense of the stir and bustle of the migration into Minnesota. "When out on the prairie again," wrote Jane Grout after leaving Jackson, "we could see three trains of emigrants besides our own, one train of eleven teams." The trains were trains of covered wagons.

Simple things are in the record, including some minor tragedies. Jane's family had to unload along the way a bureau and a chest and some heavy tools. And then worse luck. "We lost our canary bird before we reached Wyocena," she wrote. A few days later Beauty, the pet dog, was crushed under the wheels of the heavily loaded wagon. The children wept; all felt sad; the whole train stopped for the ceremony of burying Beauty at a camping ground along the trail.

There were no tourist camps. "It rained most all night," Jane recorded one day, "but our family slept in our wagons," protected by the canvas. Here is the start of a typical day: "We arose in good season – cooked our breakfast by the road side – the hogs showed their appreciation of victuals by taking a ball of butter out of my basket. Reading of scripture & prayer by Mrs. James. After our usual work of dishwashing & packing we started off."

There were no paved roads, no trunk highways. "After we left St. C[harles] we found the deepest mud we have yet seen." Sometimes there was sickness and it was promptly treated. "Thaddeus . . . felt so bad that I went to work & gave him a good thorough sweat with hot corn. Br[other] E. H. B. treated him with quinine powders." Later the diary says that Thaddeus felt better, but the reader is left to guess whether it was the sweat with hot corn or the quinine that cured him.

There was music of a kind: "We got up early & got started about half past six, cheered on by the music of the hungry mosquitoes." There were sights to be seen: "We see more frame houses than sod. When within about five miles of Jackson we met the grasshoppers which are coming from the west where they have done much damage."

And so the diary goes on, following these pioneers to their destination. There a curious thing happened. Jane Grout put the diary aside and did not use it again for fifty years. Then she found it, read it, looked back to the day of small things, and wrote a few words. What she said summed up a bigger story than her own or even than that of her community. She wrote, "I am now eightyseven years old & have seen . . . the end of our trail grow into a beautiful thriving . . . city & the entire broad prairie of beautiful Agricultural Rock County, dotted all over with fine houses & barns, surrounded by groves . . . Every family of our Emigrant train has high school graduates & College graduates among their children & Grand children."

History, like charity, begins at home. The world we first know is the home and the neighborhood. It is there we first explore history. Who has not known, in early years, the local story of the haunted house, the tale of the cellar hole in the abandoned field, how the near-by pond was named, what happened in the great blizzard? We start off with a background of local history; we share in the community memory; from the community we first look out upon life and the world. Then we learn the story of the land in which we live and of countries and nations and peoples outside, and we begin to realize that this broader history is the sum of the histories of numberless localities and communities.

So, as someone has said, "the understanding of the local contemporary scene is the prime objective of all educational endeavor." In that understanding the community is, not an isolated thing, but a living part of state, country, and world, with myriad bonds of interrelation.

One difficulty about exploring community backgrounds is that so many of the records we need to have are pushed away into attic corners or old boxes and chests, beyond our reach. What profit there might be if we could turn an entire community loose in quest of its own history—set apart a day of attic rummaging for old diaries, account books, and letters; of interviewing old settlers and recording their stories; of gathering up and filing the records of churches and schools, lodges and societies, organizations of many kinds.

On this day of attic inventory I want to collect the diaries that record our farms and homes. Someone has said that such records, more than most others, are representative of the past life of our people—the diaries kept by a "determined and faithful few, who sat down night after night to record by the flickering light of a candle or kerosene lamp the events of their daily existence." They make it possible to follow the daily life of the farmer, from plowing and seeding in the spring to harvest time and winter, year after year.

I have been turning over the pages of some farmers' diaries and have found in them stories of self-denial and privation, of experimentation with crops and livestock, of frontier farm life in all its aspects. A frontier farmer just after the Civil War wrote in his diary: "The black currants transplanted from the woods 4 or 5 years ago, having proved a failure, I dug the greater part of them up, and filled their places with the domestic varieties, of which we have now about 150 bushes. The wild black produced luxuriant bushes and little fruit. They have similarly failed with others who have tried them. They do not seem to bear cultivation." The diary records a pioneer experiment station.

A horticulturist near Owatonna, Minnesota, wrote one March day in the 1870's about his experiments with fruit trees: "Finished grafting in all over 13000 including about 60 varieties mostly for experiment." On another occasion he made a record of what he had learned about building fences. "Worked building over cow yard fence," he said. "Found Red Elm posts that had been set but 3 or 4 yrs so rotten I could break most of them off will not make any more of that kind Went to the woods & made 14 oak posts." One time, after several days of silence, he made a human entry of two words. "Comfortably sick," he wrote—and ten pages could not have told us more about his condition.

The diary of the man from Wabash who had seen the day of small things ranges over a long period. I shall pick up an entry made in 1863, in the midst of the Civil War. "I sold flour today," he wrote, "at 5:00 per bbl. which is higher than it has been for two years or more. Whilst most kinds of goods have been steadily advancing for a year produce has kept low but now wheat flour Pork &c begin to feel the effects of the abundant supply of money or the paper currency that has taken the place of money Heavy brown Sheeting 1 yd wide are held at 40c per yd which is an advance of full three hundred percent in less than two years. Sugar, that we have been buying at 8c are now bringing 15c . . . These are war times."

This farmer, whose name was Mitchell Young Jackson, was not blind to natural beauty. One day he wrote that wild flowers should be preserved, for, he said, the "plow & lowing herds are already making their paths and selecting their shades and watering places and it is plain that the native beauty must give way to the artificial." Sometimes when writing in his diary he got a bit restless, and once he wrote, "I feel quite anxious to quit these books & figures . . . and get hold of the plow again . . . I would much rather plow."

Diaries and letters have all the freshness of contemporary recording, and it is a quality that time does not erase. For revealing views of Roman life we read Cicero's epistles, and for vivid pictures of Roman ways in the time of Tacitus and the Emperor Trajan we turn to the polished letters of Pliny the Younger. For homely insight into English conditions in the seventeenth century we read the inimitable Samuel Pepys.

But I turn, not to Cicero or Pliny or Pepys, but to a plain Minnesota farmer named Allen W. Dawley, who kept a diary for more than half a century. It is doubtful that his diary will charm and delight the world, but he was brother in spirit to Pepys. Into his record went entries about the everyday life on his farm and in his community. There is little in it that is spectacular, but it is a comprehensive record of common things, with a long sequence.

Look at some items for the year 1867, when Dawley was living near Wabasha, Minnesota. He taught a country school during the winter months and he records the experience. Sometimes for lack of wood he had to dismiss his pupils; often because of cold weather attendance was meager. He "boarded around" and makes sharp comments about the various homes in which he was entertained. Sometimes he faced problems of school discipline. One January day he recorded: "Went in on my nerve on one of my scholars. Gave him a very *striking* illustration of how to behave."

Among diversions for winter evenings were dances, attendance at Methodist society meetings, sessions of the lodge of Good Templars, checkers, backgammon, and cards. The last day of school was held on March 15, and the teacher records that no tears were shed on that account. His farm now claimed his attention. On March 23 he bought twenty bushels of seed wheat at two dollars a bushel. The entry is typical, for the diary abounds in records of prices. Plowing, sowing, dragging, the digging of the first new potatoes on July 20, the picking of various kinds of berries, the developments of the harvest up to threshing, and the marketing of the grain – all these things are described in the diary.

One Sunday Dawley, who was a Puritan, felt obliged to

put up wheat, and that night his conscience did not rest until he had made this entry: "Did something that I was never guilty of before – that is working on Sunday."

So the diary goes. The diarist joins a ball club and records his satisfaction that his team was usually on the winning side in its games. He tells of buying tobacco. When he bought a new suit, he was careful to record the exact price – $23.00. A friend of his got married and Dawley wrote, "Good luck to him but I had rather it would be him than me." He tells of casting his first vote – straight Republican. He describes a county seat war and mentions that Wabasha was leading. In this connection he reports that Wabasha cast 4158 votes, and then adds, "Pretty well done considering it contains only about 1500 inhabitants."

If twenty centuries from now a student should attempt to reconstruct the everyday conditions of life in the pioneer agricultural commonwealths of the Middle West, he would be almost as pleased with the Dawley record as in our own day the historians of the Roman Empire are with the letters that Pliny wrote from his Laurentine and Tuscan villas and from Bithynia.

Gather up the diaries and other records that tell of the way of life of the farmer, and one day the historians may surprise us by writing the story of the farm and its folk, not less fascinating, and more significant to the people of today, than the story of the medieval manor. It will be a story of development from the day of small things – a story of the folk who in their toil and integrity create the great things that historians and poets and novelists search for in the human saga.

Everyday Life as Advertised

IN THE busy search of historians for materials illuminating the past, the newspaper advertisement is not infrequently neglected. It is well to be reminded by Professor Lucy M. Salmon, who has written a scholarly book on newspapers as historical sources, that the advertisement "serves the historian in every part of his effort to reconstruct the past," and that it is "an invaluable record in the reconstruction of the normal life of the past, – invaluable, because in large part unconsciously made and recording not only material conditions but even more clearly the intellectual and moral conditions from which they have sprung."

Do the advertisements in the newspapers of the frontier Northwest bear out this generalization? Is it possible, by studying and analyzing such advertisements, to reconstruct the normal life of the pioneers who were building a commonwealth nearly a hundred years ago?

To answer these questions, let me try to describe some aspects of life in Minnesota, particularly in St. Paul and St. Anthony, in the period from 1849 to 1851, when these towns were in their infancy, using as materials only the advertisements found in the papers of that time.

In many of the homely aspects of living the situation in Minnesota – and in America – about the middle of the nineteenth century presents interesting contrasts with that of the present. Not kerosene, gas, or electricity, but sperm oil, and "Sperm, Tallow and Star Candles, by the box or pound," met the lighting needs of the St. Paul housewife. In the matter of house furnishings she was doubtless interested in "Marble Mantle Pieces of every variety . . . Furniture Tops, and

Marble work of every description." At the hardware store she could buy, among other things, bed cords, mahogany knobs, sleigh bells, gridirons, and cooking stoves.

She had a fondness for shawls, and the advertisements reminded her of ample stocks of "shawls – Cashmere, Marino, blanket and delane Shawls"; and no doubt she was intrigued when she read the announcement of Freeman, Larpenteur and Company: "Muffs! Muffs! Received by the steamer Franklin, a complete assortment of ladies muffs, of the finest quality, and for sale low."

The clothing needs of her household could be met at Henry Jackson's store in St. Paul, which offered for sale satinets, Kentucky jeans, "bang up cord," cottonade stripe, laces of all kinds, corset jeans, blue drills, lawns, muslins, Swiss jaconet, cambric muslin, ginghams, delaines, bombazines, alpacas, "Gent's Cravats," silk gloves, and numerous other articles.

At Fuller and Brother a cordial – if somewhat aggressively genial – invitation was extended to the public:

> Examine, if you please, Ladies and Gentlemen, the prime staple, and firm texture of these woolen goods! Here is a "jam up" article of Sheep's Gray, for pantaloons; – or, if you want something finer, look at this Kerseymere. Here are Satinetts, which are warranted to wear like buckskin, and which we could sell for all wool, if we were not too honest. Here are Vestings hard to beat, especially, when on the back of a fighting man. Examine that bolt of Fustian, so firm that it seems like anything but "all fustian."

The institution known as the "general store" was ready to sell miscellaneous articles such as nails, shovels, window glass, playing cards, groceries, candy, nuts, mackerel, liquors, and tobacco. When a bakery was established in St. Paul, it hastened to explain that its products were not of the crude western variety: "Cakes, butter crackers, Boston crackers, hard bread and loaf bread, in the latest New York style, and all kinds of candies by wholesale or retail."

Farmers could get the best kind of implements at a St. Paul store: "Grain Cradles.—Patent Grapevine Cradles; also, Scythes, Snaths, Forks, Shovels, Spades, Hoes, etc."

If one may judge by advertisements, our grandparents were addicted to the excessive use of patent medicines. Dewey and Cavilier of St. Paul had an enormous supply:

FAMILY MEDICINES.

Anti-bilious, cathartic, vegetable, and ague pills, Coxe's hive syrup, Stoughton's bitters, Burgundy pitch, Liniment—volatile, nerve and bone, poor man's and anodyne; Am., Thompson's eye water opodeldoc, paragoric, castor oil without taste or smell, rheumatic drops, together with every article in the Drug line for sale cheap for cash.

The same firm expatiates on the marvelous qualities of Dalley and Connell's Magical Pain Extractor, Dr. McNair's Acoustic Oil for the cure of deafness, Langley's Great Western Indian Panacea (for dyspepsia and liver complaint), and addresses a special message to women.

To the Ladies.

The Genuine Balm of Columbia for Restoring Hair.

"Long Hair is a glory to woman," says Paul,
And all feel the truth of the pious quotation;
Preserve it then, ladies—your glory may fall,
Unless you protect it with this preparation.

Column after column of advertisements is devoted to medicines, though doctors were scarce in the frontier town. On May 12, 1849, Dr. N. Barbour announced a new drugstore and also declared that he would prescribe medicine "according to the Eclectic practice, as taught in the Cincinnati Reformed College of Medicine." He later made it clear to the public that in his practice he did "not use any calomel nor the steam system."

Dentists in St. Paul and St. Anthony had need, apparently, of a side line. The *Minnesota Pioneer* of May 30, 1850, announced that "Doctor Jarvis, Dentist & Daguerrean" was coming to St. Paul, not as an itinerant practitioner, but to "make Minnesota his home for life." The nature of his practice was explained in the advertisement: "His stock of materials, both in the Dental and Daguerrean line is most extensive and complete. Pictures taken in superior style, in clear and cloudy weather."

The doctor appears to have found the "daguerrean line" more profitable than the dental, for in 1851 his announcement was made simply as a "Daguerrean": "An Appropriate New-Year Present, Is a good daguerreotype likeness handsomely colored in fine case for $2. Two heads upon one plate, $2.50. Splendid gold and pearl embossed, satin, velvet and morocco cases, suitable for family groups."

Henry Fowler in St. Anthony combined dentistry with his work as a jeweler and as a repairer of guns, locks, and umbrellas.

Spirituous liquors flowed freely in the frontier towns, and their merits are given considerable space in the advertisements. Liberal amounts were available to customers. Thus "F L and Co." of St. Paul advertised "Whiskey – 50 bbls old rectified Whiskey, for sale cheap for cash," and wines, brandies, and gin were also in stock. John Orth of St. Anthony made the proud announcement: "I am now prepared to supply the citizens of the Territory with Ale and Beer, which will be found equal – yes superior – to what is brought from below. I am now demonstrating that malt liquors of the very best quality can be manufactured in Minnesota."

One St. Paul dealer exhibited a seasoned knowledge of human nature when he promised "something to smoke, a good fire to sit by, and whatever is usually called for at a well provided bar," adding "People in traveling between the landings, who get fatigued, will find here a comfortable place to rest on their way."

A somewhat mysterious advertisement announces a "Liquorary Association," with nightly meetings for the discussion of such important topics as "Oysters, Sardines, Pigs feet &c."

All was not bliss for the liquor dealer, however, for another and somewhat grimmer type of association was active. The New England element was strong in early Minnesota, and the movement for temperance reform was early begun. On May 31, 1851, the *St. Anthony Express* carried this advertisement: "Sons of Temperance. Cataract Division No. 2, St. Anthony Falls; instituted May 18th, 1850; meets every Wednesday evening at 8 o'clock precisely." An advertisement of "St. Paul Division No. 1" discloses that the Sons of Temperance were organized in St. Paul as early as May 8, 1849, and that they held their meetings at seven o'clock every Tuesday evening at Temperance Hall.

The transportation problem of the remote frontier settlements, untouched as yet by railroad lines, was not a simple one; but the Mississippi River furnished a main highway and the river boats tied Minnesota to the outer world. St. Louis, Galena, and Dubuque business firms advertised liberally in the Minnesota newspapers. A. C. Monfort, captain of a well-known boat, advertised in the *Pioneer* of November 1, 1849: "Dr. Franklin No. Two Will leave St. Paul on Thursday Nov. 8, for St. Louis, Louisville, Cincinnati and Pittsburgh. To go through direct." Orrin Smith, master of the *Nominee*, announced weekly service between Galena and St. Paul and advertised the cabin fare as six dollars for the journey upstream and five dollars for the trip down. It was harder to get into than to get out of Minnesota.

In 1850 a "Regular Semi-Weekly Line from Galena to Saint Peter's" was announced by Captains M. W. Lodwick and Orrin Smith, who listed agents at Galena, Dubuque, Prairie du Chien, St. Paul, Point Douglass, and Stillwater. They announced that their boats would "remain at St. Paul or St. Peter's sufficiently long to afford passengers an opportunity to visit the Falls of St. Anthony." These boats made connections with the "Galena and Chicago Union Rail Road," which also used the Minnesota newspapers to advertise its summer arrangements for 1850, with train service between Chicago and Elgin, and with stages between Elgin and Galena.

Transportation in another direction is described in an advertisement of the "Steamer Governor Ramsey, John Rollins, Master," which plied between St. Anthony and Sauk Rapids, leaving St. Anthony every Monday and Thursday at 1:00 P.M. Charles R. Reed advertised an express line for passengers and freight between St. Paul and Prairie du Chien, with freight charges of two dollars per hundred pounds. Burbank and Person's "Minnesota Express" made connections at Galena with the American Express Company and assured the public of "speedy and safe" transportation of valuables, with a messenger leaving St. Paul every Wednesday. A four-horse stagecoach line connected St. Paul and Stillwater. Pattison and Benson advertised a "Daily Line of splendid Hacks between St. Paul and St. Anthony, during the season of navigation, leaving each place every morning and evening regularly; making twice a day each way." A somewhat humbler mode of transportation is indicated by such an advertisement as the following: "A pair of large, well-trained Oxen, in prime condition to work, for sale cheap for cash."

The isolation of the Minnesota towns after the cold weather had closed the Mississippi for steamboat navigation led to at least one curious project that to modern ears sounds like a practical joke. Apparently it was not so intended, but seems rather to have been a sober illustration of Yankee ingenuity coupled with a somewhat too trusting faith in the coldness of the Minnesota winter.

The *Pioneer* of November 15, 1849, carried an advertisement announcing that the *Icelander*, Captain Orrin Smith, and the *Glidiator*, Captain Harris, were ready for business. They were "Locomotive Ice Trains prepared expressly for travel on the ice of the Mississippi" between Galena and St.

Anthony, "with ten cars in each train besides the engine and tender cars, with ample arrangements for meals and for sleeping." The trains "will commence running as soon as the ice is sufficiently strong." "The prices of freight and passage for the present, will be the same usually paid on steamboats in the month of September. The trains will stop at all the usual steamboat landings. As this novel enterprise is attended with great expense, it is to be hoped that the public will extend it their liberal patronage." One additional advantage is presented: "By this arrangement, tri-weekly mails will be furnished between Galena and the Falls." No further announcements of the project appeared, however, and one suspects that the ice of the river did not become "sufficiently strong."

A less chimerical arrangement was that of M. P. Ormsby for the "United States Mail Stage Line to Minnesota," announced in the *Minnesota Democrat* for December 31, 1850. It provided for the conveyance of passengers between Prairie du Chien and Stillwater, by way of Black River Falls and Chippewa, in sleighs and carriages. The stages "will leave Prairie du Chien every Wednesday and Stillwater every Thursday, and go through in six days."

Ormsby's announcement was modest: "His sleighs and carriages are covered and fitted up in a manner to render the passengers as comfortable as possible, and no pains will be spared to make the passage as pleasant as can be in a country and on a road so new as this is, and he is also happy in stating that the fare and accommodations on the road are as good as can be found on any road as new as this." Connections were made at Prairie du Chien with Galena, Madison, and Dubuque stages, and at Stillwater with St. Paul.

In the early transportation situation ferries were of considerable importance. A St. Paul newspaper, in the summer of 1849, contained in one issue advertisements of eight ferries. Other advertisements disclose the fact that several of the ferrymen were also tavern-keepers. The *Pioneer* for November 1, 1849, contains a formal notice that James M. Goodhue and Isaac N. Goodhue will apply to the board of county commissioners for a license to conduct a ferry at the lower landing in St. Paul. That the Goodhues encountered some opposition is shown by the following advertisement printed in the spring of 1850: "New Ferry. The subscriber would respectfully announce, that having procured from His Majesty Little Crow a license to keep a ferry, she is now prepared to carry passengers at the rates fixed by law, and for as much more as the public choose to give her. 'Old Betsey.' 'The connecting link between the Indians and the whites.' N. B. — This Ferry is in opposition to Goodhue."

"Proposals for carrying the mail in Minnesota Territory," called for in 1850 in a long advertisement signed by J. Collamer, the postmaster general, reveal the extent of the early mail service. Provision was to be made for three routes, all starting "From St. Paul at 6 a.m., once a week, Monday." It is interesting to know that under a federal act of 1845 routes were "let to the lowest bidder tendering sufficient guarantees for faithful performance, without other reference to the mode of transportation than may be necessary to provide for the due celerity, certainty, and security of such transportation." If a bid did not name the type of transportation proposed, the post office department assumed that it meant "horseback conveyance."

The advertisements reveal certain opportunities for entertainment and recreation, though naturally the social life of the new towns — a social life notable for its vigor and urbanity — is not reflected in the advertising columns save in exceptional cases.

The *Chronicle* for July 5, 1849, carries a notice that "The Independent Order of Odd Fellows are about establishing a Lodge at St. Paul," and the same paper for July 12, 1849, publishes an announcement of the Masonic Order. "A Splendid

Bowling Saloon," was announced by Charles Cave of St. Paul in 1849, and a similar establishment conducted by Alexis Cloutier was advertised in St. Anthony two years later.

It is a far cry from bowling saloons to church fairs, but the "Ladies of the St. Paul M. E. Church" announced a fair to be held on July 3, 1850: "The public is respectfully invited to attend the fair by candle-light. Articles useful, as well as ornamental, will be offered for sale."

Balls and "cotillion parties" were apparently popular, with announcements like the following: "The Ball Goes On! At Lott Moffatt's on the evening of February 27th, there will be a ball; at which all gentlemen with their ladies, in Minnesota, are invited to be present."

The "Minnesota Hunting Club" represents an organized attempt to cultivate a peculiarly appropriate form of frontier recreation. Its purposes were "rational amusement, the sports of the chase, and the cultivation of a taste for the history of the wild beasts, fowl, birds and fish of the West." That they might legitimately have included the hunting of a somewhat unusual species of wild animal apparently was the opinion of the individual who inserted this advertisement in the *Pioneer*: "Notice to the Hunters' Club. There is a lank old *land pirate* scouring about the wild lands near Saint Paul and Saint Anthony, robbing all the vacant tracts he can find, of rail timber. He is a regular 'wolf in sheep's clothing.'"

Occasionally professional entertainers came to town. The "American Fire King," for example, was publicly announced for an exhibition on July 6, 1849, involving the eating of live fire coals, molten lead, and other fiery substances, and the drinking of "Boiling Brandy." It is astonishing to learn that a circus found its way to remote St. Paul as early as 1850. A flaring advertisement in the *Pioneer* for July 18 of that year announced the coming of a circus for "two days' exhibitions," with a "splendid company of equestrians, gymnasts, acrobats, pantomimists, comedians, olympiads, and Herculeans."

Some light on the cultural interests of the people of St. Paul and St. Anthony is shed by the advertisements. A curious affair was a raffle arranged by Sergeant E. K. Thomas in 1850. He informed the public that he had "a copy of that celebrated painting of the Last Supper" by Da Vinci "which he was willing to dispose of in a Raffle, thirty-five chances, at one dollar each number." On another occasion the enterprising sergeant offered for sale paintings of the Sioux warrior "Wah-ah-cordah" and of the Indian maiden "We-no-na."

The earliest book advertisements were from the Galena bookstore of J. Brookes. On May 12, 1849, Brookes announced Parkman's *California and Oregon Trail*, Fredrika Bremer's *The Midnight Sun*, Bulwer-Lytton's *The Caxtons – A Family Picture*, Jerrold's *A Man Made of Money*, the London *Punch* and *Illustrated News*, and a number of historical works, including books by Macaulay, Prescott, Hallam, Bancroft, Russell, and Allison. On April 25, 1850, he announced Whittier's *Old Portraits and Modern Sketches* and Longfellow's *Seaside and Fireside*.

An early St. Paul bookstore was that kept by William G. Le Duc and known as the "Minnesota Book-Store." Le Duc did not limit himself to books. He was prepared to sell "Jenny Lind's best Songs and 100 pieces choice sheet music, Boston Melodeons, Kingsley's series of Music Books, Ethiopian Glee Books, 100 cheap Novels, Lady Willoughby's Diary, Irving's complete works," and other items. In 1851 Le Duc advertised *Dakota* by Mrs. Eastman, a *History of the Ojibway Nation* by Copway, and *American Institutions* by De Tocqueville.

A sentimentally suggestive advertisement of magazines was run in 1850 by Charles D. Elfelt of St. Paul, "St. Valentine; St. Valentine! Now is the time to subscribe to the Magazines; Graham, Godey or Sartain. A copy of either is certainly the neatest Valentine a gentleman can send a lady." An advertisement of *Godey's Lady's Book* for 1852 primly reminds readers that in this magazine "the useful and the elegant will always be kept in view." The subscription price was ten dollars a year in advance.

Under the caption of "New Class Book for Young Ladies" the following characteristic announcement was made: "The Hemans Reader for Female Schools; containing extracts in prose and poetry, selected from more than one hundred and thirty different authors." A prospectus "For Publishing a Dakota Lexicon, Under the patronage of the Historical Society of Minnesota" was announced in 1851. Early library activities in St. Anthony were reflected in an announcement in 1851 that the annual meeting of the stockholders of the St. Anthony Library Association would be held on November 24 in the office of Isaac Atwater.

Some types of religious activity are given conspicuous announcement in the advertisements. Thus the *Express* for June 7, 1851, carries a notice of an important "Bible Meeting" to be held on the following day. An address was to be delivered at the schoolhouse in St. Anthony in the morning, and a "Territorial Bible Society" was to be organized at the Methodist church in St. Paul in the evening. The announcement closes with these words: "All friends of the Bible are invited to attend both the above named meetings."

Though the University of Minnesota did not open its doors until 1869, the regents of that institution of the future were holding meetings as early as 1851. A meeting was called for June 3 of that year at the St. Charles Hotel, St. Anthony – probably to make plans for the opening of the preparatory department of the university, for in the fall of 1851, E. W. Merrill, the principal, announced that it would be opened on November 26. He made public the titles of the courses to be offered and in later advertisements listed the textbooks to be used.

Some light on the manner in which the university got its start is afforded by an advertisement signed by the treasurer,

J. W. North, calling for prompt payment of subscriptions for the university building.

A somewhat different type of school is indicated in an advertisement by Monsieur Benjamin Lessard, in the *Express* of November 22, 1851. Lessard, who had "recently arrived from Canada," proposed to give instruction in French, Latin, and other branches, including "epistolary correspondence to those sufficiently advanced." He explained that he already had some knowledge of the English language, and he hoped "in two or three months to be able to teach English classes also with profit."

The business and professional life of the two towns is reflected in many ways in the advertisements. The cards of the lawyers appeared week after week in the professional directory of the paper, supplemented from time to time by new names. Not a few of the attorneys announced that they specialized in pre-emption claims and military warrants. Some of the St. Paul lawyers had their announcements printed in both English and French. The business establishments of various kinds in the towns employed the newspapers to advertise their products and services, and in St. Paul forwarding and commission merchants were regularly and prominently listed.

The advertisements show that St. Paul and St. Anthony were beginning to feel the boom that was to place them in advance of other Minnesota settlements. Hotels catered to visitors and newly arrived settlers, and their claims to patronage were advanced without undue modesty. "Rodney Parker, Late of Massachusetts," the proprietor of the American House in St. Paul, declared that he could "satisfy even the most fastidious." His table was supplied "with the choicest viands the country afford [*sic*] and prepared by an experienced cusine [*sic*]." Visitors who desired to go to the Falls of St. Anthony or any other point could be furnished "with saddle horses, buggies or carriages at any time for that purpose." The St.

Charles House offered good accommodations to visitors at St. Anthony Falls.

The *Pioneer* for May 5, 1849, lists no less than seven "house builders" in St. Paul. Newspaper advertisements show that the sale of town lots was being rapidly promoted. David Lambert had "the exclusive agency of that beautiful portion of the town of St. Paul, owned by Vetal Guerin, adjacent to the Catholic church, and extending from the banks of the Mississippi, beyond the bluffs at the north of the town," and he announced that the "portion of this property beyond the town line is now being surveyed into *out lots* of convenient size for suburbian [*sic*] residences."

That the region was still only thinly settled is evidenced by the number of advertisements telling of stray ponies, cattle, and oxen "taken up." The *Pioneer* for November 15, 1849, contains no less than five signed announcements of this general type: "Came on to my premises, about four weeks ago, one yoke of Oxen (with yoke on)." In St. Anthony a famous scout and Indian interpreter, Pierre Bottineau, appears in the role of real estate dealer:

P. BOTTINEU,

WOULD announce to the citizens of St. Anthony, and the Territory, that he has land by the acre, and a large Number of Village Lots for sale, which he will sell *cheap for cash.*

ALSO – All kinds of farming utensils, such as ploughs, wagons, &c.

The St. Anthony Mill Company announces in the *Express* on May 31, 1851, that it has four sawmills in full operation; in the same advertisement the company gives a price list and states that its terms are "cash on delivery of the raft." An intimation of the coming pre-eminence of Minneapolis in the milling industry is afforded by the businesslike announcement of Calvin A. Tuttle in the same issue of the *Express*, a notice that also appears regularly in the St. Paul press:

GRINDING

THE UNDERSIGNED is now in readiness for grinding Corn, Rye, Oats, Peas, Buckwheat and whatever else requires grinding, including Salt, at the grist-mill on the west side of the Mississippi river at St. Anthony, for lawful rates of toll. When desired, grists will be received at the subscriber's on the east side of the river, and be returned ground at the same place.

CALVIN A. TUTTLE

The advertisement of St. Paul's first wagon maker appeared in the *Pioneer* for April 28, 1849: "I want three thousand Spokes, of good timber, for which I will pay the highest price in cash. Wm. H. Nobles." That Nobles was more than an ordinary wagon maker may be inferred from his later career, for, appointed in the 1850's by the federal government to lay out a wagon road to the Pacific, he became the discoverer of Nobles' Pass through the Rockies.

The heyday of the fur trade in Minnesota had been passed by 1849, and evidence of its declining fortunes is found in the following advertisement:

NOTICE

IS HEREBY given that the co-partnership heretofore existing between P. Chouteau, jr. & co. of St. Louis, H. H. Sibley, H. M. Rice and Sylvanus B. Lowry, under the name and style of Northern Outfit, including Sioux Outfit and Winnebago and Chippewa Outfit, is hereby dissolved by consent of the parties. The liquidation of the amounts properly due by said business or co-partnership, as well as the general adjustment of all matters appertaining thereto, will be attended to by said H. H. Sibley.

P. CHOUTEAU, Jr. & CO.,
H. H. SIBLEY

St. Paul, Oct. 12, 1849

Prairie du Chien Patriot, Galena papers, Gazette Burlington, I. and St. Louis Republican and Union, please copy.

It is interesting to note, however, that the name of a great fur company was preserved in the St. Paul firm of "W. H.

Forbes, American Fur Company, St. Paul Outfit, also Dry Goods and Groceries.—Bench Street."

Not a few of the advertisements touch upon the relations between the Indians and the whites. Nathaniel McLean, the subagent at St. Peter's, announced on February 15, 1850, that the Bureau of Indian Affairs had given him instructions "to put a stop to all trespassers upon Indian Lands, by commencing suits in all cases where proof can be obtained. No purchase of timber or firewood from an Indian chief or bands of Indians combined will be recognized as valid."

In March 1850 Alexander Ramsey advertised that he would buy at reasonable figures a hundred horses for the Sioux Indians. Proposals for the transportation of annuity goods to the "Winnebagoes, Chippewas and Pillagers" were called for by J. E. Fletcher, Indian agent, on March 15, 1850. A similar advertisement for 1849 specifies transportation from St. Paul to the Winnebago agency at Long Prairie of 32,036 pounds of annuity goods, and of 16,321 pounds to be delivered at the mouth of the Crow Wing. Another advertisement calls for bids on ninety barrels of mess pork, one hundred of flour, and three hundred bushels of shelled corn for the Winnebago agency.

A St. Paul shop popular with the children was that of B. Presley. He exhorted his customers to "Walk in and See the Hanimals," and boasted the largest assortment of toys north of St. Louis. There were wooden as well as live Indians in early Minnesota, for Presley advertises thus: "Call where the wooden Indian stands sentry at the door and you can buy a little cheaper for cash than any where else in St. Paul."

Since it is frequently assumed that the western pioneers were bearded men, it may not be amiss to note that in St. Paul their patronage seems to have kept alive the business represented by the following delicately worded advertisement:

ABSALOM LOST HIS LIFE FOR WANT OF A BARBER

WILLIAM ARMSTRONG, a Castilian by birth, continues to

smooth the countenances of the male public at the Central House, amputating the beard with the utmost facility, upon new and scientific principles. He also performs the operation of hair-cutting and hair dressing, in the latest fashion and most approved style of the art. Shampooing in the Asiatic method, as taught in Constantinople, is also his forte. It will be his delight to render these operations as agreeable as possible without the aid of chloroform.

The alleged "Castilian" is less suave in another advertisement, for he "desires to have it distinctly understood, that those who are indebted to him for his past services with razor and shears, are expected forthwith to liquidate; and that hereafter, his business will be conducted strictly upon cash principles."

The uniform emphasis upon "cash principles" in the early business announcements of the two towns is what one expects to find. Some customers appear not to have taken these "cash principles" seriously, however.

RUN AWAY

From Saint Paul, without paying his honest debts a person in the shape of a man, calling himself DOCTOR SNOW, formerly of Prairie du Chien. This is to warn all persons against this man's rascality.

GEORGE WELLS

Prairie du Chine Patriot please copy

A "St. Paul Price Current," run in the *Chronicle and Register*, furnishes valuable clues not only to economic conditions as reflected in prices but to kinds of materials being sold. Though not strictly speaking an advertisement, the price list was printed as a supplement to the advertisements. One learns from the list for September 30, 1850, that buffalo tongues sold at five dollars a dozen, pemmican at ten cents a pound, and sperm oil at $1.50 per gallon. Fresh beef was offered at seven cents a pound, pork at ten, hams were sold at twelve, eggs at twenty cents a dozen, and bread was available at four cents per pound loaf.

It is clear that the advertisements in the early newspapers contain a wealth of information about the social and economic life of the people. Often this information does not go beyond a mention, a list of articles, or an announcement of a coming event, and it needs to be supplemented by other data. Itemized lists of articles of clothing or of pieces of household furniture are not so valuable as detailed descriptions, but they afford many interesting clues.

The kinds of tools and implements used, tastes in food and drink, and tendencies in the use of medicines are suggested in the advertisements. Transportation developments are accurately reflected, and many aspects of the business and professional life of the region are faithfully recorded. Some features of the recreational and cultural activities of the people can be learned from the advertisements – for example, kinds of entertainment, lists of books and magazines available in the book shops, formal library beginnings, and tendencies in public and private education.

When the many items of information imbedded in the advertisements are dug out and brought together, they give one something of the flavor of the times, revealing manners and customs in the broad sense. Without exaggerating the historical importance of advertisements, one can claim high value for their use in reconstructing the normal life of the past.

On the Stir!

"THE whole town is on the stir," wrote a St. Paul editor in 1849. "Stores, hotels, houses, are projected and built in a few days. California is forgotten, and the whole town is rife with the exciting spirit of advancement."

Five years later another journalist exclaimed, "Enclose St. Paul, indeed! Fence in a prairie fire! Dam up Niagara! Bail out Lake Superior! Tame a wolf! Civilize Indians! Attempt any other practical thing; but not to set metes and bounds to the progress of St. Paul!"

These are typical notes from the American frontier in the middle of the nineteenth century. Growth was turbulent, rapid change was in the air, and everywhere was the infection of optimism. America was moving westward, tackling with confidence the task of transforming the wilderness, glorying in the flux of freedom of the frontier. In steamboats up the great river and in wagons, covered and uncovered, along the trails and roads winding into Minnesota came thousands of eager young people, Yankees in the van, Germans, Scandinavians, and other immigrant stocks joining in the trek, all seeking lands and homes and prosperity. In ten years, from 1850 to 1860, the population shot from 6000 to 172,000, an increase of 2730 per cent.

The pioneer Minnesotans were busy breaking land, erecting cabins, starting farms, building roads, developing towns, organizing the economic, social, and political life of the commonwealth. The community instinct, so characteristic of the Yankee stock, sometimes found expression in colonizing land companies, one of which founded Zumbrota in 1856, with church and school as community centers, and with the Puritan influence exhibited in the local prohibition of the sale of intoxicating liquors. Two years later Zumbrota advertised itself as one of the best communities in the West and proclaimed that "recklessness, intemperance, and profanity" were unknown in the town.

A writer of the 1850's, referring to the westward-moving emigrant, remarked, "In Illinois he will be met by the Illinois Central Railroad and the fever and the ague; in Iowa, by land speculators who infest the State like a famine. In Minnesota alone he will find an excellent soil, a fine climate, a healthy temperature and a pre-emption law." In 1855 the territory itself sent an emigration agent to New York to refute the allegation that Minnesota was a hyperborean region and to entice settlers.

Meanwhile every town in Minnesota considered itself a potential metropolis, and town-site speculation reached a frenzy before the panic of 1857 descended like a blight upon the territory. In three years, from 1855 to 1857 inclusive, not less than seven hundred new towns were platted in Minnesota, with lots enough for a million and a half people. Not a few of these towns prospered, survived the panic, and, if not jilted by capricious railroads, blossomed out in a later period. Others sprang up like mushrooms, enjoyed a brief day of prosperity, and then disappeared.

Nininger, sponsored by the gifted Ignatius Donnelly, was a typical city of dreams, and the editor of its newspaper, the *Emigrant Aid Journal of Minnesota*, once printed a fanciful sketch telling of an imaginary visit to America in the year 4796 A.D., when a traveler found New York to have a population of 4,892,568, then journeyed out to Nininger, the imperial city of the West, which, with 4,981,947 people, surpassed even the eastern metropolis. Alas for the prophet! Today the house of Donnelly is almost the only landmark of that hopeful frontier town.

Some stages in the economic history of the Middle West

may be suggested by the symbols of gun, trap, saw, plow, pick, and shovel. In the 1850's Minnesota, where once trap and then saw had been supreme, was being transformed by the plow into an agricultural domain. The pioneer farmer plowed the virgin soil, knew the terror of the prairie fire, braved the fury of the blizzard, felt the isolation of the frontiersman, yet labored on in his tasks, aided by his wife, a wilderness Martha, mistress of the primitive cabin.

One traveler, after visiting a frontier family, wrote, "They lived in a rude log cabin, sixteen by eighteen, plastered with mud, and with a huge fireplace and mud chimney pushed out at one end. This one small room served as kitchen, parlor, bedroom, pantry, cellar, and all other purposes. The furniture was equally rude, there being but one chair with a back to it, and that quite rickety. For seats, there was a large trunk, two stools, and two empty boxes. We ate a hearty supper of pork and potatoes, and bread and black molasses. . . . There were two beds – the settler and wife occupied one, myself and chum the other, while the children made a bunk on the floor."

Transporting supplies was sometimes a problem for the pioneer. Hans Mattson, a Swedish settler in Goodhue County, once walked from Red Wing to his cabin, a distance of fourteen miles, with a smoked ham, thirty pounds of flour, a gallon of molasses, some coffee, salt, and sugar, all strapped into a pack and carried on his shoulders. Lacking luxuries, frontier farm life was bare, yet it had amenities as the communities grew, for the pioneers were cooperative and hospitable. There were raising, husking, and quilting bees, and the church and the frontier minister played an important part in the life of the people.

A noted American scholar has commented on the "power of the pioneers to join together for a common end without the intervention of governmental institutions," and to it he traces some significant American tendencies of today. Minnesota pioneers exemplified this kind of resourcefulness in the skill with which they devised associations to protect the land claims of squatters.

Though distinctly extralegal in purpose, the claim associations were organized with constitutions and officers and paid solemn attention to parliamentary procedure. When the lands had been surveyed and were opened to government auction, the usual technique of an association was to select one member to make all its bids, then to attend the auction in a body, each member armed with a club as a warning to speculators not to interfere. This technique proved successful; the threat sufficient, no heads were broken, though occasionally a grumbler complained of the "great waste of timber."

The middlewestern talent for agricultural organization seems to hark back to the frontiersmen of the 1850's. As early as 1852 an agricultural society was formed in Benton County, Minnesota, with Oliver H. Kelley, prominent later in the Granger movement, as one of its founders. The same year saw a Ramsey County society, and in 1854 a Hennepin County society held the first agricultural fair in Minnesota. The next year witnessed a territorial fair, and in 1859 the first state fair was held.

The pioneers evidently liked such fairs, and eight thousand of them thronged the fair grounds at Fort Snelling in 1860 to hear Cassius Clay of Kentucky deliver a two-hour address, to see "Flying Dutchman" trot a mile in 4:11, and to witness an exhibition of fire-engine companies.

A frontier society exhibits in many ways the transit of ideas and culture to the pioneer West from older societies. A concrete illustration may be found in the Minnesota lumber camps and lumbering technique, which represent transfers from Maine, a state that left a marked impress especially upon Stillwater and Minneapolis.

A more general illustration is afforded by the spirit of New England piety and Puritanism that hovered over frontier Minnesota. The first legislature passed a law placing a Sunday ban on work and on such diversions, "to the disturbance of the community," as hunting, shooting, and sport, with a fine of three dollars for violation of the law. Desecration of the Sabbath by profane conduct was considered more serious, and was punishable by a ten-dollar fine. With a nice sense of the fitness of things, the legislators provided that all fines so collected should be used for the relief of the poor. Later, Minnesotans were forbidden by law to be present "at any dancing" or at public shows on Sunday. An early law was aimed against gambling, and particularly at the use of roulette and faro, but evidence indicates that this statute was not strictly enforced.

The Sons of Temperance were organized in Minnesota as early as 1849. The first territorial legislature prohibited the sale or gift of liquor to the Indians and established a license system; and three years later the legislature was prevailed upon to pass a so-called "Maine Law," which forbade the manufacture or sale of intoxicating liquors save for medicinal and "mechanical" uses. Voting down a facetious amendment to impose the death penalty for its violation, the legislators adopted an amendment to submit the act to a popular referendum. In the referendum the people supported the law by 853 votes to 662, but on a test case the district court held that the legislature had delegated its power, and, since Congress had given it no authority to do so, the statute was ruled invalid.

Later attempts to pass a Maine Law in Minnesota proved unavailing and the saloons flourished, but in 1855 a St. Anthony newspaper gave prominent space to an Illinois resolution that read: "Resolved, that we young ladies . . . pledge ourselves not to keep company, or join in the the sacred bonds of matrimony with any young gentleman who is not in favor of the Maine liquor law, or some other prohibitory law."

It has been said that newspaper editors were always in the vanguard of the westward movement, "setting up their presses and issuing their sheets before the forests had been cleared or the sod turned." James M. Goodhue, a graduate of Amherst College, reached St. Paul with his printing press before the first territorial officers got there; and on April 28, 1849, he launched the *Minnesota Pioneer*, discarding his first choice of a name, the "Epistle of St. Paul," because, he said, "we found so many little saints in the Territory, jealous of St. Paul."

A bold, intelligent, and honest exponent of personal journalism, Goodhue made his paper a cultural and political power in Minnesota. St. Paul was only a village of straggling shanties and log huts, but to Goodhue, optimist and prophet, it was more marvelous than the Seven Cities of Cibola. He glorified Minnesota, extolling its wide, blooming plains and hills, its lands as fertile as the banks of the Nile, its forests of ancient pines, its lakes of crystal water. To him California was a place of "lingering, living death," whereas Minnesota was life. Never ceasing his prophecies of greatness for the coming state, he foresaw the Indians "fading, vanishing, dissolving away," and, looking out into the future, drew a picture of thousands of farms and cottages, waving wheat fields, and "jungles of rustling maize."

In Goodhue's paper one could almost hear the rumble of trains roaring into St. Paul on the way from St. Louis to Lake Superior. He was a dreamer, but wise in his dreams. He called for bridges across the Mississippi, better roads, a railroad, better mail service, a telegraph line, and good schools. The steamboat wharf, he said, was a bad school where children graduated with diplomas from the devil.

Of a dishonest official who hastily left Minnesota, Goodhue wrote, "He stole into the Territory, he stole in the Territory, and he stole out of the Territory." As a consequence of one of his scathing editorials he was attacked one day by an opponent and stabbed twice, while he himself made the flurry more exciting by shooting his assailant.

The *Pioneer* was one of eighty-nine newspapers established

in Minnesota in its territorial period. Among these were the *Sauk Rapids Frontiersman*, the *Red Wing Republican*, the *Wasioja Gazette*, the *Hokah Chief*, the *St. Cloud Visiter*—edited by the fiery antislavery crusader, Jane Grey Swisshelm—and the *Winona Argus*. The frontier newspapers brought news of the world to the pioneers, served as a literary medium in a day when magazines were few, boosted Minnesota with extraordinary vigor, reflected in their advertisements the economic trends of the time, and by their forthright editorial methods made their leadership felt not only in politics but also in the social and cultural life of the people.

The cultural life of pioneer Minnesota was vigorous and interesting, especially in the capital and the larger towns, where lawyers, doctors, and other professional men, many of them with fine eastern traditions, gave it tone. To the pioneers of the West we owe the discovery of the idea of studying American history from the bottom up rather than from the top down, and the cultural leaders of Minnesota made their contribution by organizing in 1849 the Minnesota Historical Society.

"Let us save that which is interesting in the fleeting registers of the day," said Governor Ramsey, "and which in the years to come will be esteemed rich mines for the historian." When it is recalled that the Historical Society today possesses files of sixty Minnesota territorial newspapers, let the wisdom and foresight of this frontier statesman be praised.

Every considerable frontier town had its lyceum or library association, where essays, lectures, and debates were heard. St. Paul, indeed, boasted no less than seventeen incorporated cultural associations in the territorial period.

The pioneers liked the theater, supported dramatic associations of their own, and welcomed visiting troupes. Music lovers on the frontier heard Ole Bull in 1856 and Adelina Patti the next year, and welcomed the singing Hutchinsons whenever they gave a concert. The Turners were early on the Minnesota scene, and their gymnastic exhibitions were popular. St. Paul supported an opera company that published its own organ, the *Opera Companion*, and in one season, at the German Theatre, presented such operas as Rossini's "Cinderella," Donizetti's "Elixir of Love," Balfe's "Bohemian Girl," and Verdi's "Il Trovatore."

There was even a modest literature produced in frontier Minnesota. Harriet Bishop, the Vermont schoolteacher, published in 1857 her book, *Floral Home*. A periodical entitled the *Frontier Monthly* was brought out at Hastings in 1859. And in 1865 an anthology, *The Poets and Poetry of Minnesota*, appeared at Chicago, dedicated by the "editress," Mrs. W. J. Arnold, to Governor Stephen Miller, who himself contributed a number of poems to the volume.

The pioneers liked balls such as the one held in St. Paul at the Central House in 1850, when there were five sets of cotillions and Goodhue was inspired to write, "It was the largest collection of beauty and fashion we have ever seen in the West."

New Year's Day, Washington's Birthday, St. Valentine's Day, the Fourth of July, Thanksgiving, and Christmas were celebrated with merrymaking and gaiety. On January 1, according to Judge Flandrau, "the whole town was alive with sport. Everybody kept open house and expected everybody else to call and see them." There were social rivalries, for he adds, "A register of callers was always kept, and great was the victory of the hostess who recorded the greatest number."

A pioneer Christmas sleigh-ride party in Minneapolis was followed by a typical New England dinner, the table piled high with vegetables, jellies, cakes, pies, and puddings. At a somewhat similar feast in Winona five kinds of cake, three kinds of pies, and goose, venison, and coon were served. The pioneer considered it proper to be prepared for emergencies. A St. Paul woman wrote in 1853, "Then we have a cellar, filled with potatoes, cabbage, Turnips, Beans, Molasses, Onions, Apples, 8 Turkeys, 3 barrel flour, 20 lbs. sperm candle, 4 of chicken, 50 dozen Tallow Candle for the kitchen, 7 pound sage, 10 pound dried pumpkin, 2 bags Buckwheat, 10 dz Eggs, 30 pound butter." Such things were no doubt excellent, but a disconsolate pioneer was once heard to say, "I'm homesick to get back to Massachusetts and have a meal of good salt cod."

The day of the specialist had not yet arrived. The pioneers stood on their own feet, forced by circumstance to rely upon themselves. And so the housewife, who could run loom and spinning wheel, make soap, and manage her household, was not shocked by the St. Anthony jack-of-all-trades who genially offered to do half a dozen different tasks, from repairing a watch to tinkering with locks and umbrellas, or, if need arose, extracting a tooth.

The photographer also made it known that he was not unversed in dentistry, and the doctor was a druggist as well as a general practitioner. The lawyer could turn nonchalantly from the law to real estate or business, or, as in the case of Judge Flandrau, to military command in time of Indian trouble, and give a good account of himself. The farmer sometimes taught school in the winter; the minister might take to the plow on everydays; and few there were who were not ready at a moment's notice to plunge into the rough-and-tumble of politics.

Frontier Bookshelves

A PICNIC was held under the pines at Minnesota Point on Lake Superior one summer evening in 1856. Among the pioneers present were some who, notwithstanding a certain amount of scoffing by the citizens of the rival town of Superior, Wisconsin, anticipated the emergence of an important Minnesota city at the head of Lake Superior and were interested in finding a splendid and appropriate name for it.

The story goes that the picnic was a name-selecting conference and that those who were present drank a toast to the future of the city. Community historians disagree both as to the picnic and the toast, but they agree that one Joseph Wilson, a missionary, proposed the name "Duluth" and thereby won for himself not only a certain community distinction but also the award of two lots in the infant city.

The most interesting item in this leaf from community history is neither the picnic nor the name itself, but the record of the way in which the missionary went about the business of finding the name. An old resident writes that Wilson "set about the task" by visiting "the homes of citizens that might be expected to be possessed of a library." The phrase lingers in one's mind, for it suggests that touch of enthusiasm and even madness often associated with those for whom books have a consuming interest.

Wilson's search was successful, for he found "among some old books belonging to George E. Nettleton, an old English translation of the writings of the French Jesuits, relating to themselves and the early explorers and fur traders of the

Northwest. In this he ran across the name of Du Luth . . . who visited the head of the lake in the remote past."

This record may mean that the frontier village on the shores of Lake Superior boasted a copy of the *Jesuit Relations.* Wilson undoubtedly found it in the humble shanty where the Nettletons then lived – a hut built of such green lumber, Mrs. Nettleton later recalled, that the boards shrank, and every time it rained they had to put dishes about to catch the water. A pioneer library in a pioneer shanty! For the phrase used was "among some old books."

The book tradition in the Superior country is older than the episode of 1856, however, for men "possessed of libraries" had lived there in an earlier day. Edmund F. Ely, the missionary, was one. In 1834 he opened a Chippewa mission at Fond du Lac, the site of fur-trading activities since the eighteenth century. Among Ely's prized possessions were his books.

Let us dip into a letter written to Ely by another missionary, William T. Boutwell, in 1846. "Have sent you Townsends Commentary and kept the vol. of Comprehension," wrote Boutwell on May 26 of that year. "You recollect I sent for the 3d vol. of Bancroft . . . the complete work was sent. I send you the 2 first vols. and have kept the 3d as I have not yet read it. . . . Some of the articles in your large Box were pretty well sweetened with molasses from a little paltry jar, you had tied a paper over the top."

Thus we may add molasses to the hazards of snow, rain, river, and mud that frontier books encountered.

Many of the early missionaries in the Northwest sent regular reports to the American Board of Commissioners for Foreign Missions in Boston, telling of their hardships and work, their many disappointments and occasional successes. Frequently these reports contain long lists of necessary supplies which the missionary, his family, and his neighbors needed for the year's sustenance. Often these lists tell more about the actual conditions of the frontier than do the solemnly worded letters that accompany them, for in them are mentioned medicines, food, materials for clothing, and other needed items of everyday life.

And often, tucked in between urgent demands for food or apparel, are equally urgent requests for books. Ely in October 1835, wrote to Boston that he needed "a good *Atlas*" for the Fond du Lac mission, that a "Commentary" and "Barnes Notes on Gospels and Romans . . . would be valuable" to him, and that what Mrs. Ely needed—was this by any chance a reflection of some slight discontent with her culinary skill?—was "a copy of Mrs Childs, Dom Cookery."

Other missionaries made similar requests. Here are two lists—one made by G. T. Sproat, the other by Sherman Hall at La Pointe on Madeline Island. Sproat's list included five yards of red flannel, two pairs of small shoes for a child's second year, some Castile soap, some morphia, a dozen corset laces, one steel corset board, a toothbrush, six copies of the first part of "Emerson's Arithmetic," six copies of the "Beauties of the Bible," six inkstands, two hundred quills, two and a half dozen copies of Webster's "Spell. Book," "The Young Wife by Dr. Alcott," and the *Remains* of Mrs. Isabella Graham "(not her Memoirs) lately published by Mr. Bethune."

Hall displayed no interest in works like the *Young Wife* or Mrs. Graham's *Remains*, but sprinkled requests for church psalmodies and various religious works among such items as seven yards of "French Merino Black," one pair of "Mens Yellow Kid Gloves," and two pairs of women's high laced shoes for feet nine and one-eighth inches long.

After Sproat's request for one toothbrush, it is comforting to find that Ely in 1839 wanted, for the use of the Fond du Lac mission station, a copy of Dr. Mann's "Treatise on Preservation of Teeth," cost, six and a half cents. Ely in 1839 also wished to have Mrs. Torrey's "Ornament, or christian rules of Dress," "Dr. Bell's Lessons on the Human Frame," Dr. Humphrey's "Letters on Education," and the "Memoir of Carvosso" – the latter a name that one suspects is not a misprint for Casanova.

From these and other lists one can get an idea of the books in the wilderness log cabins: lives of famous divines, *The Christian Exemplified*, Mrs. Row's *Devout Exercises*, and the like. For the children there were the *New England Primer* and Gallaudett's *Picture Defining and Reading Book.* Ely's son had, in addition, *Youth's Penny Gazette* and an *Illustrated Almanac.*

In the same period there were other men in the Lake Superior country who had more comprehensive and liberal tastes. The fur traders have often been pictured as men of adventure, businessmen of lone frontiers, trail blazers of the West, but it is worth recalling that they sometimes were pioneers of culture, men whose bookshelves must have made the lonely winters less lonely, the isolation of the wilderness less cruel.

In modern days a farmer's wife wrote a public letter calling for "library service" and exclaimed, "If only the men had something to read after the chores are done!" Many of the fur traders of the pioneer Northwest had books to which they could turn on long winter evenings after their chores were done, especially such men as Dr. Charles W. W. Borup and Lyman Warren, traders of the American Fur Company.

Dr. Borup sometimes ordered medical treatises sent to him at his trading post in the North Country. In 1835 he wanted Lizars' *Anatomical Plates.* He requested later such religious works as *Persuasions to Piety*, *All Is Well*, or *Faith's Estimate of Affliction*, and *Saints Rest*, the well-known treatise by Richard Baxter, the seventeenth-century English divine.

Both Borup and Warren in 1837 called also for books of travel and natural history: *Discovery and Adventure in the Polar Seas*, Russell's *Ancient and Modern Egypt*, a *History of the Barbary States*, and the *Natural History of Insects.* They also requested a copy of "*Allein's Allarm.*" This title may seem to suggest some story of adventure or mystery, but it was in fact a religious work. The author was an Englishman, Joseph Alleine; the title of the book, *An Alarm to Unconverted Sinners.*

In January 1841 the fur traders ordered two volumes of Smollet, *Gil Blas* (in French), Hallam's *Middle Ages*, Gutzlaff's *Travels in China*, Prescott's *Ferdinand and Isabella*, and *Handy Andy*, an Irish novel of Samuel Lover's which, according to the *Oxford Companion to English Literature*, was not published in book form until the year after this list was written. Later in the same year Dr. Borup wanted Irving's *Sketch Book* and Mrs. Hemans' *Works*. So we know that as early as 1841 the shores of Lake Superior had a glimpse of the boy who stood on the burning deck.

These fur traders prevailed upon missionaries like Sherman Hall to send their book lists on to Boston. In one of his letters Hall expressed the true library point of view when he said, "I presume you will be willing to hand the list to some bookseller. . . . I am the more desirous to accommodate them" – he referred to Borup and Warren – "on account of introducing such books as they send for into the country." On one occasion Hall used the word *circulate* in connection with a book order. He asked for six copies of the *Life* of Harlan Page and said that it would be "a useful book to circulate in this country."

Modern readers, notwithstanding the efficiency of libraries in anticipating their wants, sometimes wait with a fever of impatience for certain books to appear on the library circulating shelf. But what of the booklovers of the early frontiers who sent their orders off to Boston, New York, or other cities in the East and then waited half a year or more for the books to come?

The Catholic Bishop Baraga in September 1842 sounded a note of despair about the North Country library system. He wrote to Ramsay Crooks, president of the American Fur

Company in New York, "I come forth once more with some commissions. Please to procure for me the two works, whose titles you find on this paper. . . . I will look for them next summer, if I live." One of the books he listed—*Ritualis Romani*—was sent on to him by Dr. Borup in June 1843, and it must be added that the good Bishop lived to see many other summers and no doubt to order and receive many other books.

Evidently he had a serene philosophy, this bishop of the frontier, for on one occasion he paid for a paper for four years in advance, and said, "If I die before, they may have the benefit, for their conducting so excellent a paper."

In many other parts of the Northwest there were pioneer booklovers for whom life on the frontier without books was unthinkable. A fur trader, John Aitken, wrote to Boutwell from a remote spot called Swan River in April 1838, asking for various supplies, including "a chip hat which one of my men will try on his head you will Receive by them 5 volumes of the History of England and the Biography of Napoleon Please also to send me a Horse saddle."

Another trader, Martin McLeod, on his way from Lake Superior to the Red River Valley, spent a day resting at the American Fur Company's post at Cass Lake on November 28, 1836, after an exhausting trek across frozen lakes. There he recorded in his diary that he read all day "The author of Cyril Thornton's Annals of the Peninsular Campaigns." His comment was: "Don't think much of the work. Not so good as Napier's." A few days later, suffering from a lame ankle, he again rested, this time at Red Lake, where he "by a wonderful chance, got hold of very old copies of 'The Lady of the Lake,' the 2d vol of the 'Scottish Chiefs' and the 2d vol of Thaddeus of Warsaw." With these "prizes," as he called them, he hoped to take his mind from the pain.

McLeod was a true lover of books. When obliged to spend the winter of 1840–41 in a "Cabin 15 by 20 with one man;

an Interpreter and his squaw . . . and 2 d—d noisy, rude children"—the "dull and monotonous" lot of a fur trader wintering at Traverse des Sioux on the Minnesota River—he wrote philosophically in his diary: "a pleasant *prospect* God wot; n'importe, I have a few books, a dog and a gun,—some patience—and *so, and so* I suppose I must be resign'd."

Byron was his favorite poet, and during that winter McLeod's journal records frequent reading of his letters and poems, with the regret that Byron "did not leave some prose work worthy of his fame." McLeod devoured Scott's *Monastery* in two days, his *Abbot* in one, while Cooper's *Pilot* kept him "up until past 1 o.c." in the morning. Locke's *Essay Concerning Human Understanding*, *Oliver Twist*, *Lalla Rookh*, and the Bible also helped him to pass the lonely winter.

Henry Hastings Sibley of Mendota as early as 1844 sent an order to New York for a little library that included Prescott's *Ferdinand and Isabella* and *Conquest of Mexico*, Sparks's *American Biography* in ten volumes, Hallam's *Middle Ages*, Thiers' *French Revolution*, Froissart's *Chronicles*, a book called *Music for the Million*, and Webster's "Dictionary Abridgement Revised Edition." He sent his order on January 2 and asked that the books be shipped out to Mendota, at the junction of the Mississippi and Minnesota rivers, in the spring.

It requires no stretch of the imagination to think of Sibley's books as a semipublic library, for his home was almost always crowded with guests, and we may be sure that many of them turned to his shelves with that glow of interest that bookshelves everywhere generate, perhaps most of all in frontier areas where books are few.

Eventually something more was needed. The story of public libraries is the story of the democratization of books. The glory of libraries is their part in the diffusion of knowledge. Both have their setting in the democracy of a free people. Not long ago James Gray, the novelist, commenting on the services of libraries to the people, said that we are "casually grateful—if we remember to be—that such services exist." It is a tribute to American freedom that the gratitude is casual, but in a world darkened by the intolerance of book burners something more than casual gratitude is necessary: to cherish our libraries, to support them as essential institutions, and to understand their relationship to our democracy.

Public libraries were created out of the need of our people just as surely as our farms and mines and cities were so created, and modern public library service was developed by experiment in response to that need. Like many things that people take for granted, the democratic public institution known as the public library was built up gradually. The pioneers took hold of an idea that seems to go back to Benjamin Franklin, the idea of subscription clubs or associations, a kind of joint-stock association. People got together, raised funds, paid fees, bought books, and enjoyed the privileges of a reading room with a much wider selection of books than they could afford individually in their own homes. This was not a public library, but it was a step toward it.

As early as October 1856 the citizens of Northfield, Minnesota, united in a library association. The minutes of its early meetings tell how the members collected $28.00 for the upkeep of a reading room. Of this sum, $11.60 went for a stove and pipe, $3.00 for a cord of hickory wood, $10.40 for a table and benches, and a small sum for a lamp. Soon the association was able to put up a building (its cost was $580.00), and on February 3, 1858, the library opened with 269 books on its shelves.

The minutes reveal some troubles over unreturned books, and there was some grumbling about the failure of papers and magazines to arrive as ordered from New York. One record runs as follows: "It is the private opinion of the Librarian (Publicly expressed) that there is hard Sledding somewhere between here and N York City, or that Mr. Orvis"—the New

York bookseller—"is a swindler." Among other things, the *Atlantic* and *Putnam's* monthlies had not arrived.

A debating society was conducted alongside this library association. Among the subjects debated were woman suffrage, the question whether or not war is ever justified, and the proposition, striking with incredible freshness across the decades since the 1850's, "That England is the guardian of Liberty in Europe."

The association of libraries with free debate is no coincidence. In many parts of the Northwest the pioneer lyceums figure in the genesis of libraries.

In 1855 the *St. Croix Union* carried a lengthy editorial on Stillwater's need of a library. The good it could do was "incalculable." It would help to keep the mischievous out of trouble and stimulate their minds "to healthful action." The editor was exasperated at those who said they had not time to read, yet spent "from one to five hours every day telling some hard yarn and spitting tobacco juice all over creation."

A New Englander living in Stillwater about the same time wrote less disparagingly of his townsmen, however. "People pay more attention to the literature of magazines and papers, than at the East," he said. "You can hardly enter a family without finding Harper, Putnam, Graham and Godey, and oftener two of these than one. The Home Journal, and Arthur's Gazette visit hundreds of log cabins, and then every body takes the Tribune. We have heard of the annexation of Hawaii and the war in Europe, and we discuss and settle these great questions as much as you do at the East, only we are about ten days behind you, that is all."

The *New York Tribune* had nearly three thousand subscribers in Minnesota Territory in 1856, more than any single paper printed in that territory. A farmer in the St. Croix Valley saw a young man working on his road crew take a copy of the *Tribune* from his pocket to read at lunch time. The farmer remarked that any young man who read that paper would "not go far wrong." The farmer, whose name was Joseph Haskell and who broke soil for what has been called the first farm in Minnesota, had a small but select collection of books and magazines in his pioneer home. He carefully preserved the volumes of the *Atlantic Monthly* from its first issue and subscribed to such other publications as the *Boston Journal of Commerce*, Orange Judd's *American Agriculturist*, and *Scribner's Magazine*.

"We have neither hotels, side-walks, gas-light nor police—as yet," declared the *Duluth Minnesotian* in its issue for June 5, 1869. "Our townsite even, is not all surveyed out. We are carving a city right out of the woods, and he is a fool who comes here expecting to see a full grown city, or even a large town. . . . we warn everybody . . . to bring two blankets. . . . Every man 'takes up his bed and walks.'"

But in the Duluth newspaper for July 10, 1869, one finds a most interesting item from a town that lacked sidewalks, gaslights, and police. The paper reports that "some of our young men are moving toward starting a Literary Society connecting it with a Library and Reading Room." How fast the young men moved may be seen by a little further inquiry. A group met and formulated plans for the new society on August 30; and on December 1 the formal opening of the new library and reading room took place.

The *Duluth Minnesotian* gives a vivid picture of the scene. The room "was quite crowded by a fashionable and intelligent audience of ladies and gentlemen, fully appreciative of the significance and purpose of the occasion. It was carpeted, and the walls were "hung with evergreen wreaths and handsome pictures." A "large and commodious reading table, filled with papers and periodicals" occupied the middle of the room; and "in the recess a most flattering commencement of a Library" was "seen, containing about 500 volumes, varied and variable." In the evening a local celebrity delivered a lecture on "Boston and the American Revolution." The newspaper expressed the hope that the reading room would be "a place of resort for the ladies as well as the gentlemen" and "conduce to social as well as mental cultivation during the long winter."

Although this pioneer library did not last long, it was succeeded by an institution set in motion by the "Ladies Library Association." A disastrous fire in 1889 destroyed the collection of that association, and a year later Duluth became "possessed" of its first public library.

The word *public* is the clue to a development that was becoming more and more marked throughout the Northwest and indeed all over the United States. For the subscription library, with shareholders and fee-paying members, did not meet the needs of a civilization in which the processes of education were being democratized. As the private academies gave way to public high schools, so the library associations gave way to public libraries. Legislators in Minnesota caught the trend of progress when in 1879 they passed a law authorizing city and village councils to establish public libraries and to levy taxes for their support.

It was one thing to pass a law, another to create and develop public libraries. They did not spring up by magic; people worked for them; and in many towns women's organizations took the lead in starting them. Often the beginnings were humble, but once started the public libraries made a place for themselves. Sometimes private gifts encouraged the better housing and administration of community book collections. A library profession emerged, and its leaders, pioneering a social frontier, saw clearly that the public library was not only an educational institution but also a social force that touched and influenced the life of an entire people. In Minnesota a state library association was formed in 1891, and by the end of that decade a state library commission was established and a traveling library system inaugurated.

Thus public libraries became a living part of the communities of the Northwest. Created by the people out of the people's needs, they became a true part of the community life, identified with special community needs and concerns, usually taking on something of the character and atmosphere of the community itself.

Sometimes community effort received encouragement from outside sources, notably from Andrew Carnegie, whose familiar account of why he became deeply interested in libraries touches the heart of the whole story. "When I was a boy in Pittsburgh," he wrote, "Colonel Anderson . . . a name that I can never speak without feelings of devotional gratitude – opened his little library of four hundred books to boys. Every Saturday afternoon he was in attendance at his house to exchange books." Carnegie never forgot "the intense longing with which the arrival of Saturday was awaited, that a new book might be had." And he said later that "it was when revelling in the treasures which he opened to us that I resolved, if ever wealth came to me, that it should be used to establish free libraries, that other poor boys might receive opportunities similar to those for which we were indebted to that noble man."

Against this general background the service of public libraries to the communities of the Northwest developed and expanded until they had become an indispensable factor in the life of the region. The pioneers needed books and were determined to have them. Their need expressed itself in private collections which, by grace of the open shelf, were shared with others. Then came cooperative efforts to make books available, at first through private associations and the sharing of costs, and later through general community action backed by local ordinance and law.

In the early era a private citizen hunted through his community for individuals "possessed of libraries." The spirit passed from individuals to communities, and ultimately an entire region became "possessed of libraries."

They Came, They Saw, They Recorded

IN THAT most famous of all essays on American history in which Frederick Jackson Turner analyzes the significance of the frontier, he invites us to stand at Cumberland Gap "and watch the procession of civilization, marching single file." In the march are Indian, fur-trader, hunter, cattle-raiser, and farmer, but one does not see the frontier scientist—the man of maps and instruments.

Yet wherever there were frontiers, whether of land or of spirit, the men of science were familiar figures. They came, they saw, they recorded; and to them we owe a singular debt of gratitude.

In the spring of 1818 Joseph Provencher, a Catholic priest, found time, on the long and hazardous canoe voyage from Quebec to the Red River Valley, to dispatch a letter to the Bishop of Quebec, telling of his plans for a mission in the West. Taking occasion to give advice to churchmen who might venture into the wilderness, he admitted that their primary purpose was the salvation of souls, but he also suggested another pursuit to which they might well give attention. This was to "take a complete and successful course of study and apply themselves to astronomy, both practical and theoretical, and to everything that concerns that subject."

Whether or not the Bishop of Quebec set his priests to studying the stars we do not know, but we do know that nearly a hundred years before Provencher's time the middle-western wilderness boasted astronomers of a kind.

In September 1727, when the wide-ranging lands of the upper Mississippi were part of New France, a pioneering French expedition established a fort on Lake Pepin—Fort

Beauharnois, near the present site of Frontenac. It was a wilderness post consisting of three log buildings surrounded by "stakes twelve feet high with two good bastions." With the French officer who commanded Fort Beauharnois were two Jesuit fathers who promptly built a chapel, the Mission of St. Michael the Archangel, the first Christian church of the North Country.

It was also the first observatory of that region, for the Jesuits had taken with them some "mathematical instruments" – "a dial plate of universal astronomy, a graduated semi-circle with the degrees indicated, a spirit level, a chain with stakes, and a telescope six or seven feet long." One of the first tasks of the priests was that of working out the latitude of Fort Beauharnois, and they placed it at 43°51′. We know today that the correct figure is 44°31′.

On many an expedition to the early West, Jesuit priests played the roles of scientists and map makers. The difficulties of exploration without such skilled aid may be illustrated by recalling the experiences of the famed Scottish trader and explorer, Sir Alexander Mackenzie. After the notable exploration which resulted in the discovery of the great river that bears his name and took him to the shores of the Arctic in 1789, he felt bitterly disappointed.

"I was not only without the necessary books and instruments," he wrote, "but also felt myself deficient in the sciences of astronomy and navigation." In order "to procure the one and acquire the other," he "undertook a winter's voyage" to England; and in London, although he might have won acclaim as a successful explorer, he remained in seclusion, studying the sciences he lacked.

Once back in the Northwest he struck out again for the Western Sea. One of the great epics of western history is the story of how he crossed the mountains, overcame incredible odds, and finally, twelve years before Lewis and Clark, reached the Pacific on a July day in 1793. There, on the shores of the Western Sea, he stopped to take observations and to inscribe a record in vermilion on a convenient rock.

"While I was taking a meridian," he writes, "two canoes . . . appeared." His Indian guide begged him to leave. "My people were panic struck, and some . . . asked if it was my determination to remain to be sacrificed? My reply was the same . . . that I would not stir till I had accomplished my object."

In Mackenzie's narrative, a classic of western exploration, he says of himself, "I do not possess the science of the naturalist; and even if the qualifications of that character had been attained by me, its curious spirit would not have been gratified. I could not stop to dig into the earth, over whose surface I was compelled to pass with rapid steps; nor could I turn aside to collect the plants which nature might have scattered on my way, when my thoughts were anxiously employed in making provision for the day that was passing over me. I had to encounter perils by land and perils by water; to watch the savage who was our guide, or to guard against those of his tribe who might meditate our destruction. I had, also, the passions and fears of others to control and subdue."

An Italian astronomer, Count Paolo Andreani of Milan, visited the Lake Superior region as early as 1791, but left such meager records of his travels that he seems almost a phantom. He was an Italian nobleman who had made the first successful balloon ascension in Italy, and when he came to America he was armed with a letter of introduction to the president of Yale University. On his Lake Superior visit he measured Thunder Mountain, near the present Canadian city of Port Arthur, and to puzzled fur traders he explained that he was interested in the admeasurement of heights and the formation of the earth at the poles.

In La Rochefoucauld Liancourt's *Travels*, published in 1799, there is a brief sketch of the western fur trade drawn from Andreani's diary, but it is merely a fragment and nobody seems to know where the original diary is.

Soon after Andreani's time the Northwest became the theater of an important enterprise, for in 1797 David Thompson set out from Grand Portage, the fur-trading post on the western shores of Lake Superior, to make a scientific investigation of the hinterland.

Born in London of impoverished Welsh parents, Thompson was put into a charity school at the age of seven. He was taught so-called "navigation" there, but his preparation was slight even though the school records describe him as a "mathematical Boy." At fourteen he was apprenticed to the Hudson's Bay Company, and by 1784 he was in the Canadian West. When he was nineteen he was at Cumberland House on the Saskatchewan River, where he kept a meteorological journal of "natural phenomena," recording thermometer readings three or four times a day, the direction and force of the wind, remarks on the climate, and astronomical observations. The "mathematical Boy" determined the location of Cumberland House almost exactly as it is today computed – no small achievement.

Thompson studied the next winter under a surveyor in the employ of the Hudson's Bay Company; and by 1797, when he left that company to join the Northwest Company, he had already accomplished some 9000 miles of surveying. He now undertook, in 1797, to determine the line of the forty-ninth parallel and the positions of the trading posts of the Northwest Company, and also, as he wrote later, "to extend my Surveys to the Missisourie River; visit the villages of the ancient agricultural Natives who dwelt there; enquire for fossil bones of large animals, and any monuments . . . that might throw light on the ancient state of the unknown countries I had to travel over and examine." He took with him "a Sextant of ten inches radius, with Quicksilver and parallel glasses, an excellent Achromatic Telescope; a lesser for common use; drawing instruments, and two Thermometers; all made by Dollond."

Thompson's trip required ten months. He followed the usual water route westward from Grand Portage. From Lake of the Woods he pushed on to Lake Winnipeg, made his way by stream and plains to the Mandan villages on the Missouri, returned to the Red River, and crossed by way of Red Lake to the headwaters of the Mississippi. He went on to Fond du Lac and Lake Superior, passed around the south shore of the lake to Sault Ste. Marie, and finally returned to Grand Portage by the north shore route. He had accomplished a "total of four thousand miles of survey through previously unsurveyed territory, a record that has rarely been equalled."

The *Dictionary of American Biography* describes Thompson as "one of the greatest land geographers of the English race."

His journals are full of vivid description. Here is one small item, a word picture of the Savanna portage: "a great Swamp of 4½ miles . . . the latter part of what may be termed bog; over which we passed by means of a few sticks laid lengthways, and when we slipped off we sunk to our waists, and with difficulty regained our footing on the sticks. No Woods grow on this great Swamp, except scattered pine shrubs of a few feet in height; yet such as it was, we had to carry our Canoe and all our things. And all the furrs, provisions, baggage and Canoes of the Mississippe have to be carried on their way to the Depot on Lake Superior, and likewise all the goods for the winter trade. It is a sad piece of work. The Person in charge of the brigade; crosses it as fast as he can, leaves the Men to take their own time, who flounce along with the packs of furrs, or pieces of goods, and 'sacre' as often as they please."

Thompson's words were chosen with care. He explained, for example, that when he wrote of "a Plain I mean lands bearing grass, but too short for the Scythe; where the grass is long enough for the Scythe, and of which Hay can be made, I name meadows."

Sometimes he philosophized about the people he observed. The exploitation of the beaver in one area of the Canadian Northwest led him to say, "For several years all these Indians were rich, the Women and Children, as well as the Men, were covered with silver brooches, Ear Rings, Wampum, Beads and other trinkets. Their mantles were of fine scarlet cloth, and all was finery and dress. The Canoes of the Furr Traders were loaded with packs of Beaver, the abundance of the article lowered the London prices. Every intelligent Man saw the poverty that would follow the destruction of the Beaver, but there were no Chiefs to controul it; all was perfect liberty and equality. For years afterwards almost the whole of these extensive countries were denuded of Beaver, the Natives became poor, and with difficulty procured the necessaries of life." He added that "the Beaver, once destroyed cannot be replaced: they were the gold coin of the country."

Most of Thompson's later explorations belong outside the Northwest country, but he did return during the decade following 1816 to survey and define the international boundary line. It was in this period that Chief Two Hearts of Rainy Lake came to Thompson and said that "his people had seen us frequently . . . as well as other canoes of palefaces, holding up pieces of shining metal to the sun.—'Have you suffered wrong from any red man? What is your purpose in rambling over our waters, and putting them into your books?' "

Mr. Thompson answered that he and his associates had not been harmed by the Indians. They were simply trying "to find how far north the shadow of the United States extended, and how far south the shadow of . . . King George." So Thompson was a diplomat as well as a geographer.

There were a few doctors in the North Country in the late eighteenth and early nineteenth centuries, the most notable among them being Dr. John McLoughlin, who later won fame as the "Father of Oregon." He was a physician, fur trader, and adventurer. Once he nearly lost his life in Lake Superior when a canoe in which he was traveling capsized and nine of his companions were drowned. Many years later a traveler on a Liverpool packet met Dr. McLoughlin on board ship and heard him say that there were no risks whatever connected with canoe travel in the New World. A few minutes later the traveler heard the doctor telling of his near-drowning. "Men . . . are fond of talking of Dangers past," wrote the traveler.

Dr. McLoughlin evidently was an entertaining talker with a rich fund of experience. His fellow traveler recorded that he "felt melancholy" when the voyage ended and the doctor departed. A trader named Harmon who spent the winter of 1807 with Dr. McLoughlin wrote in his diary that McLoughlin was "an excellent companion, and fond of conversation," a man whose company made a long winter "pleasant and profitable."

Another record from those years indicates that the doctor owned a wilderness library. His letters give details of the treatment of diseases in the new country; an unpublished treatise of his describes plant and animal as well as Indian life in northern Minnesota; he was, among other things, a farmer who planted at his northern post a garden of barley, oats, and peas. The missionary priests on the Red River told of his advice to them; an escaped captive of the Indians, John Tanner, who had been wounded, wrote that Dr. McLoughlin charged him no fee, but set him to trapping when his arm was healed and then bought the furs he collected. Dr. McLoughlin "will be wanted," wrote the trader Harmon, "as soon as he can arrive, [at Fort William] to attend on the sick."

With the opening of the American regime, army men were sent into the Northwest to explore the rich lands acquired as part of the Louisiana Purchase, to establish forts, and to learn about the resources of the region. Few of these soldiers were scientists, but they had ingenuity and courage and some of them did notable work.

The first was Lieutenant Zebulon M. Pike, who, with twenty subordinates, came up the Mississippi from St. Louis in the fall of 1805, wintered in the Minnesota country, and returned to St. Louis the following spring. In the preface to his *Explorations* he wrote, "I literally performed the duties (as far as my limited abilities permitted) of astronomer, surveyor, commanding officer, clerk, spy, guide, and hunter; frequently preceding the party for miles in order to reconnoiter, and returning in the evening, hungry and fatigued, to sit down in the open air, by firelight, to copy the notes and plot the courses of the day."

His meteorological observations, said Pike, were "very imperfect," partly because, when traveling alone, he could not carry his instruments, partly because "during the intense cold . . . the mercury of the barometer sank into the bulb." On one march in northern Minnesota his men had to stop every three miles to build fires in order to combat the cold, and Pike says that fingers, noses, and toes were frozen.

Pike admitted that he did not look at the Minnesota country "with the eye of a Linnaeus or Buffon." Nevertheless, he assembled much information about the Northwest and made it available in an excellent report.

One afternoon in May 1820 a flotilla of three bark canoes, bearing in all forty-three persons and all their equipment, with voyageurs and Indians paddling, set out from Detroit. This was the expedition of Lewis Cass, governor of Michigan Territory, who had been authorized by the Secretary of War, John C. Calhoun, to examine the western parts of that territory and, among other things, to learn about "its animal, vegetable, and mineral kingdoms."

This expedition passed through the Great Lakes, pushed into the Minnesota interior from the present site of Duluth, took the Savanna portage to Sandy Lake, then went on to Upper Red Cedar Lake, now named Cass, which the Governor thought was the "true source of the Mississippi," and then descended the river to the Falls of St. Anthony and Fort Snelling. It was the first expedition into the Minnesota country of a group of scientific explorers.

Cass was not a scientist, but he seems to have been a good expedition leader. One member of the party later recalled that the governor always had with him, in his canoe, "a well selected . . . small library," and that "when the weather permitted, some young member of the party was called upon to read aloud during a part of the forenoon. . . . the evening camp-fire . . . was always enlivened by some literary or scientific discussion, generally started by the general, and carried on by some of the savans in his suite." Henry R. Schoolcraft, another member of the party, later thanked Cass for his "zeal in the promotion of scientific objects."

The physician of the expedition was Dr. Alexander Wolcott, a Yale graduate, chosen, Cass said, because he was "a scientific man and a skilful Physician." Schoolcraft noted that Wolcott had "decidedly saturnine feelings, and a keen perception of the ridiculous." Once Cass sent Wolcott some inquiries he wanted answered. "Many a time and oft," replied Wolcott, "I have wished" your queries "at the bottom of the Red Sea, along with so many other wicked spirits, whose only object on earth was to disturb the repose of quiet, lazy people, like myself." That he finally sent off an answer at all, he added, was mainly in order "to quiet certain stirrings and twitchings somewhere about the region of the pericardium." He lacked all faith in the value of his answers and said he felt like "a man who should attempt to polish a diamond with a woodrasp." Recalling his experiences on the Indian frontier, he exclaimed, "like the Pharisee, I thank God that I am not as other men – Indian traders and dwellers on the borders of Sandy Lake."

One can almost fancy hearing the voice of this man who came to dinner with the fur traders, a voice carrying the accent of his kinsman of a hundred years later, Alexander Woolcott.

Unlike the saturnine Dr. Wolcott, Schoolcraft had utter faith in the value of his answers. He was the "mineralogist and geologist" of the expedition, which he reported in his *Narrative Journal* of 1821 – and he went on reporting expeditions as long as he lived. He was driven by a passion to explore and a fever to write. Although he was no scientist, he had a wild enthusiasm for science. He was no scholar, but he was a worker who could amass mountains of information. And he loved to write mountainous books. Even though he was far from being a scientific ethnologist, he turned out tomes on the Indian races of the Northwest which are vast storehouses of information.

There was no zoologist on the Cass expedition, and Schoolcraft, never daunted by any assignment, cheerfully undertook to serve in that capacity. Near Sault Ste. Marie he procured a specimen of the Eastern Evening Grosbeak, the first example brought to the attention of ornithologists. Dr. Thomas S. Roberts points out that Schoolcraft was mistaken in describing the Evening Grosbeak as an evening singer, but he concedes that Schoolcraft did find the bird.

Botany was represented on the Cass expedition by a veteran of the War of 1812 named David B. Douglass. He was successively instructor in several branches of science, including mathematics and engineering, at West Point. His botanical findings were drawn up and published, not by himself, but by the eminent botanist, Dr. John Torrey of New York.

Recently I found Torrey's article on the plants collected by Professor Douglass "around the Great Lakes and the upper waters of the Mississippi" in the University of Minnesota's file of the *American Journal of Science and Arts*, printed at New Haven in 1822. This article is the botanical story of the Cass expedition. Many rare species were included in the collection that Douglass sent to Dr. Torrey, notwithstanding the loss of part of the collection when a canoe capsized in the Wisconsin River.

Torrey incidentally published a letter from Douglass which contains one curious item. Douglass reported the plant *uvularia perfoliata* as "efficacious in the cure of Rattlesnake-bite."

Nearly everybody on the Cass expedition recorded his experiences, and only recently a diary of much interest and value has been discovered. This is the diary of the assistant topographer, Charles C. Trowbridge, the original of which was found by Professor Ralph Brown of the University of Minnesota, who has published it in the quarterly of the Minnesota Historical Society.

From it I shall quote only one passage, a description of the reception of the Cass party at the American Fur Company's trading post on Sandy Lake: "Immediately after our arrival at the fort we were invited [to] take supper; welcome news to us, for our provisions were exhausted before we arrived at the lake. We found on the table a plate for each person, containing each a Boiled Duck and a large slice of Buffalo meat, dried in the sun. The quantity seemed repelling, but we had learned to eat . . . and we were astonished at looking at our plates, in a little time, to find them all empty." The voyageurs, Trowbridge learned, lived chiefly on buffalo meat and wild rice.

The year 1823, four years after Fort Snelling was established at the junction of the Mississippi and Minnesota rivers, was notable in Northwest history for at least three developments. One was the arrival from St. Louis of the *Virginia*, the first steamboat to churn the waters of the upper Mississippi. The second was the visit to Minnesota, as a passenger on that boat, of Giacomo Beltrami, another of those curious, solitary Italian explorers who figure in western history. And the third was a well-organized expedition under Major Stephen H. Long sent out by the War Department to explore the Minnesota and Red rivers, a part of the vast stretch of country between the Mississippi and the Missouri. Long previously had made a trip up the Mississippi in 1817. Beltrami went out to the Red River with the Long expedition, but his connection with it was only temporary, since he quarreled with Long. Later he said that there was in Long's party only one person who deserved to be called a naturalist.

Certainly that person did deserve the title, for he was Thomas Say, the "father of descriptive entomology in America." In the official report on the Long expedition of 1823, Say supplied elaborate descriptions of Minnesota fishes, shells, leeches, and insects. They would have been fuller than they were, but, we are informed, "the skins of many birds, quadrupeds, and fish," and some shells were lost in transit.

Say also took on the duties of botanist and physician. William Keating, the editor of the general report, said that Say had undertaken the botanical work "with the diffidence with which a man will undertake a task with which he does not profess to be conversant." In his medical duties Say appeared to be less diffident, however. He suspected that one soldier whom he treated with various medicines was feigning sickness in order to escape the task of rowing in an eight-oar barge up the Mississippi. Say studied the case and then prescribed the "use of an oar as a sudorific" – and the patient was soon well.

Keating was the mineralogist, geologist, and secretary of the expedition. He was only twenty-four years old but already had a good reputation as a mineralogical chemist. Later, according to the *Dictionary of American Biography*, he was largely responsible for the discovery of eight or ten new minerals.

Like David Thompson, Keating had some difficulties with

words. In his preface he apologizes for using words "not sanctioned by the dictionaries," but too "characteristic and essential" to be omitted. Such words, he says, are *bluff* and *prairie.* He managed with some inconvenience, he said, to avoid the term *creek* and he used the word *run* but once.

At Pembina in the Red River Valley, Keating says, the travelers encountered a druggist [David Hoerner?], probably the first of his kind in the Northwest. He had come all the way from Switzerland, stocked with "aniseed, Palma Christi seed, &c.," thinking that the new western settlement would need his expert "pharmaceutical and chemical knowledge." He intended to plant a botanical garden, but his hopes "dwindled away at the necessity of handling a plough, and attending the more important cultivation of wheat, potatoes, &c."

The astronomer of the Long expedition was a young man named James E. Colhoun, whose original diary turned up in a class in American history at the University of Minnesota some years ago. It may be of interest to note that his instruments included a brass sextant of five inches' radius, made by Cary, London; a common surveyor's compass, marked to degrees, with a needle four inches long; an artificial horizon of mercury; and a patent lever watch, made by Robert Roskell of Liverpool.

Young Colhoun, who notwithstanding a small orthographic variation in name was a nephew of John C. Calhoun, had a curious interest in some of the tall stories of the frontier. He said that his good opinion of Renville, the guide, "somewhat abated" because of one story Renville told. As a boy on the Minnesota River, Renville said, he had shot a flying snake, seven or eight feet long, black, white, and yellow in color, with a deep green belly, and a red throat. It had a membrane "on each side . . . which could be folded at pleasure." Other frontiersmen told Colhoun of seeing similar reptiles in Minnesota.

The backwoodsmen were having a little fun with the astronomer. He was young but not naive and he remained skeptical about this herpetological wonder.

Major Long's original diaries, preserved by the Minnesota Historical Society, are still unpublished. They are full of survey notes, maps, and calculations, with occasional diary entries about members of the party. Beltrami, Long writes, was "an amateur traveller," and he comments on the quarrel that caused Beltrami to leave "in a very hasty and angry manner."

That Beltrami was something less than a scientist is suggested by a phrase in his own book. "*The real forms and dimensions of objects* do not differ from my descriptions," he writes, "except just so far as to prevent their appearing insipid and monotonous."

In 1832 another expedition to the headwaters of the Mississippi was organized, this time under the direction of the bustling Schoolcraft. This was the expedition that went to the source of the Mississippi and named Lake Itasca from the two Latin words *veritas* and *caput.* Among the men who accompanied it was Dr. Douglass Houghton, a physician, who vaccinated two thousand Chippewa Indians against smallpox. In his unpublished diary, which was found in Michigan a few years ago, he tells of the "wonderful dread" of the Indians for the disease and their willingness to submit to vaccination; and in an appendix to Schoolcraft's report on the trip he tells of five frightful smallpox epidemics among the Chippewa during the preceding eighty-five years.

Dr. Houghton had to take care of the members of the expedition in emergencies. After crossing a certain portage they looked, a companion wrote, "like renegades, covered with mud from head to foot. . . . Face, hands, and necks look like men scarred with the small-pox. . . . Bruised skins, sore toes and legs are gathered in good numbers around the Doctor's tent this morning. Every one will carry some mark in remembrance of this portage."

Dr. Houghton was also a botanist, and he listed ten new species in his findings of the trip, including one of the violet family at Itasca. Lieutenant James Allen was the topographer of the expedition and collected "many useful facts" on geology and mineralogy in the Lake Superior region; and Houghton reported on its copper.

I can only mention Albert Miller Lea, a topographical engineer, who, with a son of Daniel Boone as an assistant, mapped southern Minnesota in 1835; and George W. Featherstonhaugh, an English-born geologist, who toured southwestern Minnesota in the same year on appointment as United States geologist. He offended nearly everybody he met by his arrogant manner. Later he published in London a curious book called *A Canoe Voyage up the Minnay Sotor.*

But the next year, 1836, there appeared at Fort Snelling an exploring scientist who calls for more than a mention. This was Joseph Nicolas Nicollet, a well-trained French mathematician and astronomer. He pushed northward to Leech Lake, where the Indians promptly dubbed him with a Chippewa name that meant "A Frenchman of the Olden Time." Upon them, and also upon the traders, missionaries, and soldiers of frontier Minnesota, Nicollet made a profound impression as a scientist and philosopher.

His fame in western history hinges primarily upon a great map of the "Hydrographical Basin of the Upper Mississippi River" that he published in 1843. It was the basis, according to William Watts Folwell, for "all the subsequent cartography of an immense region." His report, accompanying the map, is regarded by the same authority as a classic.

Unlike some explorers of his time, Nicollet was generous and gave credit to those who had gone before him or who assisted him in his work, but a reference to Schoolcraft's discovery of Lake Itasca perhaps carries a note of mild reproof. Nicollet writes that "having devoted three days to an exploration of the sources of the Mississippi, and spent portions of the nights in making astronomical observations, I took leave of *Itasca lake,* to the examination of which the expedition that preceded me . . . had devoted but a short time." The short time referred to was two hours.

Nicollet gives us a picture of how he traveled: "I carried my sextant on my back, in a leather case, thrown over me as a knapsack; then my barometer slung over the left shoulder; my cloak, thrown over the same shoulder, confined the barometer closely against the sextant; a portfolio under the arm; a basket in hand, which contained my thermometer, chronometer, pocket-compass, artificial horizon, tape-line, &c., &c. On the right side, a spy-glass, powder-flask, and shot bag; and in my hand, a gun or an umbrella." Thus equipped, he explored the wilderness, sometimes so engrossed in protecting his instruments that he lost his way in the swamps of the portages.

He had an almost poetical appreciation of the West, and when he saw the prairies near the Red River, he spoke of their "magical influence." "To look at a prairie up or down; to ascend one of its undulations; to reach a small plateau . . . moving from wave to wave over alternate swells and depressions; and, finally, to reach the vast interminable low prairie that extends itself in front, – be it for hours, days, or weeks, one never tires; pleasurable and exhilarating sensations are all the time felt."

One of Nicollet's companions on his western trips was John C. Frémont, then a young man in his twenties. In a letter to his mother he described Nicollet as a "real Frenchman," a man "inclined to spare neither himself nor us as regards labor," an expedition leader who "takes every means to make us comfortable." "As far as regards Science," wrote Frémont, "I am improving under him daily."

Nicollet was conscious of an obligation to the botanist Torrey, "to whom," he said, "I was proud of an opportunity – brought about by the liberal and disinterested intercourse which characterizes American *savans* . . . of submitting my collection." Actual botanical work on several of Nicollet's trips was done by the Saxon, Charles Geyer of Dresden, who had come to America a few years earlier with the purpose of exploring the plant life of the New World and had first met Nicollet on a Missouri River steamboat.

One of Nicollet's daily journals of a trip up the Minnesota Valley in 1838 tells of the start of an expedition: "Leave the Sioux Crossing at 7 minutes after 11. . . . My eight men each at the head of a heavily loaded cart. LaFramboise is at the head of the file with his wife and Eugene in the barouche. I, Fremont and Geyer, in the wagon of Joseph Renville and his wife, we bring up the rear of the train to superintend the march. The flag flies in the center of the file, the son of the Chief of the Sissetons, he of the Sleepy Eyes, is alongside the flag. The heat is prostrating, but it does not prevent the company from dancing, running races, fighting and giving themselves up to battles with their whips on the beautiful greensward that we pass over."

Nicollet died in 1843. His own manuscripts were long believed to have been lost, but as a result of the moving of records in governmental buildings in Washington during the First World War, an old wooden chest turned up, on one side of it the name "Nicollet" and inside it the original Nicollet Papers.

The papers are now in the Library of Congress, which announced the acquisition of the collection in its *Report* for 1921. Fragments of two of the Nicollet diaries have been published. It should be possible now, in the light of all the printed and manuscript materials available, for someone to write a good biography of this "Frenchman of the Olden Time."

Nicollet marks the end of my story, but not of the role of science in the exploration of the frontiers of the Northwest. In 1846 another Frenchman, F. V. Lamare-Picquot, was building up a natural history museum in the wilds of Minnesota. A traveler who saw the collection reported that it included a buffalo head, elk, deer, otter, beaver, fox, and wolf as well as wild swan, pelican, eagle, and partridge. Though regarded by the natives as a sorcerer or conjuror, he was successful in his collecting and carried off numerous specimens to European museums.

Other scientists who visited the Middle West in the 1840's included the Le Conte cousins, John Lawrence and Joseph, in pursuit of entomology and geology, and the first of these joined Louis Agassiz in a trip to the north Superior shore late in the same decade. There were other expeditions in the 1840's and 1850's that have scientific interest, including the Stevens transcontinental railroad survey of 1853, and there were physicians, like the fur trader Charles W. W. Borup and the missionary Thomas Williamson, who practiced medicine on the Minnesota frontier in the 1830's and 1840's.

An exuberant young naturalist, Robert Kennicott, traveled widely in Minnesota and the Northwest in the late 1850's and early 1860's. He had a particular interest in birds, but his letters and diary reveal a wide-ranging observation that included the techniques of voyaging. He called himself *un bon voyageur*, and in one of his letters, written by the light of a buffalo-tallow candle, he said, "I can eat as much buffalo meat as would be considered sufficient for half a dozen of you poor inhabitants of shells & boxes."

In 1861 Henry David Thoreau, on a trip in vain search of health, listed in botanical Latin the flowers he found on Nicollet Island (now a part of Minneapolis), roamed the woods around Minnehaha Falls and the shores of Lake Calhoun identifying specimens of plant, animal, and bird life, and journeyed far up the Minnesota River. Among the animals in which Thoreau took particular interest was the gopher, whose name has become a nickname for Minnesotans. Its stripes reminded the naturalist of "the rude pattern of some Indian work, – porcupine quills, 'gopher-work' in baskets and pottery."

Thoreau's observations of the Middle West are recorded in letters and in his *Last Journey*.

For every part of America one could tell a similar story of the men who came, saw, and recorded. In books and reports, in maps and drawings and manuscripts, and in specimens gathered up and deposited in the museums of the world they have documented their searches and researches. They helped to make the unknown known and understood, as scientists have done in pioneering both physical frontiers and frontiers of thought through long ages of history.

From Cottage to Clinic

IT IS pleasant to recall that the institutions where men and women in white serve the sick and suffering take their name from a Latin word relating to a guest. The saga of these institutions in America and throughout the world is one of sacrifice and service and devotion in the humane tradition of hospitality, but it is more: it is also a saga of pioneering, of professional and scientific advance, and of public enlightenment. And it is bound up with folk history.

The outlines of a great national, human story that has not been told in all its richness and fullness may be suggested by tracing the development of hospitals in one state from the days of a lonely fort on the American frontier in the days of President Monroe to our own day, when more than two hundred hospitals, with nearly thirty thousand beds, offer sanctuary and care to the sick.

Minnesota was a lonely frontier of Indians, fur traders, and soldiers in 1819, when Fort Snelling was established at the junction of the Mississippi and Minnesota rivers. In June of that year the order book of a Fort Snelling lieutenant directed the surgeon of the post to "make returns . . . for such supplies of Vegetables, Poultry, Milk &c as He may think necessary for the use of the Sick."

The surgeon was one Dr. Edward Purcell, who arrived with the first troops in 1819, and a hospital was among the first buildings to be erected. By 1821 such provisions as pork, fresh beef, beans, flour, salt, vinegar, soap, and candles were being sent to the "Hospital." It is not surprising to learn that in those pre-chloroform days whisky, too, was among the standard requirements of the establishment.

A humble log structure met early needs, but the completed Fort Snelling hospital, as pictured in old maps and drawings, was a substantial stone building between the Round Tower and the Hexagonal Tower, two structures that have survived the decades and are still to be seen at Fort Snelling. One side of the hospital was the stone wall of the fort; on the other side were doors and windows; later a second-story porch was added where convalescing patients had a panoramic view of primitive Minnesota scenery at its best. For many years all the water for the fort was hauled up from a spring.

A report from a later date tells us that the hospital had three large ward rooms. On the second floor the windows and porch doors could be opened for ventilation, but on the first floor the ventilation was "entirely natural." Since there were no windows at all on the wall side, one can only conclude that it was very natural, indeed. In later years a surgeon attributed the large number of cases of pneumonia to the lack of fresh air in the fort buildings, and explained the matter by saying that the soldiers were obliged to use quarters erected in frontier times, when "it was the aim to place the largest number of soldiers into the least possible space without any regard to the demands of hygiene."

Whatever the limitations, the hospital of the pioneer fort was a busy place. It sometimes met demands from outside the military. For example, in 1827 eight Chippewa Indians who had been ambushed by hostile Sioux were brought to the fort hospital, and the surgeon did "all in his power to relieve them." One victim was Chief Hole-in-the-Day, who had been shot in the breast. His only child, a little girl, had also been wounded and finally died of her wounds. There were no nurses, but the officers' wives took turns in caring for the child.

Upon her death, her father, the chief, spoke to the American Indian agent, Major Taliaferro, with the dignity befitting a chief. "My *only child*," he said, "left me to go to the great

Spirit above last Night. Her body is all that is now left to me and her *bones* are dear to me." He would take the body, he said, to his own lands, and added, "I thank you and the white people here for the great Charity done us in our distresses, My Father." This chief's gratitude contributed to the long-continued friendship of the Chippewa nation for the whites in the Northwest.

About 1849 a second military hospital was erected, at Fort Ripley – a frame building filled in with brick, one story high, with an attic. The chapel and fort offices were in the same structure. A surgeon's report complains of the ventilation; the air in the medical ward was practically stagnant; and only a few feet in the rear of the windows were the woodhouse and latrines. The surgical ward communicated with the mess hall, from which kitchen odors permeated. This pioneer hospital had no bath, washroom, water closet, or dead house, and for lack of separate rooms the attendants slept in the wards.

A copy of a diary kept at old Fort Ripley by an army chaplain stationed there in the 1850's tells of patients with typhoid fever, soldiers with frozen arms and legs, and accident cases of various kinds. On one occasion there was a suspected murder, and an autopsy was performed by a well-known St. Paul physician, Dr. Thomas R. Potts, whose investigation brought to light twenty-six large gallstones and an affected liver, thereby disposing of the suspicion of foul play.

A third military hospital before the days of civilian hospitals was a log structure at Fort Ridgely in the Minnesota River Valley. This fort played a dramatic role in the Sioux War of 1862. The fort, which was described as "more fit for a county fair than for a fort," was not far from New Ulm. To it several hundred refugees fled when Little Crow and his warriors went on the warpath in the late summer of 1862. From August 18 to 25 the post, manned by some 180 soldiers and volunteer defenders, held out against a horde of Indian besiegers who looked upon Fort Ridgely as the "door to the valley as far as to St. Paul."

The fort's hospital soon filled with injured and with refugees suffering from exposure and shock. The post surgeon, Dr. Alfred Mueller, and his wife Eliza tended the wounded and sick with such skill and devotion that their work is mentioned in the military reports. Mrs. Mueller made coffee and carried it to the exhausted sentries. At one time, when aid was needed to synchronize a blast of the fort's cannon, she pulled open the fort doors at the signal of a dropped handkerchief.

Forty wounded men were brought to the fort after the battle of Birch Coulee, and Mrs. Mueller took care of them in the hospital. Survivors recalled long afterward that her presence was like "sunlight" in the "darkened hospital." This courageous nurse has been honored by the state of Minnesota, which has erected a monument over her grave at Fort Ridgely. She has been described as the "Florence Nightingale of Fort Ridgely."

The military hospitals of the frontier, like the pioneer forts, were of service not only to soldiers but also to the native population and white settlers. They were havens where doctors vaccinated Indians, mended the injured arms of fur traders, and advised farmers on the treatment of children stricken with disease. But as the westward march of America caught up with the Minnesota frontier, towns sprang up and soon needed civilian hospitals.

The capital city, St. Paul, in 1852 was a settlement of some 1500 people, a community built around the French Catholic Chapel of St. Paul. In the spring of that year a St. Paul newspaper, the *Minnesota Weekly Democrat*, ran a curious announcement. It was headed "St. Paul Hospital" and it stated that two men named Rey and Carlioz had "commenced building . . . a large four story building for a Hospital." This was to be "under the superintendence of Dr. Carlioz, a French physician of distinguished eminence in his profession." Later the paper said the building was making progress, but that meanwhile "Vital Guerin's house would be employed as a temporary hospital, under the charge of Dr. Carlioz and assistants."

Vital Guerin's wife was famed as a midwife in the pioneer town, and Dr. Carlioz ran an advertisement in which he described himself as a "Surgeon, Physician and Accoucher," a graduate of the universities of Paris and Turin. He even announced that he would "take pleasure in exhibiting his diploma to any one who desires to see it." And he added a final note that he had "instruments of the most approved kinds, for every surgical operation ever required."

Alas for the historian, this eminent surgeon's advertisement ran for exactly a year, then disappeared; probably he had paid for a year's run; whether he practiced in St. Paul or built the four-story hospital the records do not disclose, but his newspaper announcement smacks of frontier charlatanism.

St. Paul did not have a real hospital until two years later, in 1854. Through the encouragement of Bishop Cretin, St. Joseph's Hospital was completed that year on the same site it occupies today. The gifted Mother Seraphine and three other sisters of the order of St. Joseph of Carondelet came up from St. Louis to take charge of the new venture. Before St. Joseph's Hospital was ready for use, Asiatic cholera appeared in St. Paul, and the sisters undertook to nurse the sick in the old log chapel from which the city had taken its name.

But soon they were able to use the new hospital, a stone building seventy-two feet long and thirty-four wide, with a basement housing the kitchen, vegetable cellar, and laundry, and three stories which included everything from a chapel, wards, and assembly room to the sisters' living quarters. The attic had two rooms for what a modern writer has called "neurological cases which were usually cases of delirium tremens." But in the 1870's the attic was rearranged to include an operating room, which it was said would "relieve the patients in the several wards from the sickening scenes which they have been frequently compelled to witness before."

A humanitarian touch is disclosed by a smoking and reading room in the hospital for the benefit of convalescent "lovers of the weed," to quote a St. Paul newspaper. A force pump made spring water available on all floors. A newspaper comments admiringly on the ventilating system, which was faulty until a number of stoves "were introduced into the building . . . which by means of pipes introduced cold air from the outside," which in turn was warmed before being allowed to escape into the rooms.

The original price for private rooms, "furnished with the careful attendance of the Sister, a doctor, medicine, lights and fuel," was eight dollars a week. Charity patients were cared for at St. Joseph's, their expenses paid by the city. In 1855 the hospital took care of sixty-eight such patients. In 1870 St. Joseph's had a grand total of some two hundred and fifty patients, many of them sufferers from typhoid fever.

A newspaper of the 1850's gave special praise to the nursing sisters, who devoted, it said, "their whole time and labor to this work of practical Christianity." This paper said, "The best of nursing, clean and airy rooms, good diet, and attention have cheated the stern tyrant of many victims there, and sent them 'on their way rejoicing,' full of gratitude to those who prefer to minister over the couch of suffering, to leading a life of flaunting idleness and vanity."

Just why the alternative was so uncompromising the paper does not make clear. But the press accurately voiced a gratitude that was multiplied through the years. The institution was fittingly the scene of pioneering surgical advances, most notable of which, perhaps, was the cholecystectomy performed by Dr. Justus Ohage of St. Joseph's in 1886, the first operation of its kind in America.

It would be interesting to trace the history of other St. Paul hospitals – St. Luke's, founded in 1857, Ancker, in 1872, and Bethesda, in 1883 – or to tell of the pesthouse erected in two days in 1866 to care for cholera patients; but we must cross the river into St. Anthony, now a part of Minneapolis, to observe a phenomenon.

While St. Paulites were telling of their splendid new hospital in the 1850's, St. Anthony boasted that it had a doctor but no patients. The *Pioneer* in 1855 said that Hennepin County had two thousand people, but its doctor "had not a single patient within its limits" and, what was more, "had not heard of a single case of indisposition in the county for some weeks." A year later the *Saint Anthony Express* again referred to this doctor, Dr. A. E. Ames, a graduate in 1845 of Rush Medical College, as a man "whose familiar face is known to all of you as a neighbor and upright man, but not as a doctor – few of you ever required his services."

One can't help wondering whether the advertising of Minnesota as a health resort in early days, with a climate of super-therapeutic powers, did not contribute to the practice of Dr. Ames and other doctors. We know that many invalids came into Minnesota on the same steamers that carried crowds of settlers and land speculators.

That Dr. Ames did become known as a doctor after the middle 1850's is apparent enough. In 1871 he was able to open a free dispensary in Minneapolis. The papers, announcing that opening, added that it was hoped that the dispensary might be preparatory to opening a hospital, "an institution much needed in our city."

In the spring of that year, largely through the efforts of an Episcopal clergyman, Reverend David B. Knickerbacker, the Cottage Hospital was opened. It was a rented cottage, with eight beds, and was in some sense a cooperative enterprise, for the Masons furnished one room, the Milwaukee railroad employees another, while druggists donated the needed medicines, liquor merchants the needed liquor, and the Ladies' Society of Gethsemane Church the necessary bedding. By midsummer of its first year the hospital had cared for thirty-four patients.

The Cottage Hospital, now known as St. Barnabas, received gifts from its well-wishers. For example, one J. H. Pearl gave the hospital a twenty-pound jar of butter, and a business house presented fifty pounds of coffee. In June 1876 the hospital acknowledged gifts of one ham, two ladies' wrappers, seven boxes of strawberries, and a bottle of whisky; and yet other gifts were seventy-five cabbage plants, a gallon of blueberries, a barrel of onions, ten pairs of blankets from the North Star Woolen Mills, and cut flowers presented by a lady named Mrs. Helen Bovy.

From the beginning St. Barnabas seems to have been blessed with grateful patients, ranging from its first patient, a barber who returned weekly to shave the sick, to the man who, grateful for aid given his wife when the hospital was newly started, left a half million dollars to the institution in 1930.

After seven and a half years of service, the Cottage Hospital reported that of 662 patients admitted, 77 had died and 578 had been discharged either "cured or improved." The hospital had taken in 176 charity, 165 private, and 314 county cases. Its maintenance cost was $1,931.77 the first year and $1,932.79 the seventh year – a difference of only $1.02. Among the special items mentioned in the report was a successful operation for cataract, performed in 1877.

Occasionally the pioneer hospitals faced criticism, as in 1880 when the press reported that nine of twelve patients in this institution had come down with typhoid fever. Sometimes the hospital was the scene of sheer drama, as in 1875 when it had been persuaded with some difficulty to take the case of an unmarried expectant mother. The father, a lumberjack, returned from the woods to find the mother and newly born infant in the hospital and married her just preceding the child's baptism by the Reverend Mr. Knickerbacker. It was cases of this kind and the humane interest of women like Dr. Martha G. Ripley that gave Minneapolis ultimately its Maternity Hospital in the summer of 1887.

The day of hospitals was definitely at hand in Minneapolis: Northwestern Hospital started in 1882 as a "retreat for sick women and children"; General opened its doors in 1887; and St. Mary's was opened in 1887 by the same sisterhood that had founded St. Joseph's in St. Paul in the 1850's.

And in 1881 the Minnesota College Hospital was started. It was housed for a time in the Winslow House of old St. Anthony, a building originally erected as a summer hotel in the 1850's and then crowded, as a newspaper put it, with "dark eyed southern beauties" and "haughty southern gentlemen." But, the paper added, another life had "crept up the broad staircase" of the Winslow House. "The echoes so long regent have died away before the hurrying, slippered feet of the physician and nurse."

This hospital had more than eighty patients during its first month, about three fourths of them suffering from typhoid fever. The next year Dr. Charles Hewitt proposed to the regents of the state university the creation of a medical department, and in 1888, when medical teaching was unified at the university, the reorganized Hospital College as well as the St. Paul Medical College were drawn into the university organization.

Outside the Twin Cities, too, hospitals were appearing: in Stillwater in 1880, and in Duluth, where St. Luke's was opened in 1882 in a shack heated by a stove. Meanwhile, early agitation for the acceptance of state responsibility for asylums for the insane and other unfortunates was beginning to bear fruit. As early as 1852 the far-seeing Dr. Ames of St. Anthony had petitioned for an insane asylum; but it was not until 1866 that such an institution was established in St. Peter, marking a new step forward in state social responsibility.

As one looks at the hospital development from the days of the pioneer forts to the earlier civilian hospitals, one is struck by the humbleness of beginnings and the slimness of support the institutions at first received. Public sentiment for a long time was skeptical of the hospital as anything but an institution of charity.

For example, in 1885 Dr. Ancker reported that the death rate in the St. Paul public hospital was about 6½ per cent, which he said was very low compared with similar institutions in the country. But, he said, it was much higher than it should be, and this he attributed to the "unreasonable prejudice against a public hospital" – a prejudice so great that the "sufferer seeks it only as a last resort." Surgeons, reporting their mortality rates, asked allowances for 'the disadvantage of a hospital atmosphere,' and resort to even the best of Twin City hospitals was not given very serious consideration unless the patient was without funds or family to care for him. In extolling the benefits of St. Joseph's Hospital and its nurses, a St. Paul newspaper in 1863 spoke of them as the "nearest possible substitutes for the loving wife, the dear affectionate mother or sister." But they were thought of only as substitutes.

"By Act of God and the Sisters of St. Francis" is the title of one chapter in Helen Clapesattle's *The Doctors Mayo*. It tells the story of that tornado in Rochester in 1883 which has so often been credited with setting the course of the rise of the Mayos to fame and the fashioning of the Mayo Clinic. It assuredly did point the need for a hospital in Rochester, but much must be said for the determination and self-sacrifice which went into the founding of that hospital by the Sisters of St. Francis. Nor should one overlook the efforts and enterprise of the doctors themselves, notably the "old doctor," the elder Doctor Mayo.

Sisters, nurses, and doctors, who brought St. Mary's Hospital into being, were sharers in the great tradition of men and women who have labored for the sick. From the officers' wives at Fort Snelling who cared for the wounded daughter of Chief Hole-in-the-Day to the "Florence Nightingale of Fort Ridgely" and on to the physicians and nurses who worked in dark and crowded buildings, we come to the great hospitals and clinics of the modern state of Minnesota, in every instance achieving their greatness from days of small beginnings.

The story of the trained nurse, if told in fullness of detail, would be no less significant a saga than that of hospitals. I have mentioned the founding of Northwestern Hospital in 1882 – an institution planned and brought into existence by a group of forty-three women. In the year of its founding a nurses' training school was established there. An account of that school describes it as the twenty-fifth in the United States and, save for one in New Orleans, "probably the only one west of the Mississippi." And we are told that the hospital board spent anxious hours wondering whether enough young women could be found who would devote a whole year to training in a hospital, whether there actually would be families willing to pay as much as twelve dollars a week for the services of a trained nurse, and whether, if Northwestern turned out four nurses a year, the supply would not soon exceed the demand.

The advance of nurses' training soon indicated that these worries were misplaced, for other hospitals followed the leadership of Northwestern in establishing training schools: St. Luke's in Duluth in 1887, the State Asylum at St. Peter two years later, Asbury in Minneapolis and St. Luke's in St. Paul in 1892, Minneapolis General in 1893, St. Barnabas in Minneapolis and St. Joseph's in St. Paul in 1894, and Winona General in 1895. Dr. Ancker asked for such a school at the St. Paul public hospital in 1890, declaring that "the hour is ripe and the field is rich," and two years later one was established. According to his report in 1894, fourteen nurses were working in the hospital, their working day "at least thirteen hours," with 1006 patients for the year.

Not until 1909 did the University of Minnesota establish its school of nursing. This may seem to some a late date, but this was the first university school of nursing in the United States—and, in fact, in the world. As its bulletin announced, its purpose was to serve as "a stepping-stone to the advancement of the profession of nursing in the northwest." The organization of a school of nursing as an integral part of a university has been called "a step of the greatest consequence for nursing education. It changed the status of the fledgling nurse from that of a 'pupil nurse' to that of a student. The final step in the creation of a nursing profession had now been taken."

Dr. Richard Olding Beard spoke to a group of nurses in 1909 about the meaning of university education for nurses, and his words are significant today. He pictured a broadened function of the university. "In adjusting itself to the increasing complexity of human society," he said, "in affording a more varied means of preparation for the multiplying avocations of modern life, in specializing training for the many forms of expert service which the industrial and professional systems of today involve, in answering to the needs of the progressive many, rather than the privileged few, higher education should lose—and will lose—none of its cultural values."

He went on to say that the university is "peculiarly interested in providing for the highest and most selective training for those who are to engage in the pursuits" that affect "human life, human development, and human health. . . . It should bring the full emphasis of its nurture upon the value of human life itself." Nursing, he believed, was one of the "life-serving and life-saving callings" which "have been slow to receive the cultural care of the State and of its higher institutions of learning in America."

The fifteen-bed hospital attached to the walls of old Fort Snelling has grown to a system of some two hundred and thirty hospitals with nearly thirty thousand beds, serving the people of the Upper Midwest, and indeed of the nation and the world. The hopes of those brave souls who started with little rented cottage hospitals have been fulfilled. And from frontier days when there were no trained nurses at all or only one or two in the entire state, Minnesota has come into an age when it has an army of more than twelve thousand registered nurses.

Both pioneering and courage play roles in the saga of hospitals, and the corridor of advance stretches illimitably into the future.

I Moved among Men

THE outstanding event of the political campaign of 1860 in the Northwest was the visit of William H. Seward, the Republican leader who, defeated by Lincoln for the presidential nomination, generously took the stump for his rival in a strenuous speech-making tour.

In the party that accompanied Seward were Charles Francis Adams, who was later appointed by Lincoln United States minister to Great Britain, and his son, Charles Francis Adams, Jr., who later became a distinguished historian. The younger Adams tells in his autobiography of the visit paid by Seward to Boston and Quincy after his defeat at the Chicago convention. He was then planning a speaking tour through the Northwest, and he desired both the elder and the younger Adams to join him. "I eagerly caught at the idea," writes the son, "and prevailed on my father to fall into it. We went, and it proved a considerable episode in my life. I saw the West for the first time, and moved among men."

The Seward party reached the upper Northwest by a steamboat journey up the Mississippi from Prairie du Chien and arrived at St. Paul early in the morning of Sunday, September 16, 1860. "Mr. Seward was conducted to the International Hotel," notes a contemporary newspaper. "He attended Church at Rev. Dr. Patterson's, and we believe, was allowed to spend the day in privacy." The following day was devoted to an excursion to the Falls of St. Anthony and to Minnehaha Falls. A "grand mass meeting of the Republicans of Minnesota" was held on September 18, and this all-day celebration reached its climax when Seward delivered a speech from the steps of the State Capitol in St. Paul, to which he had been escorted by a procession of "Wide Awakes."

Seward's speech was one of the ablest delivered by him during the campaign. The elder Adams was puzzled because Seward apparently regarded the Northwest as very important in the campaign. Doubtless Seward was much pleased by the attachment the Minnesota Republicans had shown for him at the Chicago convention. But he seems to have had a conception of the role of the Northwest that Adams could scarcely understand. His theme was the political power of the West.

"We look to you of the Northwest to finally decide whether this is to be a land of slavery or of freedom," he said. "The people of the Northwest are to be the arbiters of its destiny." It is interesting to turn from this remark of Seward's and read a study by an American historian, William E. Dodd, who believes that the Northwest was the critical contested area of the 1860 election and that the contest was won by the Republicans "only on a narrow margin by the votes of the foreigners whom the railroads poured in great numbers into the contested region."

Perhaps the most interesting portion of Seward's speech was that occupied with prophecy of the future of the Northwest. On the journey up the great river, the New York statesman had apparently given much thought both to the beauty of his changing surroundings and to the destiny of the continent.

> And then that beautiful Lake Pepin scene, at the close of the day, when the autumnal green of the shores was lost in a deep blue hue that emulated that of the heavens; the moistened atmosphere reflected the golden rays of the setting sun, and the skies above seemed to come down to complete the gorgeous drapery of the scene. It was a piece of upholstery such as no hand but that of nature could have made. This magnificent Lake, I said to myself, is a fitting vestibule to the Capital of the State of Minnesota.

Minnesota to Seward was a point of vantage for a continental survey:

I find myself now, for the first time on the highlands in the centre of the continent of North America, equidistant from the waters of Hudson's Bay and the Gulf of Mexico, from the Atlantic Ocean to the ocean in which the sun sets. . . . Here is the central place where the agriculture of the richest regions of North America must begin its magnificent supplies to the whole world. (Applause.) On the East, all along the shore of Lake Superior, and on the West, stretching in one broad plain, in a belt quite across the Continent, is a country where State after State is yet to rise, and whence the productions for the support of human society in other crowded States must forever go forth. This is then a commanding field; but it is as commanding in regard to the commercial future, for power is not to reside permanently on the eastern slope of the Alleghany Mountains, nor in the sea ports of the Pacific. Seaports have always been controlled at last by the people of the interior. The people of the inland and of the upland, those who inhabit the sources of the mighty waters, are they who supply all States with the materials of wealth and power. The seaports will be the mouths by which we shall communicate and correspond with Europe, but the power that shall speak and shall communicate and express the will of men on this continent, is to be located in the Mississippi Valley, and at the source of the Mississippi and the St. Lawrence. (Loud applause.) In other days, studying what might perhaps have seemed to others a visionary subject, I have cast about for the future, the ultimate central seat of power of the North American people. I have looked at Quebec and at New Orleans, at Washington and at San Francisco, at Cincinnati and at St. Louis, and it has been the result of my best conjecture that the seat of power for North America would yet be found in the Valley of Mexico; that the glories of the Aztec Capital would be renewed, and that city would become ultimately the Capital of the United States of America. But I have corrected that view, and I now believe that the last seat of power on the great continent will be found somewhere within a radius not very far from the very spot where I stand, at the head of navigation on the Mississippi river, and on the great Mediterranean Lakes. (Loud applause.)

In this speech of 1860 Seward touched prophetically on the possible acquisition of Alaska by the United States:

Standing here and looking far off into the North-West, I see the Russian, as he busily occupies himself in establishing seaports and towns and fortifications, on the verge of this continent, as the outposts of St. Petersburg, and I can say "Go on and build up your outposts all along the coast up even to the Arctic Ocean – they will yet become the outposts of my own country – monuments of the civilization of the United States in the North-West."

Seward must have breathed the air of manifest destiny as he journeyed into the wilderness of the Northwest. His imperial vision was by no means limited to Alaska. He also took occasion in his St. Paul speech to predict the incorporation of Prince Rupert's Land and Canada into the American domain, and he even looked toward the reorganization of the South American republics "in free, equal and self governing members of the United States of America."

Seward saw the West as a harmonizer of sections and races, and he particularly commented on the place of the foreign-born in the Northwest, pointing out that

> "while society is convulsed with rivalries and jealousies between native and foreign born in our Atlantic cities and on our Pacific Coast, and tormented with the rivalries and jealousies produced by difference of birth, of language, and of religion, here, in the central point of the Republic, the German, and the Irishman, and the Italian, and the Frenchman, the Hollander and the Norwegian, becomes in spite of himself, almost completely in his own day, and entirely in his own children, an American citizen."

The documents herewith printed are records of the Seward campaign in Minnesota from the pens respectively of Charles Francis Adams and his son. In 1900 the son, then president of the Massachusetts Historical Society, participated in the exercises at the dedication in Madison of the new building of the State Historical Society of Wisconsin, and on this occasion Adams quoted a number of interesting passages both from his father's diary and from a contemporary record of his own relating to the visit made to Madison forty years earlier. Samuel R. Thayer of Minneapolis, greatly interested in these two historical records, ventured to ask Adams for copies of the passages relating to the journey beyond Madison—to the Mississippi River and to Minnesota. In a letter to Thayer written on December 3, 1900, Adams made this response:

> You may remember sometime ago expressing a wish to have the record of my father and myself made during our trip to the Northwest in 1860, being a continuation of the passages I quoted at Madison.
>
> I need not remind you that our trip was in connection with Mr. Seward's quite famous political canvass of 1860, during which he made his speech at St. Paul, prophesying the future greatness of the place.
>
> Enclosed I send you the two narratives referred to. My own was written immediately on my return home after the trip was over, partly from notes made during the trip, and partly from recollection. My father's was apparently a record made almost day by day during the experience.
>
> The records have a certain interest, and you are welcome to make such use of them, either with your Historical Society, or otherwise, as may commend itself to you.
>
> I should in any event have been glad to oblige you by making these extracts, but in my own case it came in somewhat handily, as my record was one which I was then looking over with a view to destroying it. It has, since making these extracts, been reduced to ashes, as I found it contained little worth preserving.

The story behind the destruction of his youthful diary is told by Adams in his autobiography. It appears that he kept a diary until, at the age of twenty-five, he entered the army for Civil War service. The volumes of the diary were sealed up in a package that Adams did not open until many years later. The shock of the revelation of himself as a young man caused Adams, after rereading the record, to groan over "its unmistakable, unconscious immaturity and ineptitude, its conceit, it weakness and its cant." Adams saw himself "face to face through fifty years" and was thoroughly disillusioned. "It was with difficulty I forced myself to read through that dreadful record; and, as I finished each volume, it went into the fire; and I stood over it until the last leaf was ashes."

Adams, with a spirit like that of his brother, Henry Adams, sums the matter up with the comment, "It was a tough lesson; but a useful one."

If the extract presented by Adams to Thayer and printed in these pages is a fair example of the diary, it may be doubted whether the world will agree with Adams' severe castigation of the young man who was himself some thirty or forty years earlier. It is more likely to pronounce him a shrewd observer whose journal, written with clarity, portrays both men and events with precision and vividness.

Certainly all will be thankful that the family conscience relented when Adams reached that part of his diary which tells of the Northwest journey. The original was devoured by the flames, to be sure, but a copy of the record has been preserved in the archives of the Minnesota Historical Society. It possesses an interest far transcending that of the circle of Minnesota readers. This document and also that of the elder Adams are interesting contemporary records of the national campaign that put Abraham Lincoln into the presidential chair, and the central figure in these records was the most prominent Republican in the country, save one. The two documents would possess a national interest in any case, because they are from the pens of Charles Francis Adams and Charles Francis Adams, Jr.

From the Diary of Charles Francis Adams

[Visit of William H. Seward, and party, to Minnesota, in September, 1860, during the Presidential canvass of that year.

Extracts from the Diary of Charles Francis Adams, who then accompanied Mr. Seward. In May, 1844, Mr. Adams had been at Galena, coming up the Mississippi from St. Louis, and thence had crossed to Chicago by stage, but had not revisited that region during the intervening time. On the present occasion the party had come from Chicago to Milwaukee and Madison, and thence had reached the Mississippi River at

Prairie du Chien, where they took the Steamboat for St. Paul at 9 P.M. on Thursday, September 13th. Mr. Adams's record then begins:]*

Friday, September 14, 1860: I slept very indifferently, and was up soon after five. The steamer was drawn up against the bank of the stream, waiting for a suitable hour to reach Lacrosse, the town where the Governor was to be received. This was not in the original programme, but it had been admitted on the earnest solicitation of Mr. C. C. Washburn who came with us. It is his residence; a new and small town of perhaps four thousand souls. Here the Governor was received in due form by the Wide Awakes, and escorted into the town. Carriages were then procured, and we drove out to see the vicinity, which was poor and cheerless enough. The only incident that amused us grew out of a visit at my desire to a brewery of lager beer, where we examined the whole process of manufacture, and the vaults in which the article is kept. The owner, who is a German, would not permit us to go without drinking three glasses apiece of his beer. As he is inclining to Republicanism we felt afraid to decline his civility. At last we got back to the steamer and dined. Then came the procession to the place of speaking. It was an inclosed space with a building used by the Germans for a gymnasium. A scaffolding was made against one window. The crowd, which might have consisted of twelve hundred persons, was there packed together directly under the influence of the Speakers. Governor Seward began, and made I think the most easy and agreeable address I ever heard from him. The cry was then for Mr. Nye, when I was arranged to follow.† This annoyed me as I knew the impatience people feel in having a speaker put in whom they do not want to

* This introductory material was presumably written by Charles Francis Adams, Jr.

† In addition to the two Adamses, the Seward party included George W. Patterson and James W. Nye of New York, Rufus King of Wisconsin, and various others.

hear at a time when he shuts out a favorite. So I insisted upon Gen. Nye's responding at once. He made a good deal of difficulty, but I was so earnest about it that he took precedence at last. His speech was better than usual, and satisfied the people; so I came on without any difficulty. Next came Mr. Doolittle who was clear and forcible. The meeting then adjourned until evening, and we went by invitation to dine with Mr. Washburn. The company consisted of himself, a Mr. and Mrs. Nevins and another lady, I presume his sister, Governor Seward, his daughter and Miss Perry, myself and son, Mr. Baker, Mr. Doolittle, Mr. Wilkinson, and Mr. Goodrich.* In the midst of dinner a thunder storm came on, and it continued to rain until late. No provision had been made for this, so we sat until midnight in the mortal discomfort of exhausted conversation. An omnibus then stopped for us, and we got home to the steamer at or near one o'clock.

Saturday, 15th September: We travelled all night and at about six this morning I arose, and found myself looking at an Autumn sky, with a fresh northwesterly wind, and bright sun. As the day advanced it grew warmer, and I made use of the greater part of it in observing the peculiar scenery of the river. All the way on each side are conical elevations so similar as almost to become monotonous, with more or less of timber all the way up. The water is low so that the boat had difficulty in keeping the sinuous channel. Yet the effect is far superior to anything I have seen elsewhere in the West. Occasionally we were interrupted by the sharp report of our piece of artillery, which was the signal for a visit to some town, and the usual formulas of acknowledgment from Governor Seward, Mr. Nye and myself. This happened at Winona, at Wabashaw, and at Redwing. At the entrance of Lake Pepin a sudden change took place in the atmosphere, and a thunder-

* Morton Smith Wilkinson was United States senator from Minnesota from 1859 to 1865. Aaron Goodrich was chief justice of Minnesota Territory from 1849 to 1851 and was one of the founders of the Republican party in Minnesota.

storm came on to give a striking variety to the scene. It was highly picturesque.

Sunday, 16th September: At six o'clock this morning we were in sight of Saint Paul, the most northerly point of our journey. Its position is striking; but it has a more ragged, uninviting look than even Western towns commonly have. As it was Sunday, and we came so early there was no preparation to meet us, I quietly slipped up to the Hotel before anybody knew I had started. After dressing and breakfast I attended Divine service with Governor Seward and others of our party, at the Episcopal Church. A certain Dr. or Mr. Hall officiated. The house looked fresh and neat, which is more than I could say for the streets. The place is barely ten years old, and it has of course all the aspect of newness consequent upon this cause. The hotel however is built as if intended for a city of a hundred thousand people.

Monday, 17th September: A very fine clear morning that seemed to promise steady weather, but it clouded up and rained by two o'clock with every appearance of a long storm. Yet in the evening it was bright starlight. Arrangements had been made for an excursion to the falls of St. Anthony at eight this morning, but Mr. Goodrich left everybody in the lurch except Governor Seward, and we were in danger of faring ill but for the interference of Senator Wilkinson who assigned me to the care of Mr. Acker, a well known gentleman of the place.* I went in his buggy, in advance of the rest of the party. We went up on the right bank as far as the ferry to Fort Snelling. Here we crossed in a boat swinging on a rope extended over the river, and, passing round the fort which is beautifully situated, travelled on a rich prairie to the falls of Minnehaha, a very picturesque little branch of the river, which with less power, somewhat resembles the smallest single fall at Niagara. We walked under the projection to the other bank without material inconvenience, and then drove

* William H. Acker was adjutant general of Minnesota in 1860 and 1861.

off to the town of Minneapolis, at the fall of St. Anthony. This is the residence of Mr. Aldrich, the member from Minnesota. At his house we all stopped to take luncheon, and see his friends. Then we went down to see the fall. However it might have been in past time, there is now little worth seeing. So much has the shelf work been destroyed that the depth of fall has been reduced to twenty or thirty feet only, and the various saw-mills have drawn off water so as to diminish the volume in the same proportion. I regretted I had not executed my plan sixteen years ago. It was now only the ruins of a fall. Proceeding towards the suspension bridge, we found a large assemblage of people, some of whom were firing off a salute by charging an anvil. Then an address was made to the Governor, which he answered, standing in his carriage. A call for me followed which I acknowledged in a few words; and then came General Nye. This over we proceeded over the suspension bridge to the other side, where the Wide Awakes were drawn up in expectation. But as it was beginning to rain, and we were in advance, Mr. Acker concluded with my assent to push right on, whereby I was saved from another speech. We got home by four o'clock. . . .* We all went in the evening to Governor Ramsay's. A large company with a ball and supper. I found many intelligent and pleasant people, especially some ladies.

Tuesday, September 18, 1860: Cloudy and raw, threatening rain, and looking highly unpropitious to the ceremony of the day. After breakfast, Mr. McLean came to see me and to ask me to ride to his house, situated on a high bluff as it is called here, or a hill as we should call it, though perhaps this is scarcely appropriate as the rise is commonly on the river side only, on the Southeasterly side of the city.† He is a younger brother of Judge McLean, though himself seventy

* This and all other omissions indicated in the document occur in the typewritten copy from which this is printed.

† Nathaniel McLean, a journalist, was born in New Jersey in 1787. He was Sioux agent at Fort Snelling from 1849 to 1853.

years old. He came here as a local officer in the administration of General Taylor, took up lands in the infancy of the city, and thus was induced to remain after he was removed. His position is a very fine one; and, during the rage of speculation he thought himself rich by his sales, but the revulsion came, and his lands returned to him. This is the fate of speculation in the West. There is little money capital, and there is a superfluity of land. Mortgages consequently constitute the substance of the personal property. But when based upon valuations made in the fever of speculation, they are made securities for sums which the lands do not actually represent. . . . Visit the Historical Society's rooms in the company of Governor Seward. So I went with him to the State House, where we found Governor Ramsay and a few other persons assembled. An address was here made to Mr. Seward by the English Bishop of Rupert's Land, far away to the north, which was briefly answered. Its substance was merely to hope that peace would be perpetual between the two countries. The Society is in its infancy, but it seems to be doing well under the care of the Secretary, Mr. Neill. Thus passed the morning. Then came the procession of the Wide Awakes, and the march to the same edifice. The assemblage was very large, and there was some delay and difficulty about the preliminaries. At last it was settled that the Governor should speak from the steps of the front entrance. The spot was well chosen, but the mass was much too large to be reached by any ordinary voice. Mr. Seward however held the standing body for an hour and three quarters, with the most careful and elaborate effort he has yet made. I am a little at a loss to know why he laid so much stress upon this, at present the least, the weakest and most inefficient of the Northwestern cluster of States. But it has been all along evident to me that he cherishes it with more than a mere political affection, on account of the attachment manifested by its delegates to him at the Convention at Chicago. During his speech the clouds insensibly vanished, and the declining rays of the sun shed a soft light over the crowd collected below the steps as well as on the heights of the distant landscape, which produced an almost magical effect on my senses. It seemed much like intoxication. But it was plainly no time for me to go on. The people had been kept standing for hours, and it was just sunset. Mr. Seward had closed very eloquently, and the people clamored for me. I thought it wisest, however, after consultation with the principal persons, not to strain their patience, so I merely rose to excuse myself at the moment, and to promise to speak in the evening if they desired it. I was received with extraordinary favor. I have nowhere seen such fixed attention to the words of a speaker as they paid throughout this long session exceeding two hours. Here and at Lacrosse, open air meetings were exceptions to the ordinary rule. They were really impressible bodies of men, and not a mere pageant. We rode back under the escort of the Wide Awakes, and proceeded to dine by invitation of Mr. Goodrich at the Merchants' Hotel. . . . At eight we returned to the Hotel. The Wide Awakes marched down in force, making a very imposing appearance and drew up in the street in front which was densely packed.* But the audience was by no means the same as before. It was tired, restless and noisy; so I changed my plan, and spoke only ten or fifteen minutes in the popular style. After which I went to bed, declining to go to a party at Mr. Oakes's.

St. Paul, Wednesday, 19th September: There seemed to be

* The following newspaper account gives some of the local color of this occasion:

"In the evening the Wide Awakes assembled at Market Hall, and when in line, marched through some of the principal streets. Their numbers were greatly augmented by a large number of German Republicans (700) who made a handsome appearance and this, with fire rockets, royal lights, &c., which were set off during the movement of the procession, made a splendid appearance. The procession halted at the International Hotel, where Hon. C. F. Adams, was called for and made a most effective speech. At the conclusion of his remarks, Lt. Gov. Patterson of New York, was called out and elicited unbounded enthusiasm. . . .

"Such a blaze of enthusiasm was never witnessed in this city before."

some doubt about our departure this morning, as the steamboat company had but one boat up here, and that the poorest on the line. The agent felt so ashamed of it that he wanted us to stay over, until tomorrow, but as the Governor's engagement at Dubuque was already hazarded by delay, it was decided that we should go. So at eight o'clock we took leave. The steamer "Alhambra" has been used mainly for a freight and emigrant boat. Old and bad at the best, she was now rendered still more uncomfortable by being surcharged with passengers. Yet she moved easily enough, and the day was so fine and the scenery so pleasing that I enjoyed our trip as much as any part of the whole excursion. Once indeed we ran over a log in the stream in such a manner as to make everybody on board believe she would sink forthwith. But the Captain mended the hole, assuring us that we owed our safety to our dilapidated condition; for that had the frame been stiffer so as not to yield, the consequences would have been more serious. Almost my whole day was passed on the upper deck, partly to watch the scenery, and partly because the cabin was so crowded as to admit of no comfort. . . . We had two or three stops at small towns on the river, at which the usual process of speeches, and guns and hurras took place. By dark we reached Lake Pepin, thus having the advantage of seeing by daylight all the picturesque scenery of the upper Misissippi which in going up we had passed by night.

Thursday, 20th September: The condition of the berths was so little dubious that I deemed it most prudent not to risk the reception of vermin. Hence I was awake most of the night. All the apparatus for washing, shaving was also deficient. Yet we had the opportunity of seeing by daylight all that portion of the river between Lacrosse and Prairie du Chien, which we missed by going up in the night. The only incident of any importance to us was that near Brownsville the current carried the boat into a raft, and broke it up, the timber drifting it directly upon an island in the midst of the river. At first we all supposed that the heavy timber would break in the feeble sides, but here again we were mistaken. The "Alhambra", after two hours spent in prying her off the head of the island, floated into the current again, and went on as good as new. We were not destined to be drowned in this bark, feeble though she be. I kept on deck watching the scenery, the main defect of which is its uniformity and its want of culture. Some time or other, perhaps a couple of centuries hence, this difficulty will cease to exist, and the waste intervals may become the garden of America. We had not so many calls from the shore towns today, and got on better by the diminution of the passengers landing at different points. At Prairie du Chien we bid goodbye to the company of gunners and the four pound gun which has annoyed me by its incessant bark all the way. From this point to Dubuque we went down in the dark. With all the haste that the anxious officers made, we did not reach the place until half past nine o'clock. Yet here were the inevitable Wide Awakes, and not less than a thousand people waiting on the bank to receive the Governor. It was mentioned that thousands had been waiting all day, but had been obliged to return to their houses in the country. We were placed in carriages and escorted to the Julian House, where a dense crowd had gathered, demanding Seward. A good but rather too long address was made to him, and he briefly replied. The call then went on in succession, Nye, and Patterson and myself. The people were greedy for talk, and full of pert answers, the custom of the West. But we retired, and so they were compelled to. But the solicitation to the Governor was so powerful to remain here until tomorrow afternoon, and make a real speech, that he yielded, and thus things stood at about one o'clock of

Friday, 21st. I was very tired and slept well, yet was up early. The day was cool but fine. Soon after breakfast a crowd of gentlemen came to invite us to go out and see the environs.

We drove out upon the bluff which gives a fine view of the place, and then to a shaft of a lead mine. This is the great product which sustains the place. The thing was not new to me however, as I had not only seen but had gone down into one of the shafts. The lead at Galena, which was the place of my exploit in 1844 is more generally diffused, but it is not quite so pure. The back country of Iowa is nearly all of it prairie, but what they call rolling prairie as distinguished from the flat of Illinois. The people here all look at this land for its productive quality, and expect you for that reason to admire its beauty. But flat country however fertile is to me monotonous and tiresome. At two we were at home, and the Wide Awakes escorted us to the public square, where was assembled a crowd of about two thousand people. The stand was good and the speaking was effective. The Governor spoke one hour and three quarters. Not so carefully methodized as at St. Paul, but with single passages of greater eloquence. I followed and held the people just as easily as I did at La Crosse. General Nye came next, and Governor Patterson closed. It was high time, as we had dinner to get and be off at half past seven. Thus closed my part of this excursion. I have made no prepared speech. At Kalamazoo, at Madison, at Lacrosse, at St. Paul and here I have tried to avoid repeating myself, by taking up a single topic at each place. The task has been easier than I expected. I have never wanted for words, have been able to interweave the remarks of others when they aided my object, and have invariably responded, or rather retorted, when any interpellation came from the crowd. So I feel as if I had passed the ordeal of extempore speaking, in the West.

From the Journal of Charles Francis Adams, Jr.

[Visit of William H. Seward, and his party, to Minnesota, in September, 1860, during the Presidential canvass of that year.

Written by Charles Francis Adams Jr., immediately on his return home from the journey, from recollection and notes made at the time.]

Tuesday, September 10th [*11th*],* we set out for Madison. As I was waiting at the hotel in Milwaukee to pay my bill I saw in the hall a strange, comical-looking character, carrying his thumbs in the arm-holes of a not over clean white waistcoat, and with a tall black hat perched on the back of his head, perambulating thoughtfully up and down. I recognized him as a man who, two evenings before, had been pointed out to me at Chicago as Judge Goodrich, of Minnesota, and as a warm political friend of Governor Seward. I introduced myself to the Judge, and my doing so subsequently proved quite a stroke; for the Judge developed into by all odds the most original and amusing character I encountered in the whole trip, and, moreover, he was greatly pleased at my having made his acquaintance. He never forgot it; and, from that time, I became, next to Governor Seward, his guest of distinction in the party. The Judge here joined us, and at once became the life of the company. Not witty, he had a queer, humorous, scriptural form of speech, and he expressed himself in the oddest and most unexpected fashion. Full of stories and broad fun, he only asked for an audience; and, when he secured one, the more fastidious were apt to be shocked; for the Western average man is the reverse of refined, and you are lucky if you escape those who mistake pure coarseness for wit. Judge Goodrich was not at all choice in his conversation, but he was indisputably humorous. In addition to these peculiarities, the Judge is also highly excitable, and, at bottom, I have an idea that he is not altogether sane; but he is always a Western original.

Wednesday, September 11th [*12th*], we drove out to a large farm of a Mr. Robbins, in the vicinity of Madison, a

* The dates of this and the two following entries obviously are incorrect; they should read September 11, 12, and 13.

party of some 40, passing as we went a procession of wagons on their way to the meeting, to be held that afternoon. In the vehicle in which I found myself, were Judge Goodrich and Mr. Washburn, the representative of the district in Congress, beside the gentleman who drove us out, and myself. Goodrich was great. He had come out to Minnesota from New York, where he was born, by way of Tennessee, and he now got telling us of his political experiences in the latter State, – how he used to hold "discussions" with the opposing candidate, and go to the meetings "a walking magazine", – with all his "tools" as he expressed it; – how he and his opponent used to "meet on warm days, in very full-skirted coats, well buttoned up, which, somehow, neither of them cared to unbutton." And he recounted his various adventures with so much humor and in such an original way, that I felt it a misfortune that I alone from the East was there to enjoy it. Presently we met a wagon in which was seated a tall, strong-featured, close-shaven man, wearing a tall, white hat; when, suddenly, Goodrich seemed to grow crazy, and vehemently insisted on our team hauling up. He then incontinently tumbled out of our wagon, and into that of the stranger. We saw no more of him for the rest of the drive; but at the Robbins farm we found him again, and he then made us acquainted with his white-hatted friend, who turned out to be Senator Wilkinson, of Minnesota. He had, it seemed, come down to Madison to meet Gov. Seward. Of Wilkinson I afterwards during the trip saw a great deal. He is not a man of any considerable ability, and would hardly have got into the Senate except from a newly settled State; but I took naturally to him, and he apparently took to me.

Thursday, 12th [*13th*]. Leaving Madison in the afternoon we struck the Missouri [Mississippi] at Prairie du Chien, the party being now increased to about a car full. We reached Prairie du Chien about 9 P.M. and, amid the blaze of the "Wide-awake" torches, and the cheers of the assembled crowd, I followed Gov. Seward under the flaming beacon-lights of the steamboat "Milwaukee", and, for the first time in my life, found myself on the deck of a Mississippi steamboat. After the speeches were delivered and the cheers had subsided, we fairly started up stream. To me, it all seemed strange and unreal, almost weird, – the broad river bottom, deep in shadow, with the high bluffs rising dim in the starlight. Presently I saw them wood-up while in motion, and the bright lights and deep shadows were wonderfully picturesque. A large flat-boat, piled up with wood, was lashed alongside, and, as the steamer pushed steadily up stream, the logs were thrown on board. As the hands, dressed in their red flannel shirts, hurried backward and forward, shipping the wood, the lurid flickerings from the steamer's "beacon-lights" cast a strong glare over their forms and faces, lighting up steamer, flat-boat and river, and bringing every feature and garment out in strong relief.

Saturday, 15th. A heavy rain during the night of the 14th was followed by as glorious a morning as ever broke on the upper Mississippi. The day proved bright and warm, with an almost cloudless sky; though, as evening approached and we were passing up Lake Pepin, there came on a shower. On the slope of the bluffs, and on the spurs and in the ravines, the foliage, just touched by the early frosts, was mellowed in tint, while the atmosphere shone with golden haze. I have rarely enjoyed a day more intensely. Morning strengthened into noon, and noon grew to evening; and the closing day found us still laboring up towards St. Paul. It was twilight before we were clear of Lake Pepin, where we encountered a thunder-shower; and then evening fell.

Sunday, 16th. We touched the levee at St. Paul at 6 o'clock of a gray, chill, September morning, dirty, cross and hungry; and at once hurried up to the hotel. In the afternoon I was taken out to drive across the unfenced and still half-settled prairie. Yet it is a beautiful country, and everything bears a highly prosperous aspect. Though the people are obviously not rich, none seem very poor. The city is well enough, though built mostly of wood; but business blocks of stone are in course of erection, while building material seems abundant. Had I money to invest, I certainly should not fear to put it in corner lots in St. Paul; for, though the city at the head waters of the Mississippi will never be of the first class, much less what Seward in his speech here predicted, yet with its peculiar location and back country it can hardly fail to be permanently prosperous.

Monday, 17th. The party was driven over to the Falls of St. Anthony. I started out in a wagon with Senator Wilkinson, but at Minnehaha was shifted over into a wagon driven by Gen. King. Minnehaha is a picturesque little falls; but it looked tame and lifeless to one who only a few days before had been taking in Niagara. We all lunched at Col. Aldrich's; after which followed speeches, and then the drive back to St. Paul through the rain, – chill and dull.* In the evening there was a reception at Gov. Ramsay's, at which, of course, Gov. Seward was the centre of attraction.

Tuesday, 18th. This date was set apart for Seward's St. Paul speech. The day and audience were both good, but of the speech I heard only the earlier portion, that in which he predicted the great future of St. Paul. We were all to dine with Judge Goodrich, a dinner in honor of Gov. Seward. At the close of his speech I joined the party in Gov. Ramsay's room, and we were all marched off through an admiring throng to the hotel, where we were to dine. It was 6 o'clock

* Cyrus Aldrich, who came to Minnesota in 1855, was a representative in Congress from 1859 to 1863.

Characteristically Adams either neglected to enter in his original journal or else he omits from this copy a report of a speech that he delivered in St. Paul after returning from the trip to the Falls of St. Anthony. "Notwithstanding the unpropitious state of the weather last evening," reports the *Times* on September 18, "the Wide Awakes met at their Headquarters at Market Hall, where after being called to order, they were addressed by Charles F. Adams, Jr., son of Hon. Charles F. Adams, in a very neat and pertinent speech, which called out rapturous applause."

when we got there, and we had to wait an hour and a half. I never saw Gov. Seward more elated than during that hour and a half. As was his custom when exhausted by speaking, he drank brandy and water, with some lumps of sugar in it, and he seemed overflowing with good-fellowship. He declared himself, and evidently was, well pleased with his speech and with its reception; and he told us that, since the day of the Chicago Convention he had not felt so much solicitude as to what he should say, and how express himself, as he had that morning. After dinner the "Wide-awakes" marched to the hotel, and we had more speeches and more enthusiasm. Finally we finished the evening at a small party given to the ladies of Gov. Seward's party, by Col. Oakes.

Wednesday, 19th. At 8 o'clock we bade farewell to St. Paul; and I must say that for hospitality and that generous spirit of welcome, which, however roughly expressed, go so far to make life pleasant, I have yet to meet the people who equal the Minnesotans. It seemed as if they could not do enough for us; and on a trip during which all were generous of their hospitalities, the people of Minnesota were most generous of all.

During the 18th and 19th we steamed down the river in the "Alhambra". The boat was in every respect a wretched one, – old, dirty, and full of vermin. All day we glided down the river, sometimes grounding on a sandbank, and then again fouling a raft. The night was glorious, and the river not less so. The air was damp and chill; but, in a heavy overcoat I kept the deck till 3 A.M. briskly walking in the bright starlight. I saw the Great Bear drop to the horizon, and Castor and Pollux came forth with the sword of Orion; and, finally, Venus towards morning get brighter and brighter, till, when at last I left the guards, she cast my shadow distinctly against the white side of the steamer, much like a twilight moon. Finally we had a performance worth seeing, a boat-race on the Mississippi. We had left St. Paul that morning about ten minutes before the "Winona" of the opposition line, – and the competition was then bitter. Neither our boat nor the "Winona", – both old stern-wheelers, – could boast of much speed, and the only question between them was as to which was the worst. They were, nevertheless, good for a scrub race; and that we soon found. It was quite exciting. A little after 2 o'clock A.M. we heard strange noises behind us, and, looking over the stern of our boat, we made out the "Winona", close behind us and in full chase. There were her colored lanterns, her three tiers of lights, and from time to time when her furnace doors were opened to replenish her fires, lurid flashes lit up the river. The stream was so low and the channel so narrow that it was largely a question of pilotage; and, for some time, the two boats sped along in line. Then, as the channel widened somewhat, the "Winona" tried to pass us. She did not succeed this time; for she only lapped the "Alhambra", and was again pushed, cut, and forced to fall behind. Again the channel widened, and now the "Winona" got half way by; and the two boats, both running at the top of their speed, moved along side by side, at times close together, at times thirty or forty feet apart, – sometimes one apparently gaining and sometimes the other. At last, as the channel broadened, the two got fairly alongside of each other, neck and neck, and so kept it up, slowly converging until separated by only some twelve or fifteen feet; and then they would again separate. Finally the channel apparently narrowed, and the interval was closed rapidly up until, with a bump, the two boats collided heavily, almost throwing me from my feet. The guards seemed to groan and tremble, but neither boat gave; and so the two rushed along with rubbing sides. I suddenly found myself standing face to face with a passenger on the other boat, and, somewhat apparently to his surprise, extended my hand, and wished him good morning. He shook my hand, remarking that he proposed to leave us; and so on the two boats went. I think we must have rushed along in this way for several minutes; but, finally, they shouldered us out of the channel, and, giving a triumphant whistle, shot ahead and down the river, leaving us to follow. Shortly after, being thoroughly tired, I rolled, overcoat and all, into my berth, and incontinently fell asleep. An hour or two later I was awakened by a loud noise of cracking and breaking. We had run into an immense lumber raft, smashing it to bits; while, to return the compliment, the raft had forced our boat hard aground.

The following day (20th) it was a very used-up party,—sleepy, peevish, unwashed. Even Judge Goodrich was under a cloud. I was the most philosophical; for, as the sun gained power, I rolled myself in my cloak, and dozed away several hours, lying on the deck with a log for a pillow. Finally, the Captain of the boat, in great mortification, woke me up and tried to insist on my taking his room. He couldn't express the regret he felt at our being on his boat. I politely declined his offer; and we steamed along. Still it was undeniably monotonous, and the hours passed slowly; but evening came at last, and at 10 o'clock we were all pleased when we heard the roaring of a cannon and saw the long line of "Wide-awake" torches which told of our approach to Dubuque. Landing here, the party was escorted to a hotel, and the usual speeches followed. It was one o'clock before we were permitted to go to bed.

The party left Dubuque on the evening of the 22d, and at Mendota I saw the last of Judge Goodrich;* for my record says "he had come with us thus far on the road to Kansas; but for some days he had plainly been unwell, and his liveliness was departed. During the night, feeling very much the reverse of well, he got into a berth in the wretched device then doing service as a sleeping-car; and, when the party changed trains

* The quotation marks and interpolated matter in this last paragraph are printed without change from the copy of the document supplied by Thayer.

at Mendota he was left quietly asleep. We saw him no more. He and a Mr. Baker, who acted as Gov. Seward's secretary, had been left together. "The first we knew of them was a telegraphic message next morning, informing us that they were left, and pathetically asking 'when and where they should overtake us.' Mr. Baker caught up with us at Leavenworth; but poor Goodrich, – after cursing the conductor of the train on which he was left asleep with strange oaths, hurting himself in jumping from the car, running in the night time and in his slippers half a mile across country, having in his hurry forgotten to put on his boots, – felt discouraged as well as ill; so, after airing his whole varied stock of expletives, he gave up the chase in despair, and returned first to Chicago, and thence to St. Paul, – that "Apostolic City of his adoption", – as he was wont to term it."

A WIDENING PROVINCE

A Bid for Cooperation

AS EARLY as 1908 Clarence Walworth Alvord, a statesman of scholarship gifted with imagination, asked American historians to give heed to the richness and variety of subjects that still needed "to be worked over, especially outside the military and political fields."

He urged them to investigate institutional development and economic life. He called for studies of agriculture, manufacture, and the means of communication. Pointing out the need for critical histories of immigrant groups, he drew attention to the importance of tracing "the transformation of foreign communities into American." Trained in the history of the Renaissance, he had the vision of the historian whose concern was to understand American civilization.

The passing decades have witnessed the advance of American historical scholarship on a wide front, but the challenge of "manifold subjects to be worked over" is constant and presses upon every generation. In the 1930's the American Historical Association sponsored conferences that pointed to significant but neglected areas in our national history, notably the area of social history. Among many subjects then in need of study were urbanization, rural life, the family, legal history, technological changes, science and pseudo science, the uses of leisure, architecture and the fine arts, journalism, and the professions.

In the 1940's the Mississippi Valley Historical Association set up a committee on "American History and Culture" which called attention to such subjects as the fusion of cultures in the Middle West, speech and idiom, public health, population movements and folkways, social-economic institutions such as the country store, science on the frontier and in later times, and the wide sweep of our intellectual history.

I sometimes wonder why we have neglected the fundamental subject of how people work together. Everybody knows that we are great joiners and that joining is an American art. It is an old saying that three Americans falling from a balloon would be organized—with a president, secretary, and treasurer—before striking ground. Why haven't we a history of American joining?

The trend in human affairs seems to be toward more, not less, cooperative activity, and yet we have not examined realistically the ways in which people work together to accomplish their purposes—the ways they organize, manage, and direct. We have left that job, rich as it is for social and economic history, to the political scientists. Of course we want to know how political parties and governments are run, but it is very important also to know how people work together in church, in education, in business, and in meeting the recurrent crises of war and peace. What lies back of our present ways of organizing and functioning? Why do we invariably conduct our meetings according to Robert's *Rules of Order*? We have always been interested in *what* was done. Good administrative history can help us to understand *how* things were done.

We have given some attention to the story of science and medicine, but historians have not attacked the problem on a wide front, either for region or for nation, notwithstanding its importance for modern America. Science is but one aspect of our broader social and intellectual history. Although this wider story has been told by Professor Curti in *The Growth of American Thought*, a book of unusual distinction, he will be the first to admit the need for a vast number of studies looking to a more comprehensive synthesis that would immeasurably help Americans to understand themselves. His studies emphasize the need for good histories of American colleges and universities, of which we have astonishingly few;

for studies of the various intellectual disciplines and professions; for investigations of the anti-intellectualism that persists in our national history; for studies of the moderates who have stood between extreme champions and extreme opponents of ideas; and for further studies of culture groups, notably those represented by the newer immigrants.

One item emphasized by Professor Curti is the need, which I have stressed for many years, for cultural histories of communities: studies that would yield information about the backgrounds and education of settlers and later citizens; cleavages in communities and their various effects upon community institutions; the roles played by church, school, and press; the forces, too little studied, which differentiate one community from another; and the relations of Main Street to the world. Here is a field in which lay historians can join hands with professional scholars, pursuing the doctrine that history, like charity, begins at home. Here the vigorous local interest that is sometimes channeled into antiquarian backwaters can join deep historical currents.

The community in turn is part of state and region, which still invite innumerable studies essential both to regional and to national understanding. Regional investigations of the processes of immigrant transition, of speech and social custom, of minority group problems, of press and education, of industry and agriculture, of creative work in the arts, of fiction and life, of everyday conditions, and of interregional migration and influence are not only rich in promise but necessary to any really "valid and properly proportioned national synthesis" – a synthesis that will do justice to the abundant variety of American culture. And they confront us with a need that outstrips the power of the historian, for we shall not fully understand our regions until they have been interpreted through many arts and disciplines – those of the novelist, poet, essayist, painter, musician, and sculptor, as well as of the historian and biographer.

Thus far I have referred chiefly to needs in social and cultural history and have emphasized subjects that have been relatively neglected. But we must not close our eyes to another kind of topical need, perhaps equally fundamental. This is the need for filling gaps in large subjects that have already been considerably exploited.

One would suppose that by this time the history of lumbering and the American forest would have passed the stage of special studies and yielded an adequate comprehensive work. But according to specialists, we have as yet only fragments, however symmetrical, and the large synthesis is still receding like the white pine of the North Woods. In various parts of the country scholars have been aware of the richness of original materials concerning missions and missionaries, but this awareness has thus far been translated only into stray chapters of the total gospel. Singularly promising as is the field of the advance of geographical knowledge in America, we have not yet seen its complete outline, and our work is merely patches of blue and green on the map. Even so alluring a theme as the fur trade has been attacked mainly at lonely posts. The great synthesis, making full use of the vast wealth of fur trade papers, is as far away as a wilderness portage.

Our needs are many and various in fields bounded by the cement roads and billboards of the present but stretching away in the distance to the split-rail fences of the pioneers. They are in fact so diverse and far-reaching that they may yet yield new orientation in our whole approach to American history. We are interpreters of the past, but unless we relate the past to the present we interpret in a vacuum. The compelling motive behind the exploration of social and intellectual history is a need for true understanding – a need of the present and for the future. It is a need, critically important to modern Americans, to understand the "growth of American thought" – to understand, in fact, the development of American life in its full range.

We face the necessity on the one hand of recognizing the widening province of historians in terms of the subject with which they deal, and on the other, of closing the gap between past and present. Carl Becker in his essay, "Everyman His Own Historian," rests his case for history on the parallel between history and the memory of the individual man. Man needs and uses his memory of recent events and transactions and thought in his own business and life in order to meet effectively the problems of the present and to plan for the future. If we neglect large areas of our recent history, are we not a little like a man of forty who, emerging partially from the blankness of amnesia, remembers his life clearly up to the age of thirty but cannot fill in the intervening years? Amnesia in historical understanding is almost always partial, not total.

There are several possible approaches to the problems of our widening province. I wonder if it is not time for a better integration of our monographic work than in the past, so that many studies on phases of one broad subject may provide the material for a full-range interpretation of the subject. American historical scholarship needs an effective clearinghouse for significant questions and topics on which research should be forwarded. It needs an effective way of answering—for the benefit of students, trained scholars, and writers everywhere—the basic question: What do we need to know in the realm of American history?

We do cooperate now in many ways—in reporting research in progress and in listing thesis titles, and we usually have a good, if delayed, picture of what is going on. But there is relatively little cooperation or leadership in charting needs, in surveying possibilities, and particularly in formulating large patterns of knowledge by which the writings of individuals can be fitted in with the writings of many others, working toward an end design.

The choice of subject matter, not alone for doctoral theses, but for books and special studies by historians is often curious, haphazard, unmotivated by significant needs. Often the choice results from chance knowledge of unexploited or little used original materials. Back in 1912 some historical society received the papers, let us say, of John Q. Jones, for four years a representative in the state legislature and for one term a congressman. He was a politician of the 1840's, a man of unimpeachable party regularity. After his death his widow sat before his desk and lovingly examined his papers – with a fireplace close by. The expurgated collection lay in the desk until the death of the congressman's granddaughter, when the historical society acquired the treasure trove.

There they are, near at hand, inviting exploration, a body of material that will accustom the neophyte to working with manuscripts and will set him on the path to many collateral contemporary sources, including the *Congressional Globe*. Undoubtedly they are materials that can be used in learning the techniques of research. If the subject seems perchance a trifle dull, it may be redeemed by an arresting title – not just "John Q. Jones," but "John Q. Jones: Tilter for Tariffs." And so a thesis is born, a book is written. Nobody has explored, in a doctor's thesis, the sinuosities of how doctoral thesis subjects are chosen, and as a graduate dean, living in a glass house, I had better leave this fascinating topic to another.

Without denying possible values in the haphazard choice, we may still inquire about other approaches that conceivably might lead to topics just as accessible, particularly in this magic day of microfilm, and definitely significant, fitting the choice to ascertained needs. Such an approach is in fact made by many individual advisers of doctoral candidates the country over, but I believe these advisers would be aided and American history benefited by having a clearinghouse which, whatever its precise mechanics, should have ways of communicating the pooled findings of American historians to scholars and writers within and beyond academic circles.

Urgent needs in social and intellectual history should be specifically defined, as well as those in scores of other fields. With an effective clearinghouse established through cooperative action and maintained over a long period of years, it is at least possible that we should gain the wide integration that we now conspicuously lack. It is not difficult to imagine scholars and writers in fifty different universities, as well as off-campus writers, professional and lay, moving toward the filling of gaps, completing significant long-range jobs of value to society, attacking on a wide front important problems of historical scholarship that no one scholar can grapple with alone.

Every graduate adviser is, of course, a clearinghouse with respect to the students who seek his advice, but for the most part he works individually. Fortunately some scholars do reach out with their ideas of needed work to students and writers everywhere. Alvord was one of these, Frederick Jackson Turner another. Turner never ceased to tell us what our needs of knowledge were. His fertility of suggestion, richness of idea, and generosity in proposing significant research topics account in large part for his influence upon historical thinking and writing.

Occasionally established organizations have recognized the need, as Dr. Jameson once put it, in sonorous Jamesonian phrase, "of a little more careful planning in the endeavor to see that work is directed toward things that are suffering to be done, and away from fields already cultivated to the point of diminishing returns." A leader of the Agricultural History Society, sensitive to the obligations of his craft to American democracy, has set up research objectives for a quarter of a century in the future, with a wide range of subjects, including labor, tenancy, the effect of technological changes on rural life, and a score of topics centering upon farmers as social beings.

American historians are grappling in long-range plan with

the problem of recording and writing the complex history of World War II, using through cooperation the diverse and mountainous records of what has been called "the most systematically documented war in history." A scholar of vision in the Pacific Northwest sees the historian as fact-finder and interpreter of long-range trends, and he formulates a program of research, not as a luxury but as a practical attempt to make regional human experience serve the people of his area. He turns aside from lone pioneering and calls for organization, collaboration, and well-integrated projects.

The tradition of scholarship is individualistic. But we cannot close our eyes to the expanding universe of materials. Still valuing the driving power of individual initiative and enterprise, we know that scholars must take advantage of new techniques, of technology, of film and photostat and calendar and index. They must often fit their plans into larger patterns of cooperation if they are to be more than plans.

Scholars in the past have been reluctant to set forth itemized analyses of needs, but the regimentation they have feared seems not to be a real danger. Both within and beyond the range of defined significant needs there would be freedom of choice for the individual, whether amateur, neophyte, or trained scholar. One cannot reasonably argue that formulating our needs is regimentation. No matter how clever or wise the formulation, many individuals would inevitably go beyond its scope. But many writers, no less free in their choice, might welcome and profit by the pooled wisdom of the profession concerning this fundamental and, to our generation, crucial problem of what we need to know. If the profession exposes its needs, it will expose more than the needs of scholars alone. They will be the needs of education and of society in meeting the intricate problems of our age.

If the historical profession gave to historical study and writing the imaginative leadership I have suggested, it would have to do a much better job than it has done in the control of materials. We need those controls for the sake of wide use. In this field we have a good tradition of leadership and planning. Men like Turner and Jameson more than thirty-five years ago planned documentary publication by the United States on a majestic scale. They worked out this plan to meet the needs of the government, of historians, and of the public. And they had the courage and vision to call for a national archives. At the time they may have seemed visionaries rather than men of vision, but today we have a National Archives, and its establishment is the greatest advance of this generation in the province of American historical materials.

Much has been done about historical materials. We have had archival and historical records surveys. Anarchy is yielding to democratic controls. And we are digging into kinds of historical materials that were not much used a generation ago. But we need to use modern techniques in grappling with scattered and diverse bodies of records to which we have no master key.

We have only touched the film-edge of microcopying. In the years ahead scores of research centers will have on deposit edited file microcopies of significant bodies of archives and manuscripts, however distant the originals may be. The published volumes of the *Territorial Papers* are a splendid achievement, but we should also plan a vast program of documentary subpublication. And I believe we should use the microcopy for many theses and monographs that do not warrant, by their character and limited use, the dress of print and binding—even though we shed a sympathetic tear for the author denied the thrill of leafing through his own book.

I have mentioned a master key. By that I mean a great central inventory of archives and manuscripts, a key that will open closed doors—in fact, doors that many of us do not even know exist. We need some way of really knowing what has been preserved out of the past in the hundreds of collections throughout the land. Heroic efforts have been made by the

Historical Records Survey to gather up information as to where our materials actually are, but we lack the master key: a national guide or inventory. Neither the Library of Congress nor any other great central institution has given it to us.

I do not know what form it will take. Perhaps it will be an index to a thousand guides prepared after the best models we have been able to devise; perhaps it will be a master union guide. Certainly it will be a flexible scheme, controlling what has been done in amassing historical treasures and keeping abreast of current growth. As to methods and place and budgets, let us turn to the experts. Scholars and lay historians look to the objective. We want the key that will unlock the treasures. As the Pennsylvania Dutch say, "we want in."

One thing is fundamental to that objective – improvement in administering historical collecting in many parts of the land. Many collections are still unhappily distinguished, not for their symmetry and availability, but for their chaos and disorganization. Few institutions have taken full advantage of the science of historical records administration which has been growing up without fanfare in recent years. We need manuals along a dozen lines that will make this science understood and help to harvest its fruits for all our societies. We need wise professional leadership in historical work. Our state and regional historical consciousness has been magnificently creative for American history, but alongside it there must be a raising of professional standards. And always we covet the interest and drive of the lovers of history – their number is legion – who sustain the organized societies that have engendered much of our effort to make the recaptured past significant for the present.

Many of the needs now coming into clear focus relate to American culture. The urgency for understanding what American culture really is, for "clarifying our conception of American society," can't be mistaken; and the domain has already been charted. As we study the chart we are beginning to understand the necessity of what someone has called the "multi-disciplinary approach." The phrase is big and impressive, like "that blessed word Mesopotamia," but its meaning is simple. Our interest in American culture is shared by scholars in many other disciplines, and they all have contributions to make. I mean such disciplines as literature, the fine arts, philosophy, cultural anthropology, economics, science, and medicine. They need history. We need to lay hold of the things they can tell us. How can we understand folk culture without their help and the help of their techniques?

How shall we forward this "multi-disciplinary approach"? How shall we get these disciplines together? Perhaps we need the advice of the historian of how to work together. It is a problem of American scholarship. We must lay our departmental pistols down, go in for discussion and conference, and look to the "human and humane values" of American culture for American education and life.

But our needs go beyond the multi-disciplinary approach. They are greater than cooperative effort, control of materials, and the use of techniques. Let us have formulations of "the things that are suffering to be done," but our needs transcend clearinghouses. Even new areas of such engaging importance as American culture are not the whole story. These are servants in the House of History, but they are not enough.

We face the compelling need of making the past significant for the present—the fundamental imperative of individual scholarship that unites professional skill with imagination and courage, that sees it as our task to make an impact upon our people and our times. The design is one of scholarship and education in close association with the life of today. Into it we must fit our enterprise from beginning to end.

While staking out claims in their widening province, historians should give thought to narrowing the gap between the people and the scholars. Undeniably much significant writing reaches beyond the historical profession to the American public, but too many scholars, engulfed by their specialization, seem to write mainly, if not only, for their long-suffering colleagues—yet curiously cherish the hope that the public will buy their books. Clear, simple, interesting writing can carry our findings effectively to scholars and public alike. The nature of our subject is not a court sentence either to write for a sharply restricted audience or to employ formidable, awkward, dull, lifeless prose.

Some scholars damn the good writer as a "popularizer" and even make a virtue of clothing scholarship in too heavy, ill-fitting dress. Mr. Guedalla has made the biting remark that historians' English is not a style, but an industrial disease. Many scholars mistakenly identify simplification and clarity of style with oversimplification of thought. I believe in good writing, even popular writing, that can be read with pleasure by lay readers. I do not propose that we should reduce American history to the scanty wardrobe of Basic English, but why should we not use the total resources of good scholarship, good subjects, and good writing?

None of us can boast a blueprint for making the past alive and significant for the present, but all of us can profit, if our reach exceeds our grasp, by keeping the aim before our eyes. We can profit by accepting a functional concept of the values of American history to a civilization that desperately needs to understand its present and plan for its future in the light of its heritage. We can profit by thinking of history as re-creative in purpose, a vital process that deals with life in its human actuality, its human meaning, its human color and episode.

The question of *what* we need to know is important, but back of it is the question of *why* and *for whom* we need to know. We cannot escape a sense of the importance of the task of interpreting the history of the American people, for that task centers in a nation and folk whose understanding and thought and action are profoundly significant to the present and future of mankind.

Acknowledgments

THE ideas expressed and illustrated in this book have developed in my thinking over a period of years, and the several chapters represent research and writing done at different times for different purposes. Some of the chapters were first composed as lectures, some for publication as papers and articles. In the case of these latter, I am grateful to the original publishers for permission to reprint them here. I have made revisions in titles and phrasing and sometimes in content, and I have omitted all footnotes except those necessary for understanding the text. Anyone interested in knowing the sources of my facts and illustrative material will find full citations in the original publications.

INVERTED PROVINCIALISM. This chapter is based upon notes for a talk first given in 1945 at the University of Minnesota and later at the University of California in Berkeley and before the Illinois Historical Society and the Philosophical and Historical Society of Ohio.

LITERATURE OF THE UNLETTERED. This was a lecture given on the Charles M. and Martha Hitchcock Foundation at the University of California in Berkeley on January 23, 1946.

SINGING IMMIGRANTS. This talk was given originally in St. Louis at the thirtieth annual meeting of the Mississippi Valley Historical Association on April 30, 1937. It was also presented to the National Council for the Social Studies in Syracuse, New York, on November 22, 1940, and as one of the lectures on the Charles M. and Martha Hitchcock Foundation at the University of California in Berkeley on January 21, 1946.

THE AMERICA BOOK. This address was delivered at St. Olaf College, May 15, 1937, at a celebration commemorating the centennial of Ole Rynning's coming to America. For fuller detail on Rynning, see Theodore C. Blegen, *Ole Rynning's True Account of America* (Minneapolis, 1926).

IMMIGRANT MARTHAS. Reprinted from *Norwegian-American Studies and Records*, 5:14–29 (1930). The Endreson letter was brought out by the author in *Minnesota History*, 10:425–30 (December 1929).

PIONEER FOLKWAYS. This is reprinted with some revision from Theodore C. Blegen, *Norwegian Migration to America: The American Transition* (Norwegian-American Historical Association, Northfield, Minnesota, 1940), chapter 7.

HALFWAY HOUSE. A lecture given on the Charles M. and Martha Hitchcock Foundation at the University of California in Berkeley on January 16, 1946. The chapter condenses some of the material in my *Norwegian Migration to America: The American Transition*, and I have incorporated some passages from that book.

THE FASHIONABLE TOUR. This article, reprinted from the December 1939 issue of *Minnesota History*, also appears in John T. Flanagan, *America Is West: An Anthology of Middlewestern Life and Literature* (University of Minnesota Press, 1945).

WORD HUNTERS. This account of the Pond brothers was first published in *Minnesota History* as an address presented in Minneapolis on July 14, 1934, as part of a "Pond Centennial Program" under the auspices of the Minnesota Historical Society.

EVERYDAY LIFE AS ADVERTISED. The sources used in this chapter are cited in the article as published in *Minnesota History*, 7:99–121 (June 1926).

ON THE STIR! Reprinted with revisions from *Minnesota History*, 14:134–42 (June 1933).

FRONTIER BOOKSHELVES. This was an address given in Duluth, Minnesota, on September 25, 1940, at the celebration of the fiftieth anniversary of the founding of the Duluth Public Library. It is reprinted from *Minnesota History*, 22:351–66 (December 1941).

FROM COTTAGE TO CLINIC. This chapter is reprinted from *Hospitals: The Journal of the American Hospital Association* for August and September 1943.

I MOVED AMONG MEN. Reprinted from *Minnesota History*, 8:150–71 (June 1927).

A BID FOR COOPERATION. This is drawn from the presidential address of the Mississippi Valley Historical Association that I gave in St. Louis on April 20, 1944. The complete text of the address is published in the *Mississippi Valley Historical Review* for June 1944.

Index